Lecture Notes in Computer Science   1924
Edited by G. Goos, J. Hartmanis and J. van Leeuwen

Springer
Berlin
Heidelberg
New York
Barcelona
Hong Kong
London
Milan
Paris
Singapore
Tokyo

Walid Taha (Ed.)

Semantics, Applications, and Implementation of Program Generation

International Workshop, SAIG 2000
Montreal, Canada, September 20, 2000
Proceedings

 Springer

Series Editors

Gerhard Goos, Karlsruhe University, Germany
Juris Hartmanis, Cornell University, NY, USA
Jan van Leeuwen, Utrecht University, The Netherlands

Volume Editor

Walid Taha
Chalmers University of Technology
Department of Computer Science
Eklandagatan 86, 412 96 Gothenburg, Sweden
E-mail: taha@cs.chalmers.se

Cataloging-in-Publication Data applied for

Die Deutsche Bibliothek - CIP-Einheitsaufnahme

Semantics, applications, and implementation of program generation :
international workshop ; proceedings / SAIG 2000, Montreal, Canada,
September 20, 2000. Walid Taha (ed.). - Berlin ; Heidelberg ; New York ;
Barcelona ; Hong Kong ; London ; Milan ; Paris ; Singapore ; Tokyo :
Springer, 2000
    (Lecture notes in computer science ; 1924)
    ISBN 3-540-41054-6

CR Subject Classification (1998): D.3, F.3, D.1, F.4.1, D.2

ISSN 0302-9743
ISBN 3-540-41054-6 Springer-Verlag Berlin Heidelberg New York

Springer-Verlag Berlin Heidelberg New York
a member of BertelsmannSpringer Science+Business Media GmbH
© Springer-Verlag Berlin Heidelberg 2000
Printed in Germany

Typesetting: Camera-ready by author
Printed on acid-free paper   SPIN 10722858   06/3142   5 4 3 2 1 0

Preface

This volume constitutes the proceedings of the workshop on Semantics, Applications, and Implementation of Program Generation (SAIG 2000) held on 20 September, 2000, in Montreal, Canada. The workshop was held as a satellite event of the ACM International Conference on Principles, Logics, and Implementations of high-level programming languages (PLI).

SAIG aims at promoting the development and the application of foundational techniques for supporting automatic program construction. As the commercial production of software systems moves further from being an art and closer to being a traditional industry, automation will necessarily play a more substantial role in the production of software, much in the same way that automation plays a crucial role in the production of other commodities, such as garments, automobiles, chemicals, and electronics.

Four prominent contributers to the area of program generation kindly agreed to deliver invited talks at SAIG 2000: Don Batory (U. Texas), Richard Kieburtz (OGI), Gilles Muller (IRISA/INRIA), and Frank Pfenning (CMU). The proceedings include abstracts of these talks.

Seven technical papers and four position papers were presented at SAIG 2000. The technical papers covered a wide spectrum of topics, including:

- Multi-stage programmi ng languages (*Calcagno and Moggi*)
- Compilation of domain-specific languages and module systems (*Elliott, Finne, and de Moore*, and *Helsen and Thiemann*)
- Novel program transformations addressing problems specific to program generation (*Makholm*)
- Low-level program generation (*Kamin, Callahan, and Clausen*)
- Formal specification of program transformations (*Fischbach and Hannan*)
- Termination analysis (*Song and Futamura*)

The position papers also cover a broad variety of aspects of program generation, including:

- Lessons learned from previous research systems (*Ramsey*)
- Generation of high-performance scientific applications (*Vuduc and Demmel*, and *Fischer, Schumann, and Pressburger*)
- Type-based analysis (*Berardi, Coppo, Damiani, and Giannini*)

SAIG 2000 would have not been possible without the support of the PLI organizers. We would especially like to thank Amy Felty for all her effort in coordinating the PLI workshops.

July 2000   W alid Taha

Review Process

A call for papers was announced on several mailing lists and newsgroups. Twenty submissions were received, including sixteen technical submissions, and four position papers. In total, 90 reviews were written, either by Program Committee members or by the external reviewers, and each paper received at least two written reviews. The final decisions were made collectively by the Program Committee on the basis of the collected reviews. In cases where Program Committee discussions were of benefit to the authors, the discussions were summarized and included with the reviews. All submissions were of very high quality, and time constraints on the workshop were the primary reason for exclusion. In a few cases, technically outstanding papers were excluded on the basis of relevance.

Program Committee

Cliff Click (Sun)   Suresh Jagannathan (NEC)
Rowan Davies (CMU)   Tim Sheard (OGI)
Julia Lawall (DIKU)   Walid Taha (Chalmers)
Torben Mogensen (DIKU)

External Review ers

Johan Agat   Jörgen Gustavsson   Gilles Muller
David A. Basin   Andreas Hamfelt   Jörgen Fischer Nilsson
Don Batory   Reiner Hänle   Dino Oliva
Zino Benaissa   John Hatcliff   Karol Ostrovsky
Peter Bertelsen   Rogardt Heldal   Matthew J. Saffell
Mathias Blume   Erik Hilsdale   Peter Sestoft
Magnus Carlsson   Luke Hornof   Yannis Smaragdakis
Koen Claessen   Neil Jones   Andrew Tolmach
Thierry Coquand   Sam Kamin   Philippas Tsigas
Patrick Cousout   Gregor Kiczales   Hongwei Xi
Peter Dybjer   Michael Leuschel
Marc Feeley   Manolis Marak akis

.

Table of Contents

Invited Talks

Technical Papers

Position Papers

Implementing Closed Domain-Specific Languages
Abstract of Invited Talk

Richard B. Kieburtz

Oregon Graduate Institute
20000 NW Walker Road
Beaverton, OR 97006 USA
dick@cse.ogi.edu

Abstract. A closed domain-specific language (DSL) is a stand-alone, declarative language designed to provide powerful and flexible software solutions specialized to a particular application domain. The users of a closed DSL are expected to be engineers or designers expert in the theory and techniques of their application domain, but who may be naive as programmers and who may not have the expertise, time, or inclination to design their own software. A good DSL will capture both the nomenclature and the semantics of the application domain.

We contrast *closed* DSL's with *open* DSL's, which are also useful, but for a different community of users. An open DSL denotes crucial abstractions of an application domain directly in the notation of a wide-spectrum programming language, possibly enriched with syntactic extensions. It supports the semantics of the application domain through a specialized library of combinators, usually written in the host language, although they may also be provided by linkage to a foreign-language library.

Open DSL's are popular with computer scientists, for whom the ability to extend the DSL by writing new combinators has a high value, and for whom the syntactic quirks of the host language and the nuances of its type system present little difficulty. For domain experts who are not computer scientists, the benefits of programming "under the hood" have less attraction and an invitation to interpret an obfuscatory error message can be daunting. Hence, interest in techniques by which closed DSL's can be easily implemented remains high.

We advocate defining the semantics of a closed DSL in terms of a universal set of semantics combinators which form a structure algebra over a suitable domain. The combinator set may include constructors and destructors of algebraic data types. By exchanging the domain of the combinator algebra for a domain of abstract machine states, one automatically derives an implementation of the DSL in terms of byte code instructions for an abstract machine. The correctness of this implementation is proved by showing coherence of the operational, abstract machine semantics with the denotational semantics.

Advantages of this approach are that the "library" of semantics combinators is independent of the particular DSL to be implemented. The effort required to implement a semantics combinator library and to prove its coherence with respect to a denotational semantics can be amortized over

W. Taha (Ed.): SAIG 2000, LNCS 1924, pp. 1–2, 2000.

multiple uses to implement a variety of DSL's. A combinator-based implementation is also amenable to improvement by aggressive, automatic program transformation. Furthermore, the underlying abstract machine can easily be implemented on a new host architecture or via a platform-independent assembly language such as 'C'.

We compare this approach with several other approaches that have been taken to implement DSL's. The design of suitable type systems and intelligible error reporting remains a challenging issue. Users of a DSL are less interested in a programmer's notion of types, which abstract the underlying computational semantics of the DSL, than in types that characterize the crucial abstractions of their application domain.

Refinements and Product Line Architectures
Abstract of Invited Talk

Don Batory

Department of Computer Sciences
University of Texas at Austin, Austin, Texas 78712
batory@cs.utexas.edu

Abstract. Models of software are generally too low level, exposing classes, methods, and objects as the focal point of discourse in software design and implementation. This makes it very difficult, if not impossible, to reason about software architectures (also known as "application designs"); to have simple, elegant, and easy to understand specifications of applications; and to be able to design or critique software designs automatically given a set of high-level requirements.

These problems come to the forefront in the area of product-line architectures. The goal is to build families of related applications from components. Ideally, one should have simple ways to specify a particular application (its design and implementation) and differentiate it from others. It must be possible to reason about an application in terms of its components, in order to differentiate "bad" designs from "good" designs. And it should be possible to optimize designs automatically given a set of constraints. For all this to be possible, it is necessary that components encapsulate individual features that can be shared by many applications in a product-line. Knowing that a component/feature is present (or absent) provides critical knowledge about the behavior of an application. However, expressing individual features as individual components requires a concept of encapsulation that is quite different from that offered by conventional component technologies — e.g., CORBA, COM, and Java Packages.

In this presentation, I will outline a model of software that has been demonstrated in many different domains by several researchers over the last decade. The core ideas are programs are values and building blocks (what others call "components") are functions that take a program as input and produce a new program as output — the new program is the input program with an additional feature. Such functions are refinements; they add new capabilities to a program. Function composition (which corresponds to component composition) follows the age-old precepts of step-wise refinement — the idea of progressively building programs by adding one detail or feature at a time. The difference between our version of step-wise refinement and traditional work is the scale: our refinements impact many classes of an application. Moreover, expressing software design and implementation in this manner is conducive to optimization: applications are modeled as equations, which are compositions of functions. Equation optimization can be accomplished through rewrite rules

W. Taha (Ed.): SAIG 2000, LNCS 1924, pp. 3–4, 2000.

that capture equivalence relationships between interchangeable functions (components).

References

1. Y. Smaragdakis, *Implementing Large-Scale Object-Oriented Components*, Ph.D. dissertation, September 1999, The Department of Computer Sciences, The University of Texas at Austin.
2. D. Batory, C. Johnson, B. MacDonald, and Dale von Heeder, Achieving Extensibility Through Product-Lines and Domain-Specific Languages, In *Proceedings of the Int. Conference on Software Reuse*, Vienna, Austria, 2000.
3. D. Batory and S. O'Malley. The Design and Implementation of Hierarchical Software Systems with Reusable Components, *ACM Trans. Soft. Eng. and Method.*, 1(4):355-398, October 1992.

Reasoning about Staged Computation
Abstract of Invited Talk

Frank Pfenning

Department of Computer Science
Carnegie Mellon University
Pittsburgh PA 15213, USA
fp@cs.cmu.edu,
http://www.cs.cmu.edu/~fp

Abstract. We report on recent progress in the design of modal dependent type theories that integrate specifications into languages for expressing staged computation.

Recently, type systems based on constructive modal logic have been proposed as an expressive basis for run-time code generation [DP96,WLPD98], partial evaluation [Dav96], and general meta-programming [MTBS99,DPS97]. In each case, we obtain a pure λ-calculus via a Curry-Howard correspondence between constructive proofs and functional programs. This is then extended to a full programming language through additions such as general recursion.

In this talk we generalize this approach from simple to dependent types, in essence allowing us to reason about staged computation within a type theory. We follow the methodology of Martin-Löf [ML96], separating judgments from propositions. This has already been applied successfully as a foundation for propositional modal logic [PD00], providing new insights into constructive S4, lax logic [FM97] and the monadic metalanguage [Mog91].

The discipline of the approach brings a number of issues into sharp focus. For example, the choice between intensional and extensional interpretations of modal operators determines the nature of definitional equality and vice versa. Constant and varying domain interpretations of modal logic relate to the question of persistence of code between computation stages and can be unified in the semantic framework. We illustrate these issues by means of examples and report on our current understanding of modal type theories and their meta-theory.

W. Taha (Ed.): SAIG 2000, LNCS 1924, pp. 5–6, 2000.

References

[Dav96]   Rowan Davies. A temporal logic approach to binding-time analysis. In E. Clarke, editor, *Proceedings of the Eleventh Annual Symposium on Logic in Computer Science*, pages 184–195, New Brunswick, New Jersey, July 1996. IEEE Computer Society Press.

[DP96]   Rowan Davies and Frank Pfenning. A modal analysis of staged computation. In Guy Steele, Jr., editor, *Proceedings of the 23rd Annual Symposium on Principles of Programming Languages*, pages 258–270, St. Petersburg Beach, Florida, January 1996. ACM Press.

[DPS97]   Joëlle Despeyroux, Frank Pfenning, and Carsten Schürmann. Primitive recursion for higher-order abstract syntax. In R. Hindley, editor, *Proceedings of the Third International Conference on Typed Lambda Calculus and Applications (TLCA'97)*, pages 147–163, Nancy, France, April 1997. Springer-Verlag LNCS 1210. An extended version is available as Technical Report CMU-CS-96-172, Carnegie Mellon University.

[FM97]   M. Fairtlough and M.V. Mendler. Propositional lax logic. *Information and Computation*, 137(1):1–33, August 1997.

[ML96]   Per Martin-Löf. On the meanings of the logical constants and the justifications of the logical laws. *Nordic Journal of Philosophical Logic*, 1(1):11–60, 1996.

[Mog91]   Eugenio Moggi. Notions of computation and monads. *Information and Computation*, 93(1):55–92, 1991.

[MTBS99]   Eugenio Moggi, Walid Taha, Zine-El-Abidine Benaissa, and Tim Sheard. An idealized MetaML: Simpler, and more expressive. In S. D. Swierstra, editor, *Proceedings of the 8th European Symposium on Programming (ESOP'99)*, pages 193–207, Amsterdam, The Netherlands, March 1999. Springer-Verlag LNCS 1576.

[PD00]   Frank Pfenning and Rowan Davies. A judgmental reconstruction of modal logic. *Mathematical Structures in Computer Science*, 2000. To appear. Notes for an invited talk at the *Workshop on Intuitionistic Modal Logics and Applications* (IMLA'99), Trento, Italy, July 1999.

[WLPD98]   Philip Wickline, Peter Lee, Frank Pfenning, and Rowan Davies. Modal types as staging specifications for run-time code generation. *ACM Computing Surveys*, 30(3es), September 1998.

Specialization of Systems Programs: Lessons and Perspectives
Abstract of Invited Talk

Gilles Muller

IRISA/INRIA
INRIA/IRISA, Campus de Beaulieu, 35042 Rennes, France
Gilles.Muller@irisa.fr

Abstract. Systems programs are often highly generic so as to adapt to changing environement and needs. A conventional way to achieve adaptation consists of structuring systems in terms of modules and layers to enable various functionalities to be added. However, what seems to be an adequate strategy at the design level often leads to performance problems in the implementation.

Program specialization is a technique that consists of adapting a generic program component to a given usage context. Specialization is aimed at evaluating in advance the computations that depend only on the information provided by the usage context. Therefore, this process can lead to considerable performance gains. In the Compose group, we have developed program specializers for C and Java, named Tempo [1,2] and JSpec [6] respectively, that have been specifically targeted to systems programs.

We present three successful experiments in specializing systems programs: the Sun remote procedure call [4,5], a domain-specific language interpreter for active networks [7] and an incremental checkpointer for Java programs [3]. We analyse the structure of these programs and detail the opportunities for specialization. We conclude by drawing lessons for our experiments and by presenting perspectives in using program specialization on systems design.

References

1. C. Consel, L. Hornof, J. Lawall, R. Marlet, G. Muller, J. Noyé, S. Thibault, and N. Volanschi. Tempo: Specializing systems applications and beyond. *ACM Computing Surveys, Symposium on Partial Evaluation*, 30(3), 1998.
2. C. Consel, L. Hornof, F. Noël, J. Noyé, and E.N. Volanschi. A uniform approach for compile-time and run-time specialization. In O. Danvy, R. Glück, and P. Thiemann, editors, *Partial Evaluation, International Seminar, Dagstuhl Castle* , number 1110 in Lecture Notes in Computer Science, pages 54–72, February 1996.
3. J.L. Lawall and G. Muller. Efficient incremental checkpointing of Java programs. In *Proceedings of the International Conference on Dependable Systems and Networks* , pages 61–70, New York, NY, USA, June 2000. IEEE.

W. Taha (Ed.): SAIG 2000, LNCS 1924, pp. 7–8, 2000.

4. G. Muller, R. Marlet, and E.N. Volanschi. Accurate program analyses for successful specialization of legacy system software. *Theoretical Computer Science*, 248(1–2), 2000.
5. G. Muller, R. Marlet, E.N. Volanschi, C. Consel, C. Pu, and A. Goel. Fast, optimized Sun RPC using automatic program specialization. In *Proceedings of the 18th International Conference on Distributed Computing Systems* , pages 240–249, Amsterdam, The Netherlands, May 1998. IEEE Computer Society Press.
6. U. Schultz, J. Lawall, C. Consel, and G. Muller. Towards automatic specialization of Java programs. In *Proceedings of the European Conference on Object-oriented Programming (ECOOP'99)*, volume 1628 of *Lecture Notes in Computer Science*, pages 367–390, Lisbon, Portugal, June 1999.
7. S. Thibault, C. Consel, and G. Muller. Safe and efficient active network programming. In *17th IEEE Symposium on Reliable Distributed Systems* , pages 135–143, West Lafayette, Indiana, October 1998.

Compiling Embedded Languages

Conal Elliott[1], Sigbjørn Finne[1], and Oege de Moor[2]

[1] Microsoft Research
One Microsoft Way, Redmond, WA 98052, USA
[2] Oxford University Computing Laboratory
Wolfson Building, Parks Road, Oxford, OX1 3QD, England

Abstract. Functional languages are particularly well-suited to the implementation of interpreters for domain-specific embedded languages (DSELs). We describe an implemented technique for producing *optimizing compilers* for DSELs, based on Kamin's idea of DSELs for program generation. The technique uses a data type of syntax for basic types, a set of smart constructors that perform rewriting over those types, some code motion transformations, and a back-end code generator. Domain-specific optimization results from chains of rewrites on basic types. New DSELs are defined directly in terms of the basic syntactic types, plus host language functions and tuples. This definition style makes compilers easy to write and, in fact, almost identical to the simplest embedded interpreters. We illustrate this technique with a language *Pan* for the computationally intensive domain of image synthesis and manipulation.

1   Introduction

The "embedded" approach has proved an excellent technique for specifying and prototyping domain-specific languages (DSLs) [8]. The essential idea is to augment a "host" programming language with a domain-specific library. Modern functional host languages are flexible enough that the resulting combination has more the feel of a new language than a library. Most of the work required to design, implement and document a language is inherited from the host language. Often, performance is either relatively unimportant, or is adequate because the domain primitives encapsulate large blocks of work. When speed is of the essence, however, the embedded approach is problematic. It tends to yield inefficient *interpretive* implementations. Worse, these interpreters tend to perform redundant computation.

We have implemented a language *Pan* for image synthesis and manipulation, a computationally demanding problem domain. A straightforward embedded implementation would not perform well enough, but we did not want to incur the expense of introducing an entirely new language. Our solution is to embed an *optimizing compiler* rather than an interpreter. Embedding a compiler requires some techniques not normally needed in embedded language implementations, and we report on these techniques here. Pleasantly, we have been able to retain a simple programming interface, almost unaffected by the compiled nature of

W. Taha (Ed.): SAIG 2000, LNCS 1924, pp. 9–26, 2000.

the implementation. The generated code runs very fast, and there is still much room for improvement.

Our compiler consists of a relatively small set of domain definitions, on top of a larger domain-independent framework. The framework may be adapted for compiling other DSLs, and handles (a) optimization of expressions over numbers and Booleans, (b) code motion, and (c) code generation. A new DSL is specified and implemented by defining the key domain types and operations in terms of the primitive types provided by the framework and host language. Moreover, these definitions are almost identical to what one would write for a very simple interpretive DSL implementation.

Although a user of our embedded language writes in Haskell, we do not have to parse, type-check, or compile Haskell programs. Instead, the user *runs* his/her Haskell program to produce an optimized program in a simple target language that is first-order, call-by-value, and mostly functional. Generated target language programs are then given to a simple compiler (also implemented in Haskell) for code motion and back-end code generation. In this way, the host language (Haskell here) acts as a powerful macro (or *program generator*) language, but is completely out of the picture at run-time. Unlike most macro languages, however, Haskell is statically typed and higher order, and is more expressive and convenient than the underlying target language.

Because of this embedded compiler approach, integration of the DSEL with the host language (Haskell) is not quite as fluid and general as in conventionally implemented DSELs. Some host language features, like lists, recursion, and higher-order functions are not available to the final executing program. These features may be used in source programs, but disappear during the compilation process. For some application areas, this strict separation of features between a full-featured compilation language and a less rich runtime language may be undesirable, but in our domain, at least, it appears to be perfectly acceptable. In fact, we typically write programs without being conscious of the difference.

The contributions of this paper are as follows:

- We present a general technique for implementing embedded *optimizing* compilers, extending Kamin's approach [10] with algebraic manipulation.
- We identify a key problem with the approach, efficient handling of sharing, and present techniques to solve it (bottom-up optimization and common subexpression elimination).
- We illustrate the application of our technique to a demanding problem domain, namely image synthesis and manipulation.

While this paper mainly discusses embedded language compilation, a companion paper goes into more detail for the Pan language [4]. That paper contains many more visual examples, as does [2].

2   Language Embedding

The embedding approach to DSL construction goes back at least to Landin's famous "next 700" paper [12]. The essential idea is to use a single existing "host" programming language that provides useful generic infrastructure (grammar, scoping, typing, function- and data-abstraction, etc), and augment it with a domain-specific vocabulary consisting of one or more data types and functions over those types. Thus the design, implementation, and documentation work required for a new "language" is kept to a minimum, while the result has plenty of room to grow. These merits and some drawbacks are discussed, e.g., in [3,8].

One particularly elegant realization of the embedding idea is the use of a modern functional programming language such as ML or Haskell as the host. In this setting, the domain-specific portions can sometimes be implemented as a simple denotational semantics, as suggested in [11, Section 3]. For example, consider the problem domain of image synthesis and manipulation. A simple semantics for images is function from continuous 2D space to colors. The representation of colors includes blue, green, red, and opacity ("alpha") components:

$$\textbf{type } Image \;=\; Point \;\rightarrow\; Color$$
$$\textbf{type } Point \;\;=\; (Float, Float)$$
$$\textbf{type } Color \;\;=\; (Float, Float, Float, Float)$$

It is easy to implement operations like image overlay (with partial opacity), assuming a corresponding function, $cOver$, on color values:

$$a \text{ `over` } b \;=\; \lambda\, p \;\rightarrow\; a\, p \text{ `cOver` } b\, p$$

Another useful type is spatial transformation, which may be defined simply as a mapping from 2D space to itself:

$$\textbf{type } Transform \;=\; Point \;\rightarrow\; Point$$

This model makes it easy to define some familiar transformations:

$$translate\,(dx,\; dy) \;=\; \lambda\,(x, y) \;\rightarrow\; (x \,+\, dx,\; y \,+\, dy)$$
$$scale\,(sx,\; sy) \;\;\;\;= \;\lambda\,(x, y) \;\rightarrow\; (sx \,*\, x,\; sy \,*\, y)$$
$$rotate\;ang \;\;\;\;\;\;\;\;= \;\lambda\,(x, y) \;\rightarrow\; (x \,*\, c \,-\, y \,*\, s,\; y \,*\, c \,+\, x \,*\, s)$$
$$\quad\textbf{where}$$
$$\quad\quad c \;=\; cos\;ang$$
$$\quad\quad s \;=\; sin\;ang$$

While these definitions can be directly executed as Haskell programs, performance is not good enough for practical use. Our first attempt to cope with this problem was to use the Glasgow Haskell compiler's facility for stating transformations as rewrite rules in source code [15]. Unfortunately, we found that the interaction of such rewrite rules with the general optimizer is hard to predict: in particular, we often wish to inline function definitions that would normally not have been inlined. Furthermore, there are a number of transformations (if-floating, certain array optimizations) that are not easy to state as rewrite rules. We therefore abandoned use of the Haskell compiler, and decided to build a dedicated compiler instead. We will discuss this decision further in Section 10.

3   Embedding a Compiler

In spite of our choice to implement a dedicated compiler, we would like to retain most of the benefits of the embedded approach. We resolve this dilemma by applying Kamin's idea of DSELs for program generation [10]. That is, replace the *values* in our representations by *program fragments* that represent these values. While Kamin used strings to represent program fragments, algebraic data types greatly facilitate our goal of compile-time optimization. For instance, an expression type for *Float* would contain literals, arithmetic operators, and other primitive functions that return *Float*.

> **data** *FloatE* =
>   *LitFloat Float*
> | *AddF FloatE FloatE* | *MulF FloatE FloatE* | ...
> | *Sin FloatE* | *Sqrt FloatE* | ...

We can define expression types *IntE* and *BoolE* similarly.

What about tuples and functions? Following Kamin, we simply adopt the host language's tuple and functions, rather than creating new syntactic representations for them. Since optimization requires inspection, representing functions as functions poses a problem. The solution we use is to extend the base types to support "variables". Then to inspect a function, apply it to a new variable (or tuple of variables as needed), and look at the result.

> **data** *FloatE* = ... | *VarFloat String*   — named variable

These observations lead to a hybrid representation. Our *Image* type will still be represented as a function, but over *syntactic* points, rather than actual ones. Moreover, these syntactic points are represented not as expressions over number pairs, but rather as pairs of expressions over numbers. Similarly for colors. Thus:

> **type** *ImageE*   = *PointE* → *ColorE*
> **type** *TransformE* = *PointE* → *PointE*
> **type** *PointE*   = (*FloatE*, *FloatE*)
> **type** *ColorE*   = (*FloatE*, *FloatE*, *FloatE*, *FloatE*)

The definitions of operations over these types can often be made identical to the ones for the non-expression representation, thanks to overloading. For instance *translate*, *scale*, and *rotate* have precisely the definitions given in Section 2 above. The *meaning* of these definitions, however, is quite different. The arithmetic operators and the functions *cos*, *sin* as well as several others have been overloaded. The *over* function is also defined exactly as before. Only the types *BoolE*, *IntE*, and *FloatE* of expressions over the usual "scalar" value types *Bool*, *Int*, and *Float*, are represented as expressions, using constructors for their primitive operations. Assuming that these base types are adequate, a DSL is just as easy to define and extend as with a simple, non-optimizing embedded interpreter. Otherwise new syntactic types and/or primitive operators may be added.

As an example of how the hybrid technique works in practice, consider rotating by an angle of $\pi/2$. Using the definition of *rotate* plus a bit of simplification on number expressions (*FloatE*), the compiler simplifies *rotate* $(\pi/2)\,(x,y)$ to $(-y, x)$.

Admittedly, the picture might not always be this rosy. For instance, some properties of high-level types require clever or inductive proofs. Formulating these properties as high-level rules would eliminate the need for a generic compiler to rediscover them. So far this has not been a problem for our image manipulation language, but we expect that for more substantial applications, it may be necessary to layer the compilation into a number of distinct abstract levels. In higher levels, domain types and operators like *Image* and *over* would be treated as opaque and rewritten according to domain-specific rules, while in lower levels, they would be seen as defined and expanded in terms of simpler types like *Point* and *Color*. Those simpler types would themselves be expanded at lower levels of abstraction.

4   Inlining and the Sharing Problem

The style of embedding described above has the effect of *inlining* all definitions, and β-reducing resulting function applications, before simplification. This inlining is beneficial in that it creates many opportunities for rewriting. A resulting problem, however, is that uncontrolled inlining often causes a great deal of code replication. To appreciate this problem, consider the following example spatial transform. It rotates each point about the origin, through an angle proportional to the point's distance from the origin. The parameter r is the distance at which an entire revolution (2π radians) is made.

$$swirling \;::\; FloatE \;\rightarrow\; TransformE$$
$$swirling\;r \;=\; \lambda\,p \;\rightarrow\; rotate\,(distO\;p \,*\, (2\,\pi\,/\,r))\;p$$

$$distO \;::\; PointE \;\rightarrow\; FloatE$$
$$distO\,(x, y) \;=\; sqrt\,(x \,*\, x \,+\, y \,*\, y)$$

Evaluating *swirling* $r\,(x, y)$ yields an expression with much redundancy.

$$\begin{aligned}
(\; & x \,*\, cos\,(sqrt\,(x \,*\, x \,+\, y \,*\, y) \,*\, 2\,\pi\,/\,r) \\
  - \;& y \,*\, sin\,(sqrt\,(x \,*\, x \,+\, y \,*\, y) \,*\, 2\,\pi\,/\,r) \\
, \;\; & y \,*\, cos\,(sqrt\,(x \,*\, x \,+\, y \,*\, y) \,*\, 2\,\pi\,/\,r) \\
  + \;& x \,*\, sin\,(sqrt\,(x \,*\, x \,+\, y \,*\, y) \,*\, 2\,\pi\,/\,r)\;)
\end{aligned}$$

The problem here is that *rotate* uses its argument four times (twice via each of *cos* and *sin*) in constructing its results. Thus expressions passed to *rotate* get replicated in the output. In our experience with Pan, the trees resulting from inlining and simplification tend to be enormous, compared to their underlying representation as graphs. If *swirling r* were composed with *scale* (u, v) before being applied to (x, y), the two multiplications due to *scale* would each be appear twice in the argument to *sqrt*, and hence eight times in the final result.

In an interpretive implementation, we would have to take care not to evaluate shared expressions redundantly. Memoization is a reasonable way to avoid such redundance. For a compiler, memoization is not adequate, because it must produce an external representation that captures the sharing. What we really want is to generate local definitions when helpful. To produce these local definitions, our compiler performs common subexpression elimination (CSE), as described briefly in Section 8 and in more detail in [5].

5   Static Typing

Should there be one expression data type per value type (*Int*, *Float*, *Bool*, etc) as suggested above, or one for all value types? Separate expression types make the implementation more statically typed, and thus prevent many bugs in implementation and use. Unfortunately, they also lead to redundance for variables, binding, and polymorphically and overloaded expression operators (e.g., if-then-else and addition, respectively), as well as polymorphic compiler-internal operations on terms (e.g., substitution and CSE).

Instead, we use a single all-encompassing expression data type *DExp* of "dynamically typed expressions":

data *DExp* =
    LitInt Int | *LitFloat Float* | *LitBool Bool*
    | *Var Id Type* | *Let Id Type DExp* | *If DExp DExp DExp*
    | *Add DExp DExp* | *Mul DExp DExp* | ...
    | *Sin DExp* | *Sqrt DExp* | ...
    | *Or DExp DExp* | *And DExp DExp* | *Not DExp* | ...

It is unfortunate that the choice of a single *DExp* type means that one cannot simply add another module containing a new primitive type and its constructors and rewrite rules. For now we are willing to accept this limitation, but future work may suggest improvements.

The *DExp* representation removes redundance from representation and supporting code, but loses type safety. To combine advantages of both approaches, we augment the dynamically typed representation with the technique of "phantom types" [13]. The idea is to define a type constructor (*Exp* below) whose parameter is not used, and then to restrict types of some functions to applications of the type constructor. For convenience, define abbreviations for the three supported types as well:

data *Exp* α = *E DExp*

type *BoolE* = *Exp Bool*
type *IntE*   = *Exp Int*
type *FloatE* = *Exp Float*

For static typing, it is vital that $Exp\ \alpha$ be a new type, rather than just a type synonym of $DExp$.

Statically typed functions are conveniently defined via the following functionals, where typ_n turns an n-ary $DExp$ function into an n-ary Exp function.

$$typ_1 :: (DExp \to DExp) \to (Exp\ a \to Exp\ b)$$
$$typ_2 :: (DExp \to DExp \to DExp) \to (Exp\ a \to Exp\ b \to Exp\ c)$$

$$typ_1\ f\ (E\ e_1) \qquad\quad = E\ (f\ e_1)$$
$$typ_2\ f\ (E\ e_1)\ (E\ e_2) = E\ (f\ e_1\ e_2)$$

and so on for typ_3, typ_4, etc. The type-safe friendly names $+$, $*$, etc., come from applications of these static typing functionals in type class instances:

instance $Num\ IntE$
   where
      $(+) \qquad\quad = typ_2\ Add$
      $(*) \qquad\qquad = typ_2\ Mul$
      $negate \qquad = typ_1\ Negate$
      $fromInteger = E\ .\ LitInt\ .\ fromInteger$

Type constraints inherited from the Num class ensure that the newly defined functions be applied only to Int expressions and result in Int expressions. For instance, here

$$(+) :: IntE \to IntE \to IntE$$

The important point here is that we do not rely on type inference, which would deduce too general a type for functions like "$+$" on Exp values. Instead we state restricted type signatures.

Other definitions provide a convenient and type-safe primitive vocabulary for $FloatE$. Unfortunately, the $Bool$ type is wired into the signatures of operations like $\geq$ and $||$. Pan therefore provides alternative names ending in a distinguished character, which is "E" for alphanumeric names (e.g., "$notE$") and "$*$" for non-alphanumeric names (e.g., "$<*$").

6 Algebraic Optimization and Smart Constructors

An early Pan implementation was based on the Mag program transformation system [1]. Generation in this implementation was much too slow, mainly because Mag redundantly rewrote shared subterms. To avoid this problem, we now do all optimization *bottom-up*, as part of the construction of expressions. Then the host language's evaluate-once operational semantics prevents redundant optimization. Non-optimized expressions are never constructed. The main drawback is that optimization is context-free. (An optimization can, however, delve arbitrarily far into an argument term.)

— Type-safe smart constructor
$(\&\&*) :: BoolE \rightarrow BoolE \rightarrow BoolE$
$(\&\&*) = typ_2\ andD$

— Non-type-safe smart constructor
$andD :: DExp \rightarrow DExp \rightarrow DExp$
— Constant folding
$andD\ (LitBool\ a)\ (LitBool\ b)\ =\ LitBool\ (a\ \&\&\ b)$
— If-floating
$andD\ (If\ c\ a\ b)\ e_2\ =\ ifD\ c\ (andD\ a\ e_2)\ (andD\ b\ e_2)$
$andD\ e_1\ (If\ c\ a\ b)\ =\ ifD\ c\ (andD\ e_1\ a)\ (andD\ e_1\ b)$
— Cancellation rules
$andD\ e\ (LitBool\ False)\ =\ false$
$andD\ (LitBool\ False)\ e\ =\ false$
$andD\ e\ (LitBool\ True)\ \ =\ e$
$andD\ (LitBool\ True)\ e\ \ =\ e$
— Others
$andD\ (Not\ e)\ (Not\ e')\ \ \ \ =\ notE\ (e\ ||*\ e')$
$andD\ e\ e'\ |\ e\ ==\ e'\ \ \ \ =\ e$
$andD\ e\ e'\ |\ e\ ==\ notE\ e'\ =\ false$
— Finally, the data type constructor
$andD\ e\ e'\ =\ And\ e\ e'$

Fig. 1. Simplification Rules for Conjunction

Optimization is packaged up in "smart constructors", each of which accomplishes the following:

– constant-folding;
– if-floating;
– constructor-specific rewrites such as identities and cancellation rules;
– data type constructor application when no optimizations apply; and
– providing a statically typed interface.

As an example, Figure 1 shows a smart constructor for conjunction over expressions. In fact, because all smart constructors perform constant folding and if-floating, the real definition is more factored, but it does the same work.

Because if-then-else is not overloadable, Pan uses *ifE* for syntactic conditionals, based on an underlying dynamically typed *ifD*.

$ifD :: DExp \rightarrow DExp \rightarrow DExp \rightarrow DExp$

$ifD\ (LitBool\ True\ )\ a\ b\ =\ a$
$ifD\ (LitBool\ False)\ a\ b\ =\ b$
$ifD\ (Not\ c)\ a\ b\ \ \ \ \ \ \ \ \ =\ ifD\ c\ b\ a$
$ifD\ (If\ c\ d\ e)\ a\ b\ \ \ \ \ \ =\ ifD\ c\ (ifD\ d\ a\ b)\ (ifD\ e\ a\ b)$
$ifD\ c\ a\ b\ \ \ \ \ \ \ \ \ \ \ \ \ \ =\ ifZ\ c\ a\ b$

The function *ifZ* simplifies redundant or impossible conditions.

The statically typed *ifE* function is overloaded.

class *Syntactic a* **where** *ifE* :: *BoolE* → *a* → *a* → *a*

instance *Syntactic* (*Exp a*) **where** *ifE* = *typ₃ ifD*

Other overloadings include functions and tuples. In the latter case, conditions are pushed downward. Later when the resulting tuple is consumed to form a single (scalar-valued) expression, if-floating typically causes the redundant conditions to float, to form a cascade of redundant conditionals, which are coalesced by *ifZ*.

As an example of if-floating, consider the following example (given in familiar concrete syntax, for clarity):

sin ((**if** *x* < 0 **then** 0 **else** *x*) / 2)

If-floating without simplification would yield

if *x* < 0 **then** *sin*(0/2) **else** *sin*(*a*/2)

Replacement followed by two constant foldings (0/2 and *sin* 0) results in

if *x* < 0 **then** 0 **else** *sin*(*a*/2)

If-floating causes code replication, sometimes a great deal of it. CSE factors out the "first-order" replication, i.e., multiple occurrences of expressions, as with e_2 for the first if-floating clause in Figure 1. There is also a *second-order* replication going on, as seen above before simplification. The context *sin* (•/ 2) appears twice. Fortunately for this example, one instance of this context simplifies to 0. In other cases, there may be little or no simplification. We will return to this issue in Section 10.

We should stress at this point that we intend the algebraic optimizations to be *refinements*: upon evaluation, the optimized version of an expression *e* should yield the same value as *e* *whenever evaluation of e terminates*. It is possible, however, for simplified version to yield a well-defined result when *e* does not. This could happen for example when a boolean expression *e* &&∗ *false* would raise a division-by-zero exception, while the simplified version would instead evaluate to *false*.

7 Adding Context

More optimization becomes possible when the usage context of a DSL computation becomes visible to the compiler. For instance, after composing an image, a user generally wants to display it in a window. The representation of images as *PointE* → *ColorE* suggests iteratively sampling at a finite grid of pixel locations, converting each pixel color to an integer for the display device. (For a faithful presentation, images need to be antialiased, but that topic is beyond

```
type TimeE  =  FloatE
type Anim  =  TimeE  →  ImageE
type DisplayFun  =  TimeE  →  VTrans  →  VSize  →  IntE  →  ActionE
type VSize  =  (IntE, IntE)    — view size: width & height in pixels
type VTrans  =  (FloatE, FloatE, FloatE)    — view transform: pan XY, zoom


display :: Anim  →  DisplayFun
display anim  =  λ t (panX, panY, zoom) (w, h) output  →
  loop h (λ j  →
    loop w (λ i  →
      setInt (output + 4 ∗ (j ∗ w + i)) (
        toBGR24 (
          anim t (
            zoom ∗ i2f (i − w 'div' 2) + panX,
            zoom ∗ i2f (j − h 'div' 2) + panY )))))
```

Fig. 2. Animation Display Function

the scope of the present paper and not yet addressed in our implementation.)
Our first Pan compiler implementation took this approach, that is it generated
machine code for a function that maps a pixel location to a 32-bit color encoding. While this version was much faster than an interpretive implementation,
its efficiency was not satisfactory. For one thing, it requires a function call per
pixel. More seriously, it prevent any optimization across several pixels or rows
of pixels.

To address the shortcomings of the first compiler, we made visible to the
optimizer the two-dimensional iteration that samples and stores pixel values. In
fact, to get more use out of compilation, we decided to compile the display of
not simply static images, but animations, represented as functions from time
to image. (We go even further, generating code for nearly arbitrarily parameterized images, with automatic generation of user interfaces for the run-time
parameters.)

The main function *display*, defined in Figure 2, converts an animation into a
"display function" that is to be invoked just once per frame. A display function
consumes a time, window size, viewing transform (zoom factor and *XY* pan),
and a pointer to an output pixel array. It is the job of the viewer to come up
with all these parameters and pass them into the display function code.

The critical point here is that (a) the *display* function is expressed in the
embedded language, and (b) *display* is applied to its *anim* parameter (of type
TimeE → *Image*) at *compile time*. This compile-time application allows the
code for *display* and *anim* to be combined and optimized, and lets some computations be moved outside of the inner or outer loop. (In fact, our compiler goes

further, allowing focused recomputations when only some display parameters change, thanks to a simple dependency analysis.)

The *ActionE* type represents an action that yields no value, much like Haskell's type *IO* (). It is supported by a small number of *DExp* constructors and corresponding statically typed, optimizing wrapper functions. The first takes an address (represented as an integer) and an integer value, and it performs the corresponding assignment. The second is like a for-loop. It takes an upper bound, and a loop body that is a function from the loop variable to an action. The loop body is executed for every value from zero up to (but not including) the upper bound.

$$setInt \ :: \ IntE \ \to \ IntE \ \to \ ActionE$$
$$loop \ \ :: \ IntE \ \to \ (IntE \ \to \ ActionE) \ \to \ ActionE$$

According to *display*, a generated display function will loop over Y and X, and set the appropriate member of its output array to a 32-bit (thus multiplication by four) color value. Aside from calculating the destination memory address, the inner loop body samples the animation at the given time and position. The spatial sampling point is computed from the loop indices by placing the image's origin in the center of the window (thus the subtraction of half the window width or height) and then applying the user-specified dynamic zoom and pan (using *i2f* for int-to-float conversion). In fact, the optimized code is much more efficient, thanks to code motion techniques described briefly in Section 8 and illustrated in Appendix A.

8   Code Motion and Code Generation

Once context is added and all of the above optimizations have been applied, the result is an expression tree (of type *DExp*). As explained in Section 4, this tree contains a great deal of sharing, mostly because of the inlining and rewriting process. The next step in compilation is to make the sharing structure explicit using let-bindings, i.e., performing a common subexpression elimination (CSE). Another very important form of code motion is hoisting evaluation out of loops when independent of the loop variable. Finally, we also sometimes synthesize arrays of values that depend on an inner loop variable but not an outer one. For details see [5], where some subtle strictness issues are also discussed.

Having performed code motion and loop hoisting, we are in good shape to start generating some code. The output of the code motion pass could either be interpreted or compiled, but we choose to compile. The resulting *DExp* is converted into a C function. This translation is reasonably straightforward, but requires a little bit of care in places, to account for the fact that C does not have expression level variable binding support or array initialization. The generated C code is then compiled and linked into a viewer that displays the specified image effect.

9   Related Work

There are many other examples of embedded DSLs, for music, two- and three-dimensional geometry, animation, hardware design, document manipulation, and many other domains. See [8] for an overview and references. In almost all cases, the implementations were interpretive. Several characteristics of functional programming languages that lend themselves toward the role of host language are enumerated in [3].

Kamin's work on embedded languages for program generation is in the same spirit as our own [10]. As in our approach, Kamin uses host language functions and tuples to represent the embedded language's functions and tuples, and he uses overloading so that the generators look like the code they are generating. His applications use a functional host language (ML) and generate imperative programs. The main difference is that Kamin did not perform optimization or CSE. Both would be difficult, given his choice of strings to represent programs.

Leijen and Meijer's HaskellDB [13] provides an embedded language for database queries and an implementation that compiles search specifications into optimized SQL query strings for further processing. After trying several unsuccessful designs, we imitated their use of an untyped algebraic data type and a phantom type wrapper for type-safety.

Our approach to compiling embedded languages can be regarded as an instance of *partial evaluation*, which has a considerable literature (see, e.g., [7,9]). In this light, our compiler is a handwritten *cogen* (as opposed to one generated automatically through self-application). The main contrasting characteristic of our work is the embedding in a strongly typed meta-language (Haskell). This embedding makes particular use of Haskell type-class-based overloading so that the concrete syntax of meta-programs is almost identical to that of object-programs, and it achieves inlining for free (perhaps too much of it). It also exploits meta-language type inference to perform object-language type inference (except on the optimization rules, which are expressed at the type-unsafe level). Another closely related methodology is multi-stage programming with explicit annotations, as supported by MetaML [14], a polymorphic statically typed meta-language for ML-style programs.

FFTW is a successful, portable C library for computing discrete Fourier transforms of varying dimensions and sizes [6]. Its numerical procedures are generated by a special purpose compiler, *fftgen*, written in Objective Caml and are better in almost all cases than previously existing libraries. The compiler has some of the same features as our own, performing some algebraic simplification and CSE. One small technical difference is that, while fftgen does memoized simplification, our compiler does bottom-up simplifying construction. It appears that the results are the same. Because the application domain is so specialized, fftgen is more focused than our compiler.

Veldhuizen and others have been using advanced C++ programming techniques to embed a simple functional language into C++ *types* [16,17]. Functional evaluation is done by the C++ compiler during type-checking and template instantiation. Code fragments specified in inlined static methods are chosen and combined at compile-time to produce specialized, optimized low-level code.

10   Future Work

More efficient and powerful rewriting. Our optimizer uses a simple syntactic approach to rewriting. To obtain better results, rewriting and CSE should make use of associative-commutative (AC) matching and comparison, respectively, while still exploiting representation sharing, which is critical for compile-time efficiency.

CSE cleans up after inlining, recapturing what sharing still remains after rewriting. However, where inlining does *higher-order* substitution (in the case of functions), CSE is only first-order, so higher-order redundancy remains. Ideally, inlining, if-floating, and CSE would all work cooperatively and efficiently with rewriting. Inlining and if-floating would happen only where rewarded with additional rewrites. Fundamentally, this cooperation seems precluded by the embedded nature of the language implementation, which forces full inlining as the first step, before the DSEL compiler gets to look at the representation.

Invisible compilation. The techniques described in this paper turn compositional specifications into efficient implementations. Image editing applications also allow non-programmers to manipulate images by composing operations. Imagine that such an application were to use abstract syntax trees as its internal editable representation and invisibly invoke an incremental optimizing compiler in response to the user's actions. Then a conventional point-and-click user interface would serve as a "gestural concrete syntax". The display representation would then be one or more bitmaps augmented by custom-generated machine code.

Embeddable Compilation. By embedding our language in Haskell, we were able to save some of the work of compiler implementation, namely lexing, parsing, type checking, supporting generic scalar types, functions and tuples. However, it should be possible to eliminate still more of the work. Suppose that the host language's compiler were extended with optimization rules so that it could work much like the one described in this paper. We tried precisely this approach with GHC [15], with partial success. The main obstacle was that the compiler was too conservative about inlining and rewriting. It takes care never to slow down a program, whereas we have found that it is worth taking some backward steps in order to end up with a fast program in the end. Because we do not (yet) work with recursively defined images, laziness in a host language appears not to be vital in this case. It might be worthwhile to try the exercise with an ML compiler.

11   Conclusions

Embedding is an easy way to design and implement DSLs, inheriting many benefits from a suitable host language. Most such implementations tend to be interpretive, and so are too slow for computationally intensive domains like interactive image processing. Building on ideas from Kamin and from Leijen and Meijer, we have shown how to replace embedded interpreters with optimizing compilers, by using a set of syntax-manipulating base types. The result is much better performance with a very small impact on the languages. Moreover, given a reusable DSL compiler framework such as we have implemented, an embedded DSL interpreter can be turned into a compiler with very small changes (thanks to overloading). In our Pan compiler, the rewriting-based optimizations helped speed considerably, as of course does eliminating the considerable overhead imposed by interpretative implementation.

We have produced many examples with our compiler, as may be seen in [2,4], but more work is needed to make the compiler itself fast and producing even better code. We hope that the compiler's speed can be improved to the point of invisibility so that it can be used by non-programmers in image editors.

Acknowledgements

Brian Guenter originally suggested to us the idea of an optimizing compiler for image processing, and has collaborated on the project. Erik Meijer helped to sort out the many representation possibilities and suggested the approach that we now use.

References

1. Oege de Moor and Ganesh Sittampalam. Generic program transformation. In *Proceedings of the third International Summer School on Advanced Functional Programming*, Springer Lecture Notes in Computer Science, 1999. `http://users.comlab.ox.ac.uk/oege.demoor/papers/braga.ps.gz`.
2. Conal Elliott. A Pan image gallery. `http://research.microsoft.com/~conal/pan/Gallery`.
3. Conal Elliott. An embedded modeling language approach to interactive 3D and multimedia animation. *IEEE Transactions on Software Engineering*, 25(3):291–308, May/June 1999. Special Section: Domain-Specific Languages (DSL). `http://research.microsoft.com/~conal/papers/tse-modeled-animation`.
4. Conal Elliott. Functional images, unpublished, March 2000. `http://research.microsoft.com/~conal/papers/fip`.
5. Conal Elliott, Sigbjørn Finne, and Oege de Moor. Compiling embedded languages (extended version). Technical report, Microsoft Research, May 2000. `http://research.microsoft.com/scripts/pubs/view.asp?TR_ID=MSR-TR-2000-52`.
6. Matteo Frigo. A fast Fourier transform compiler. In *Proceedings of the ACM SIGPLAN'99 Conference on Programming Language Design and Implementation*, pages 169–180, 1999. `http://www.acm.org/pubs/articles/proceedings/pldi/301618/p169-frigo/p169-frigo.pdf`.
7. John Hatcliff, Torben Mogensen, and Peter Thiemann, editors. *Partial Evaluation: Practice and Theory*, volume 1706. Springer-Verlag, 1999.

8. Paul Hudak. Modular domain specific languages and tools. In P. Devanbu and J. Poulin, editors, *Proceedings: Fifth International Conference on Software Reuse*, pages 134–142. IEEE Computer Society Press, 1998.

9. Neil D. Jones, Carsten K. Gomard, and Peter Sestoft. *Partial Evaluation and Automatic Program Generation*. Prentice Hall International, International Series in Computer Science, June 1993. `http://www.dina.kvl.dk/~sestoft/pebook/pebook.html`.

10. Samuel Kamin. Standard ML as a meta-programming language. Technical report, University of Illinois at Urbana-Champaign, September 1996. `http://www-sal.cs.uiuc.edu/~kamin/pubs/ml-meta.ps`.

11. Samuel Kamin and David Hyatt. A special-purpose language for picture-drawing. In USENIX, editor, *Proceedings of the Conference on Domain-Specific Languages, October 15–17, 1997, Santa Barbara, California*, pages 297–310, 1997. `http://www-sal.cs.uiuc.edu/~kamin/fpic/doc/fpic-paper.ps`.

12. Peter J. Landin. The next 700 programming languages. *Communications of the ACM*, 9(3):157–164, March 1966. Originally presented at the Proceedings of the ACM Programming Language and Pragmatics Conference, August 8–12, 1965.

13. Daan Leijen and Erik Meijer. Domain specific embedded compilers. In *2nd Conference on Domain-Specific Languages (DSL)*, Austin TX, USA, October 1999. USENIX. `http://www.cs.uu.nl/people/daan/papers/dsec.ps`.

14. Walid Taha and Tim Sheard. MetaML and multi-stage programming with explicit annotations. *Journal of Theoretical Computer Science*, 2000. To appear. `http://www.cs.chalmers.se/~taha/publications/journal/tcs00.ps`.

15. GHC Team. The Glasgow Haskell compiler. `http://haskell.org/ghc`.

16. Todd Veldhuizen. Expression templates. *C++ Report*, 7(5):26–31, June 1995. `http://extreme.indiana.edu/~tveldhui/papers/pepm99.ps`. Reprinted in *C++ Gems*, ed. Stanley Lippman.

17. Todd Veldhuizen. C++ templates as partial evaluation. In *Workshop on Partial Evaluation and Semantics-Based Program Manipulation (PEPM'99)*. ACM Sigplan, 1999. `http://extreme.indiana.edu/~tveldhui/papers/pepm99.ps`.

A   Optimization Example

To illustrate the compilation techniques described in this paper, Figure 3 shows snapshots of a sample animation whose specification and supporting definitions are given in Figure 4. Note that *ImageE* is really a type *constructor*, parameterized over the "pixel" type. Visual images have type *ImageE ColorE*, while what one might call "regions" have type *ImageE BoolE*.

As a building block, *checker* is a Boolean image checker that alternates between true and false on a one-pixel checkerboard. The trick is to convert the pixel coordinates from floating point to integer (using the floor function) and test whether the sum is even or odd.

The *checkerBoard* image function takes a square size s and two colors c_1 and c_2. It chooses between the given colors, depending on whether the input point, scaled down by s falls into a true or false square of *checker*.

To finish the example, *swirlBoard* swirls a black and white checker board, using the *swirling* function defined in Section 4.

Fig. 3. Snapshots of *swirlBoard*, Defined in Figure 4

$swirlBoard :: TimeE \rightarrow ImageE\ ColorE$
$swirlBoard\ t\ =\ swirl\ (100 * tan\ t)\ (checkerBoard\ 10\ black\ white)$

$swirl :: Syntactic\ c \Rightarrow FloatE \rightarrow ImageE\ c \rightarrow ImageE\ c$
$swirl\ r\ im\ =\ im\ .\ swirling\ r$ — Image swirling function

$checker :: ImageE\ BoolE$ — Unit square boolean checker board
$checker\ =\ \lambda\,(x, y) \rightarrow evenE\,(\lfloor x \rfloor + \lfloor y \rfloor)$

$checkerBoard :: FloatE \rightarrow \alpha \rightarrow \alpha \rightarrow ImageE\ \alpha$
$checkerBoard\ sqSize\ c_1\ c_2\ =$
  $ustretch\ sqSize\,(cond\ checker\,(const\ c_1)\,(const\ c_2))$

— Some useful Pan functions:

$cond :: Syntactic\ a \Rightarrow BoolE \rightarrow Exp\ a \rightarrow Exp\ a \rightarrow Exp\ a$
$cond\ =\ lift_3\ ifE$ — pointwise conditional
— uniform image stretch
$ustretch :: Syntactic\ c \Rightarrow FloatE \rightarrow ImageE\ c \rightarrow ImageE\ c$
$ustretch\ s\ im\ =\ im\ .\ scale\,(1/s, 1/s)$

Fig. 4. Definitions for Figure 3

$\lambda\, t\ (panX, panY, zoom)\ (width, height)\ output\ \rightarrow$
$loop\ height\ (\lambda\, j\ \rightarrow$
$\quad loop\ width\ (\lambda\, i\ \rightarrow$
$\qquad \mathbf{let}$
$\qquad\quad a\ =\ 2\,\pi\ /\ (100\ *\ sin\ t\ /\ cos\ t)$
$\qquad\quad b\ =\ -(height\ `div`\ 2)$
$\qquad\quad c\ =\ zoom\ *\ i2f\ (j\ +\ b)\ +\ panY$
$\qquad\quad d\ =\ c\ *\ c$
$\qquad\quad e\ =\ -(width\ `div`\ 2)$
$\qquad\quad f\ =\ zoom\ *\ i2f\ (i\ +\ e)\ +\ panX$
$\qquad\quad g\ =\ sqrt\ (f\ *\ f\ +\ d)\ *\ a$
$\qquad\quad h\ =\ sin\ g$
$\qquad\quad k\ =\ cos\ g$
$\qquad\quad m\ =\ 1\ /\ 10$
$\qquad\quad n\ =\ m\ *\ (c\ *\ k\ +\ f\ *\ h)$
$\qquad\quad p\ =\ m\ *\ (f\ *\ k\ -\ c\ *\ h)$
$\qquad\quad q\ =\ \mathbf{if}\ (\lfloor p \rfloor\ +\ \lfloor n \rfloor)\,.\&.\,1\ ==\ 0\ \mathbf{then}$
$\qquad\qquad\qquad 0$
$\qquad\qquad\quad \mathbf{else}$
$\qquad\qquad\qquad 1$
$\qquad\quad r\ =\ \lfloor q\ *\ 255 \rfloor$
$\qquad\quad s\ =\ 0\ <\!<\!<\ 8$
$\qquad\quad u\ =\ output\ +\ 4\ *\ j\ *\ width$
$\qquad \mathbf{in}$
$\qquad setInt\ (u\ +\ 4\ *\ i)$
$\qquad\qquad (((s\,.|.\,r)\ <\!<\!<\ 8\,.|.\,r)\ <\!<\!<\ 8\,.|.\,r)))$

Fig. 5. Inlined, Unoptimized Code for Figure 4

As a relatively simple example of compilation, Figure 5 shows the result of *display swirlBoard* after inlining definitions and performing CSE, but without optimization.

Simplification involves application of a few dozen rewrite rules, together with constant folding, if-floating, and code motion. The result for our example is shown in Figure 6.

Note how the CSE, scalar hoisting, and array promotion have produced three phases of computation. The first block is calculated once per frame of the displayed animation, the second once per line, and the third once per pixel. As an example of the potential benefit of AC-based code motion, note that in the definition of n in Figure 6, the compiler failed to hoist the expression $e * 6.28319$. The reason is simply that the products are left-associated, so this hoisting candidate is not recognized as a sub-expression.

```
λ t (panX, panY, zoom) (width, height) output →
let
   a  =  −(width 'div' 2)
   b  =  mkArr width (λ c → zoom ∗ i2f (c + a) + panX)
   d  =  −(height 'div' 2)
   e  =  recip (sin t / cos t ∗ 100.0)
in
loop height (λ j →
   let
      f  =  j ∗ width
      g  =  zoom ∗ i2f (j + d) + panY
      h  =  g ∗ g
   in
   loop width (λ i →
      let
         k  =  (f + i) ∗ 4 + output
         m  =  readArr b i
         n  =  sqrt (m ∗ m + h) ∗ e ∗ 6.28319
         p  =  sin n
         q  =  cos n
         r  =  g ∗ q + m ∗ p
         s  =  m ∗ q + g ∗ −p
      in
      if (⌊s ∗ 0.1⌋ + ⌊r ∗ 0.1⌋) .&. 1 == 0 then
         setInt k  0
      else
         setInt k  16777215))
```

Fig. 6. Optimized Version of Code from Figure 5

Lightweight and Generative Components II: Binary-Level Components

Sam Kamin*, Miranda Callahan, and Lars Clausen

Computer Science Department
University of Illinois at Urbana-Champaign
Urbana, IL 61801
{s-kamin,lrclause,mcallaha}@uiuc.edu

Abstract. Most software component technologies fail to account for *lightweight* components (those for which a function call is too inefficient or semantically inappropriate) or *generative* components (those in which the component embodies a *method* of constructing code rather than actual code). Macro-based systems such as the C++ Standard Template Library are exceptions. They, however, have the disadvantage that components must be delivered largely in source form. In this paper, we present a component technology in which lightweight and generative components can be delivered in binary form. The technology is conceptually simple and is easily implemented with existing programming languages. Our basic idea was explained in part I of this paper: By giving a *compositional* semantics for a source language in a domain of meanings *Code*, components can be *written* in the form of macros, but *communicated* in terms of meanings. In the companion paper, we showed how higher-order values over *Code* can be used to write lightweight, generative components. There, we took *Code* to be `string`, so our components amounted to higher-order macros. In this paper, we define *Code* more abstractly, allowing components to be delivered in a form that does not resemble syntax, yet allows for them to be loaded dynamically and execute efficiently.

1 Introduction

The ideal software component technology would automate the use of common programming idioms. It would admit both lightweight components — those for which a function call is too inefficient or semantically inappropriate — and *generative* components — those in which the component embodies a *method* of constructing code rather than actual code. At the same time, its use would be as efficient and non-bureaucratic as subroutine libraries.

Perhaps the closest approach to this ideal is the C++ standard template library (STL), which "provides reusable, interchangeable, components adaptable to many different uses without sacrificing efficiency" [13, back cover text]. The

---

* Partial support for the first and third authors was received from NSF under grant CCR-9619644.

W. Taha (Ed.): SAIG 2000, LNCS 1924, pp. 28–49, 2000.

remarkable feature of the STL is that a single client program, with no change except to invoke one or another implementation of a given type of component, can yield two very different binaries: for one implementation, it might invoke a set of subroutines, as in traditional component technologies; for another, it might create in-line code with no subroutine calls at all (what we have referred to as "lightweight" components). The present paper describes a component technology that has this same feature, plus one more: components are delivered as binaries.

The ability to deliver components in binary is important for several reasons. One is the well-known unwillingness of many individuals and organizations to deliver source code. Another is that source code components introduce extra compilation cost (STL is an example of this). The most important reason is that binaries tend to be simpler and less bureaucratic to use, probably because their execution environment is more stable. The STL is the exception that proves the rule: After the STL was first introduced, it took several years before all the major C++ compilers were able to compile it. The problem is fundamental because it is *non*-technical. In principle, we could all agree once and for all on the definition of C++ and its pre-processor, and write components to that definition. In practice, we never can. However, we can — or rather, must — agree on basic conventions for using machine-language components.

Note that in referring to "source code," we include abstract syntax trees. These are more abstract than source code itself, but still subject to the objections raised in the previous paragraph. ¿From our point of view, AST representations are still too concrete.

How, then, can we write generative components without manipulating any concrete version of the source code? How, for example, can we substitute arguments to functions into the functions themselves (perform "inlining")? The answer is that, by using a *compositional* semantic map — in which the meaning of any structured fragment is a function of the meanings of its constituents — we can replace *textual substitution* by *abstraction* and *application*. Suppose component C needs to obtain an integer n from the client, after which it can generate code that is especially efficient for problems of size n. If C were a macro, we would substitute a number, say 100, into C and compile the result. On the other hand, if the language has a compositional semantic function $[\![\cdot]\!]$, then we can create a representation of the function $F = \lambda n.[\![C[n]]\!]$ and send that representation to the client. The client would then perform the application $F[\![100]\!]$, obtaining a value that can be compiled and executed. In fact, if we choose the semantic domain carefully, this compilation process can be made very simple.

All that is required to make this work is an appropriate semantic domain, which we will call *Code*, a compositional semantics $[\![\cdot]\!]$:*Source* $\rightarrow$ *Code*, and a function *compile* from *Code* to machine language. In this framework, a *component* is any value that somehow includes *Code*; we have found that *higher-order values*, such as functions from *Code* to *Code*, are particularly useful. A *client* is simply a function from a component to *Code*. In a companion paper [11], we have argued that a functional *meta-language* augmented with a *Code* type representing the meanings of program fragments in a conventional *object language*, provides a convenient notation for expressing component and client values. The component is written as a higher-order value over *Code*; the client is a function of type *ComponentType* → *Code*; the loader applies the client to the component, converts the resulting value of type *Code* to machine language, and executes that machine language. That is — and this is the fundamental idea of this approach — *the loader is essentially an evaluator of meta-language expressions of type Code.*

What, then, is an appropriate definition of the domain *Code*? Roughly speaking, in this paper we use

$$Code \ = \ Env \ \rightarrow \ (MachineLanguage \ \times \ Env)$$

where *Env* provides the types and locations of variables. The conversion from *Code* to executable is now very simple: apply the *Code* value to an initial environment and then extract the first element of the resulting pair. Components are compiled to *Code* values on the server — that is, they are the binaries compiled from meta-language expressions of type *Code* — and the conversion to machine language is performed by the loader after applying the client to the component. Figure 1 illustrates this idea for a component consisting of a pair of functions, f and g. The meta-language is called JR, a functional language similar to ML,[1] and the object language is Java.

Note that we cannot take *Code* to be simply *MachineLanguage*. In a phenomenon familiar from denotational semantics, that type is not rich enough to produce a *compositional* semantics of components.

In this paper, we describe and illustrate a proof-of-concept implementation of this idea. The next section gives a set of introductory examples. Section 3 gives the technical details; it begins by discussing a hypothetical simplified language and target machine, and then goes into our prototype. Section 4 gives another example, and section 5 discusses the relationship of this approach to previous work. We have implemented the key aspects of Figure 1, but many technical problems remain to be solved before we have a complete and robust implementation of our ideas; some of these are mentioned in the conclusions.

2   An Introductory Example

In this section, we build a sorting component to illustrate our approach. This example is virtually identical to the one presented in [11].

Before presenting it, however, we need to give a brief introduction to the meta-language and discuss a few other details relevant to the examples.

All syntactic fragments of Java correspond to values of type *Code*. There is no distinction made between different kinds of values: expressions, statements, etc. However, for clarity of exposition, we will use subscripts to indicate the

---

[1] One syntactic difference that appears in this figure is that square brackets are used for tupling.

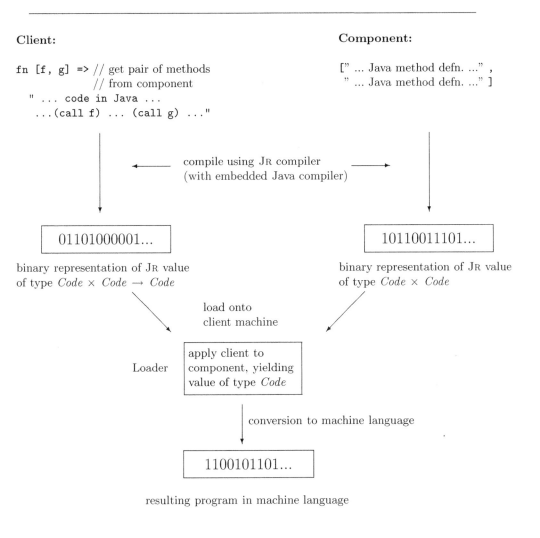

Fig. 1. Combining Clients with Components

intended kind of value. Bear in mind that *there is only one type of Code*; the subscripts are merely comments.

In this implementation, the meta-language is JR. and the object language is Java. Since we have only a bytecode interpreter for JR, and not a compiler, the "binary representation of JR values" in Figure 1 is actually a program in JR bytecode form. The programs produced by the "conversion" step are in assembly language rather than binary form. And the object language is actually a subset of Java, containing only simple types and arrays (whose semantics is actually closer to that of C arrays), with the usual expressions, statements, and function definitions, but no objects. We trust the reader will have no trouble envisioning how this implementation could be made to match Figure 1 precisely.

JR is similar to Standard ML. There are some minor syntactic differences, but the main one is JR's anti-quotation mechanism, inspired by the one in MetaML [16]. Within JR programs, items occurring in double angle brackets << · · · >> are fragments in the object language (Java); these fragments are JR expressions of type *Code*. They may in turn contain variable, "anti-quoted" parts, introduced by a backquote (`) followed by a syntax category (required for the multiple-entry parser); these anti-quoted parts are JR expressions of type *Code*, which are spliced into the larger *Code* value.

A simple example is this "code template:"

```
fn whatToPrint =>
   << public static void main (String[] args) {
         System.out.println(`Exp(whatToPrint));
      }
   >>
end
```

This is a function from *Code* (specifically, the code for a Java expression of type `String`) to *Code* (a Java function definition). In other words, it has type $Code_{expr\ of\ type\ \texttt{String}} \rightarrow Code_{fundef}$. We could apply it to an expression like <<"Hello, world.">>, or something more elaborate, like <<args.length>0 ? args[0] : "">>.

To get back to the sorting component, the simplest version consists of a single procedure:

```
// Component:
val sortcomp =
<<class sortClass {
     static void sort (int[] A, int length) {
        int i=1;
        while (i<A.length) {
           int temp = A[i], j = i-1;
           while (j >= 0)
              if (temp < A[j]) { A[j+1] = A[j]; j--; } else break;
           A[j+1] = temp;
           i++;
        }
     }
  }
>>;
```

A client obtains this component (we have nothing to say about *how* it is obtained — possibly it is in a local library, or perhaps it is on a remote component server), and converts it to machine language by calling make_dll. make_dll converts *Code* values to machine language, and places externally-visible names into a table from which other object code can access them, as usual. Thus, the component can now be used like any other class:

```
// Client:
let val _ = make_dll sortcomp
in
  <<class SortClient {
      static void useSortComponent () {
          int[] keys; ...  sortClass.sort(keys); ...
      }
   }
  >>
end;
```

One way in which the component needs to be more general is in allowing for the specification of different sort orderings. The conventional solution is for the client to provide the ordering as an argument to the sort function. But this solution is verbose and inefficient. We need to define a new class containing the sort function, pass an object to the sort function each time it is called, and invoke an instance method for each comparison. Instead, we can define the component in such a way that the comparison function can be in-lined. Since the client cannot know what the arguments to the comparison function will be, it must provide a function from arguments to *Code*:

$$SortComponentType$$
$$= (Code_{arg1} \times Code_{arg2} \rightarrow Code)_{comparison} \rightarrow Code_{sort\ function}$$

and, as always, $ClientType = SortComponentType \rightarrow Code$.
The component looks like (note the comparison `temp < A[j]` in the sort method above, from which we are abstracting):

```
fun sortcomp comparisonFun =
  << ...
       if ('Exp(comparisonFun <<temp>> <<A[j]>>))
       ...
  >>;
```

and the client:

```
let val _ = mk_dll (sortcomp (fn e1 e2 => <<'Exp(e1) < 'Exp(e2)>> end))
in ...
end
```

As delivered to the client, the component is an executable that represents the compiled version of the JR function. When provided with the code for the comparison function, it generates the binary for the Java function just as if the "less than" function had appeared in the body of the sort routine all along. This solution is both less verbose (the client does not need to define any new classes or methods) and more efficient (the comparison is inlined) than the conventional one.

This approach can also accommodate extremely lightweight uses, as when the user is sorting only a few elements and doesn't want to pay the cost of a function call. To do this, the user provides the same arguments as above, but the component returns two things: a sort procedure (optionally) and a piece of code to be placed at the point of the sort procedure call. The latter may be replaced either by an actual call or by code to do the sorting in-line. Just as the comparison function provided by the client must take two arguments, so the calling code provided by the component must take an argument, namely the array to be sorted. Thus,

$$SortComponentType \ = \\ (Code \ \times \ Code \ \rightarrow \ Code)_{comparison\ function} \ \rightarrow \ int_{size} \\ \rightarrow \ (Code_{optional\ sort\ method} \ \times \ (Code_{array\ arg} \ \rightarrow \ Code_{call\ to\ sort}))$$

and, as always, $ClientType \ = \ SortComponentType \ \rightarrow \ Code.$

```
// Component:
  fun sortcomp comparefun size =
  if (size == 2) // place in-line
  then [[],          // no auxiliary class in this case
        fn A => <<if (!('Exp(comparefun <<'Exp(A)[0]>> <<'Exp(A)[1]>>))) {
                    int temp = 'Exp(A)[0];
                    'Exp(A)[0] = 'Exp(A)[1];
                    'Exp(A)[1] = temp;
                 }>>
        ]
  else
    [<<class sortClass { ... as above ... } >>,
     fn arg => << sort('Exp(arg)); >> end ];
```

We note that the use of higher-order functions — in particular, the ability of the component to return a function to the client — is crucial. It is the main reason why we believe the meta-language should be a higher-order language.

3   What Is *Code*?

The quoted Java syntax in our examples is simply syntactic sugar for expressions built from abstract syntax operators. These operators are given definitions relative to the chosen *Code* type. For example, **while** has type $Code_{Expr} \ \times \ Code_{Stmt} \ \rightarrow \ Code_{Stmt}$ and **plus** has type $Code_{Expr} \times Code_{Expr} \ \rightarrow \ Code_{Expr}.$ These define a compositional semantics for the language, in which *Code* is the domain of meanings.

We have argued that any compositional semantics can be used as the basis for a component system. The components and clients look like macros, but they can be communicated in terms of representations of their *meanings*, not their syntactic representations.

In this view, the key technical decision to be made to create a component system is the definition of *Code*. In this section, we describe our prototype implementation. This definition of *Code* is useful for delivering Java components to Sparc machines. It is by no means the final word on this topic, but it demonstrates the feasibility of the approach.

The prototype definition is, however, necessarily quite complicated. Therefore, we first explain the idea by way of a greatly simplified language and target architecture. This is the topic of the following section; the explanation of the prototype follows it.

3.1   A Simple Language and Architecture

Consider a language consisting only of simple variables, assignment, and the addition operator; the abstract syntax operators are **ident**: $string \rightarrow Code_{Expr}$, **asgn**: $string \times Code_{Expr} \rightarrow Code_{Expr}$, and **plus**: $Code_{Expr} \times Code_{Expr} \rightarrow Code_{Expr}$. Furthermore, the target architecture is a stack machine with instructions LOAD, STORE, and PLUS.

Given a client or component written in this language, we first eliminate the quotes and antiquotes by a using these transformation rules repeatedly (the basic idea is standard [2]):

$<< x = e >> \rightarrow$ **asgn** "x" $<< e >>$
$<< e + e' >> \rightarrow$ **plus** $<< e >> << e' >>$
$<< x >> \qquad \rightarrow$ **ident** "x"
$<< \text{'}e >> \qquad \rightarrow e$

For example, suppose we have the following component, of type $Code \rightarrow Code$:

```
Component = fn arg => <<'arg + 'arg>>
```

and this client of type $(Code \rightarrow Code) \rightarrow Code$:

```
Client = fn comp => <<x = '(comp <<y>>)>>
```

Eliminating the syntactic sugar by the above transformation rules, these become:

```
val Component = fn arg => plus arg arg
val Client = fn comp => asgn "x" (comp (ident "y"))
```

We can now define the abstract syntax operators using our chosen definition of $Code$. Since we are compiling for a stack machine, and will ignore the issue of declarations (assuming all identifiers to be declared by some other mechanism), we can use a particularly simple definition:

$$Code = Environment \rightarrow MachineLang$$
$$Environment = string \rightarrow string$$
$$MachineLang = string$$

The environment maps identifiers to the names of memory locations. A *MachineLang* value is simply a sequence of machine language instructions, regarded as a string. Again, our machine has three instructions: PLUS takes two arguments off the stack and puts one result back on it, LOAD places a value on the stack, and STORE removes a value.

Now we can define the semantics of our language (carat is the string concatenation operator):

```
fun ident s // : string -> Code
       = fn rho => "LOAD " ^ (rho s) ^ "\n" end
fun asgn s C // : string x Code -> Code
       = fn rho => (C rho) ^ "STORE " ^ (rho s) ^ "\n" end
fun plus C1 C2 // : Code x Code -> Code
       = fn rho => (C1 rho) ^ (C2 rho) ^ "PLUS\n" end
```

Applying these definitions to our example, we have:

```
val Component = fn arg => fn rho =>
        (arg rho) ^ (arg rho) ^ "PLUS\n" end end
val Client = fn comp => fn rho =>
        (comp (ident "y") rho)
          ^ "STORE " ^ (rho "x") ^ "\n" end end
```

The component and client are not *transformed* into this form. Like any other expression, they are *compiled* into machine language code that has these meanings. The loader loads them both and applies the client to the component; that is, it sets up the run-time state that JR code needs for an application.

When complete, this application will leave the (binary representation of the) value:

```
fn rho => "LOAD " ^ (rho "y") ^ "\n" ^ "LOAD " ^ (rho "y")
           ^ "PLUS\n" ^ "STORE " ^ (rho "x") ^ "\n"
```

Finally, the loader may supply an initial environment to transform this value of type *Code* to a value of type *MachineLang*. Let us finish the example by assuming the loader provides the environment { "x" → "Lx", "y" → "Ly" }. The resulting machine language code:

```
LOAD Ly
LOAD Ly
PLUS
STORE Lx
```

can now be executed by the machine.

3.2   Java Components for the Sparc Architecture

We have implemented a prototype for writing components for (a compiled version of a subset of) Java, to run on Sparc architectures. The set of abstract syntax operations and the translation from the antiquote notation to these constructors is much more complicated than in the simple example, but it is conceptually similar and we will not go into detail. More to the point, the definition of *Code* and the definitions of the operations are also much more complicated, and on these we will elaborate.

Evaluating expressions of type *Code* should be an efficient process and should produce efficient code. Both forms of efficiency depend crucially on the exact definition of the *Code* type. The meanings of syntactic phrases — that is, values of type *Code* — can carry a great deal of structure, allowing the relatively slow generation of efficient code, or very little (as in the simple example above), allowing the rapid generation of inefficient code. Another dimension of variability is the amount of preprocessing performed on components: one extreme example is to let *Code* = *string*, so that components are just macros and code generation is compilation. At the other extreme is the work we present here, in which components are fully compiled to target machine language.

We have designed our definition of *Code* to allow for reasonably good code generation. The definition below makes use of a "register status" value that allows for a simple but useful register allocation process during the conversion from *Code* to machine language. For simplicity, this single *Code* type represents the meaning of any kind of syntactic fragment — expression, statement, declaration, etc. This means that some parts of each value may be irrelevant, such as the return location of a value representing the meaning of a statement.

$$Code \quad = Env \rightarrow (MachLang \times Locator \times Type) \times Env$$

$$MachLang = MachLangFrag_{l\text{-}value} \times MachLangFrag_{r\text{-}value} \times MachLangFrag_{decl}$$

$$Env \quad = (Var \rightarrow Type \times Size \times Locator) \times StackOffset \times RegStatus$$

$$Locator \quad = temp\text{-}addr + live\text{-}addr + synch\text{-}addr$$

$$RegStatus = (RegNum \cup \{Nowhere\}) \leftrightarrow (Locator \cup \{Empty\})$$

(The double arrow denotes a relation.)

Given an environment, each *Code* value produces some machine language and a "locator" and type, which give the location and type of the value returned by this bit of machine language (if any); for declarations, the piece of code might alter the environment, so a new environment is passed back as well. The machine language part of the value is actually three sequences of machine instructions, one to calculate the l-value, one for the r-value, and one for constants that are to be placed into the data segment. (In our prototype, we represent the machine language sequences by strings, in the form of assembler input.)

The environment has three parts: a table giving information about the variables, the next available stack location for future variable declarations, and the current availability of registers. For each variable, the provided information is its type, size, and location. Locations are of three types: live, temporary, and synchronized. These distinctions are important to the register allocator, as we will explain.

The environment provided to each *Code* value includes a table, called *RegStatus*, giving the contents of the registers. This table relates register numbers to locations: a given register number can contain a value that is also in a location, or it may contain nothing; similarly, the value contained in a location may also be in a register, or not. The allocation of registers depends upon the register status and also on the type of locators used in the code being compiled. A register containing a temporary value can be recycled once that value is used; a live value needs to be stored back on the stack if its register is to be used for anything else; and a synchronized location is one which is currently stored in a register, so that spilling that register is a no-op.

To illustrate the effect of this definition, consider this client and component:

```
fun client exp = <<int x = 2; int y = x+5; 'Exp(exp);>>;
val component = <<(x+y)*(x-y)>>;
```

The application of the client to the component yields the following machine language:

```
    setsw 2, %i0
    setsw 5, %i1
    add %i0, %i1, %i1
    add %i0, %i1, %i2
    sub %i0, %i1, %i3
    mulx %i2, %i3, %i2
```

This code uses an efficient register allocation scheme. It is the kind of code that might have been produced by a compiler that was given the entire, non-componentized, statement.

Figures 2 and 3 contain representative examples of combinator definitions: addition[2] and sequencing. In this implementation, "machine language" means "assembly language." Fragments of assembly language are represented by strings, so that constructing code from fragments involves a lot of string concatenation; carat (^) is the string concatenation operator.

Consider the addition operator. Its left operand produces some machine code (only the r-value, rcf1, is of interest), and may modify the environment (in particular, the stack configuration and register status). The right operand does likewise. After the right operand has been compiled, the triple [e,s,R] represents the environment, that is, the variable map, stack offset, and register status. The register allocator uses the register status, the stack offset, and the locations of the two operands to find a location for the sum; this is r3, and R' is the register status after it has been used. The register allocator may also need to generate some spill code; this is cf3. The code generated for the addition is the r-value code for both operands, the spill code (if any), and then the add instruction. The result has locator TEMP s, indicating that its home, if it needs to be spilled, is at that offset of the stack, and that it is temporary. The stack top is updated and R' is returned as the new register status.

---

[2] restricted to integers. The actual definition handles floats as well, using the *Type* of its arguments to determine the type of op-code to emit.

```
fun add opnd1 opnd2 =
  fn E =>
    let val [[[lcf1, rcf1, df1], l1, t1], E'] = opnd1 E
        val [[[lcf2, rcf2, df2], l2, t2], [e,s,R]] = opnd2 E'
        val [[r1, r2], r3, cf3, R'] = getreg R [(TEMP s)] [l1, l2]
    in
        [[["", rcf1^rcf2^cf3^"        add "^r1^","^r2^","^r3, df1^df2],
         TEMP s, ["int", 0]], [e, s+(stacksizeof "int"), R']]
    end
  end;
```

Fig. 2. The Addition Combinator (Restricted to Integers)

```
fun seq op1 op2 =
  fn E =>
    let val dummy = if trace then print "seq" else ""
        val [[[lcf1, rcf1, df1], l1, t1], [e,s,[locnos, regnos]]] =
            op1 E
        val R' = if (istemp l1)
        then freereg (regof (lookup regnos (locof l1))) [locnos, regnos]
        else [locnos,regnos]
        val [[[lcf2, rcf2, df2], l2, t2], E''] = op2 [e,s,R']
    in
      [[["", rcf1^rcf2, df1^df2], l2, t2], E'']
    end
  end;
```

Fig. 3. The Sequencing ("semicolon") Combinator

The total cost of using a component consists of the cost of code generation and the cost of executing the generated code. To be worthwhile, these costs must be lower than the cost of using a non-generative component. In our prototype, the cost of code generation is unrealistically high, because we have only an interpretive implementation of JR, and because *Code* uses assembly language programs, represented as strings, for the generated machine language. A compiled meta-language directly generating machine code would be more realistic. Thus, we cannot give meaningful results concerning the combined costs. Just to illustrate the potential gain, we give an example whose execution-time speed-up is unusually great. This example is a component that adds a cache to a function [11]. The trick to doing this is that the function may contain *recursive* calls that need to be changed to call the new, caching version of the function. For this reason, a caching component cannot have type *Code* → *Code*, but must instead have type (*string* → *Code*) → *Code*. That is, the client presents a function with a missing function call. The component fills it in with a call to the caching version of the function.

The code is given in the appendix. The function computes the ith Fibonacci number using the simple recursive definition. We give two different components. One incorporates a fixed-size cache of ten integers; this should give a significant speed-up for calculating Fibonacci numbers from 0 to 10, after which the exponential nature of the algorithm will reappear. The other incorporates a two-element cache, one for even arguments and one for odd arguments; by the nature of the algorithm, this cache is effective for all arguments. We also give a control example that uses a non-caching component.

The results show that the caching components work as we would expect. Times are in seconds, and include code generation and a single execution of the indicated function call:

Function call	No cache	10-element cache	Even-odd cache
fib(10)	.02	0.180	0.180
fib(20)	.02	0.180	0.200
fib(30)	.29	0.250	0.170
fib(40)	33.47	6.99	0.210

As just mentioned, this implementation is very inefficient in producing code. Code generation overhead dominates the times for the first three rows; we can see this because the completely linear version — the one with the even-odd cache — shows no consistent change in execution speed. However, the times for fib(30) and fib(40) show the time increase for either the uncached or the 10-element cached version. In short, even counting the overheads of our prototype — overheads which could be reduced to a fraction of their current values — we can still see a speed-up relative to the uncached version of the code.

In one sense, this example is unfair: few components will turn an exponential algorithm into a linear one. On the other hand, the example does illustrate a genuine advantage of our method: no non-generative technology can possibly produce such a speed-up. This points toward the possibility of constructing programs out of programming *methods* that are supplied as components.

4   A Search-and-Replace Component

Many editors contain a regular-expression matching facility with a "submatch" facility. That is, the pattern can contain sub-patterns, usually within escaped parentheses ("\(" and "\)"). When the pattern has matched an object string, the parts of that string that were matched by these subpatterns can be referred to by sequence number. For example, in the Unix ex editor, the command s/\(a*\)b\(c*\)/\2b\1/ finds a sequence of a's followed by a b followed by a sequence of c's, and swaps the a's and c's; thus, if the object string is aaaaabccdef, this command will change it to ccbaaaaadef.

Patterns like this are among the features that make languages like Awk and Perl preferable to Java for simple text-processing. Although C has a library subroutine that does regular expression matching, it is awkward to use because there is no simple way to define actions that can be attached to the regular expressions.

The component shown in Figures 4 and 5 offers such a facility to the Java programmer. In addition to the usual pattern-forming operations like repetition (here represented by the function `star`) and concatenation (the infix operator `**`), the (infix) operator `==>` adds an action to any pattern, which is to be executed when the pattern is matched. `==>` has type

$$Pattern \times (Code_{start\ of\ match} \rightarrow Code_{end\ of\ match} \rightarrow Code_{action}) \rightarrow Pattern$$

As an example, if a client were to include this expression:

```
'((star ((plus (oneof <<"0123456789">>) ==>
              (fn s e => <<sum = sum+convertdec(input,'s,'e-1);>> end))
       ** (star (oneof <<" ">>)))))
   <<input>> <<0>> <<z>>)
```

it would do the following: Within the string `input`, starting at position 0, it would find runs of integers separated by spaces, and add their values to the variable `sum`; then it would assign to `z` the position just past the end of the match.

5   Related Work

Efforts to componentize software in non-traditional ways include Kiczales's aspect-oriented programming, Engler's 'C and Magik systems, and the C++ template-based approaches, including the STL and the template meta-programming method of Veldhuizen, Czarnecki, and Eisenecker. Also relevant is the work on the "explicitly staged" language MetaML.

The idea behind aspect-oriented programming (AOP) [12] is to separate *algorithms* from certain details of their implementation — like data layout, exception behavior, synchronization — that notoriously complicate programs. Each such detail, or *aspect*, is described in a specification distinct from the algorithm. An aspect *weaver* combines the algorithm and the various aspect specifications into an efficient program. Our approach can account for these details as well, but it is not as convenient notationally because the client programmer has to know about, and plan for, the use of components. On the positive side, our approach is fundamentally simpler in that it requires little new technology. The most serious problem with AOP is that it provides only a conceptual framework. Each set of aspect languages and their associated weaver is *sui generis*. Our method uses conventional functional languages to write all components.

Engler's 'C ("tick-see") [7] is a C extension that includes a *Code* type and run-time macros. Engler's goal differs from ours — in his examples, the extension is mainly used to achieve increased efficiency, à la partial evaluation. The main technical difference from the current work is that the meta-language is C rather than a functional language; one consequence is the absence of higher-order functions, which are fundamental in our approach. Engler has also written a system

```
val namecnt = 0;
fun newname x = (namecnt := namecnt+1; x^(tostring namecnt));

fun str S =
  fn buff startpos endpos =>
    let val i = newname "i"
    in <<int 'i = 0;
         while ('S['i] != '\0' &&
                'buff['startpos+'i] != '\0' &&
                'S['i] == 'buff['startpos+'i])
           'i++;
         if ('S['i] == '\0') // match succeeded
           'endpos = 'startpos+'i;
         else
           'endpos = -1;
       >>
    end
  end;

fun oneof S =
  fn buff startpos endpos =>
    let val i = newname "i"
    in <<int 'i = 0;
         if ('buff['startpos] == '\0')
           'endpos = -1;
         else {
           while ('S['i] != '\0' &&
                  'S['i] != 'buff['startpos])
             'i++;
           if ('S['i] == 'buff['startpos]) // match succeeded
             'endpos = 'startpos+1;
           else
             'endpos = -1;
         }
       >>
    end
  end;
```

Fig. 4. A Search-and-Replace Component (Part 1)

called Magik [6], in which one can create language extensions by programming
transformations of abstract syntax trees. Magik is extremely powerful, but is
inherently a compile-time system, and is in general much harder to use than a
system that can be programmed at the source level (such as 'C or ours).

Most generative component systems are compile-time. Simonyi's Intentional
Programming [14] approach is another. Sirkin et al's Predator [15] data structure precompiler is specialized to the production of efficient data structure-

```
infixl 4 "**"
fun ** r1 r2 =
  fn buff startpos endpos =>
     let val i = newname "i"
     in <<int 'i;
           '(r1 buff startpos endpos)
           if ('endpos != -1) {
             'i = 'endpos;
             '(r2 buff i endpos)
           }
         >>
     end
  end;

fun star r =
  fn buff startpos endpos =>
     let val i = newname "i"
     in <<int 'i = 'startpos;
           while ('i != -1) {
             'endpos = 'i;
             '(r buff endpos i)
           }
         >>
     end
  end;

fun plus r = r ** (star r);

infixl 5 "==>"
fun ==> r S =
  fn buff startpos endpos =>
    <<{'(r buff startpos endpos)
       if ('endpos != -1)
         '(S startpos endpos)
      }
     >>
  end;
```

Fig. 5. A Search-and-Replace Component (Part 2)

manipulating code, and as such goes beyond anything we have attempted. Batory's Jakarta Tool Suite [1] is a set of tools for the generation of domain-specific languages; domain-specific optimizations are performed at the AST level. Access to concrete representations of programs always provides for greater power and flexibility. The extent to which the power of these other component systems could be realized at the binary level is an interesting question for further study.

The approaches based on aggressive use of the C++ template mechanism are an interesting contrast to ours. Stepanov's Standard Template Library (STL) [13] accounts for lightweight components, based on the `infix` mechanism of C++. Veldhuizen [17] and Czarnecki and Eisenecker [4,5] take this idea even further. Observing that the template mechanism actually provides a Turing-complete *compile-time* language embedded in C++, they show how to create "template metaprograms," thereby accounting for generative components as well. Furthermore, the integration of the static and dynamic languages has definite benefits, including a cleaner syntax in many cases. However, the static language provided by the template mechanism is a rather awkward one, and writing template metaprograms is a tour-de-force. Furthermore, the entire template approach is subject to the criticism that all components must be provided in source form. Our approach yields many of the benefits of these approaches, uses a more powerful meta-language, and permits component distribution in binary form.

In MetaML [16], one writes in a single language, but explicitly indicates where partial evaluation can be performed; that is, the dynamic parts of a program are specially bracketed, just as the Java parts of our components and clients are. This approach is simpler for the programmer, especially inasmuch as the language permits some type-checking of *generated* code to be performed at compile-time. Such a feature would make our system much easier to use, but we have not yet explored this possibility. As a general-purpose component mechanism, our system offers two advantages. First, we have greater control over the representation of the generated programs. Second, by distinguishing the meta-language from the object language, we can choose an object language that reflects a simpler, more realistic, machine model than the meta-language, so that it can be compiled more efficiently. For example, when using Java, the absence of "upward function values" allows us to place on the stack some values that, if we remained in MetaML, would have to go into the heap. In other words, programs in MetaML are made more efficient by eliminating static computations, but what remains are still programs in MetaML and can only be compiled as efficiently as MetaML. Therefore, the differing compilation models of the two languages is, for us, a crucial distinction.

6   Conclusions

To us, a "software component" is simply a value — usually, a higher-order value — that contains *Code*. This definition is both general and conceptually simple. It admits conventional "ADT-style" components, but also includes lightweight (inlined) and generative components. Based on ideas that are well-known in the functional programming community, it is relatively easy to implement because the basics are found in existing functional languages. All that is needed is an implementation of *Code* constructors, plus, in practice, a multiple-entry parser for the quotation mechanism. Our prototype implementation demonstrates that this notion is workable.

The major problem we have observed is the difficulty of writing components and clients. The semantic mismatch between meta-language and object language is the primary culprit. In staged languages like MetaML [16] where the languages at every stage are identical, there is no such problem. On a superficial level, however, it may be possible to simplify the uses of quotation and anti-quotation by, to some extent, inferring their proper placement. Since the object language and meta-languages are distinct, the "stage" of any subexpression can be determined syntactically. Nonetheless, we see no way to fundamentally simplify the construction of components. One possibility is to type-check components as is done in MetaML. This appears to be much more difficult to do in our setting, because the program-constructing operations (in the meta-language) have no semantic connection to the constructed programs (in the object language). However, we have not attempted a systematic study of this problem.

The heart of the matter is the definition of *Code* and the implementation of the component system. How efficiently can a well-engineered loader evaluate *Code* expressions? Should *Code* values carry more information than the register state to allow for higher quality code to be generated, or will the increase in *Code* evaluation time increase overall system response time? Would it be better to eliminate the register state entirely, relying on run-time code generation techniques to improve code efficiency? Although our principal goal is increased programmer productivity rather than efficiency, the method cannot achieve widespread use if it is overly costly in execution speed.

The cost of evaluation of *Code* values also depends upon how much of the value can be pre-computed. This is a challenging partial evaluation problem. In a client `fn e => <<... 'Exp(e)...>> end`, it is likely that much of the code surrounding the use of e could be pre-calculated. However, in `fn t => <<'Id(t) x; int y; ...x...y...>> end`, where the parameter is a type, it may be difficult to pre-compile very much of the program at all, because the location of y is not known. Register allocation adds considerably to the difficulties: a statement or expression abstracted from the program makes it difficult to do register allocation for the code that follows. Our prototype implementation does no such pre-compilation, and we consider this a particularly important area for study. (It is worth emphasizing that we do not advocate passing abstract syntax trees as components. In addition to the disadvantages mentioned in the introduction, there is another crucial problem with this representation: AST's are, in principle, impossible to pre-compile, because there is always the possibility that they will be modified before conversion to machine language.)

Our components are in no sense portable across architectures. However, there is an alternative approach: instead of taking the *MachLang* type to be Sparc code, we could have it be code for some virtual machine. The conversion from *Code* to machine language would then be more involved: the loader would provide some initial environment and extract the *MachLang* portion of the result (as now), and then compile the virtual machine code to actual machine code. Obviously, this is being done now on a daily basis by the "just-in-time" compilers for Java [9]. We would only remark that the Java virtual machine is perhaps not the best intermediate language for our purpose — a three-address code would seem more appropriate — and that the efforts to add annotations to Java virtual machine code to help the code generator [10,8] seem particularly apposite here.

Another key area for study is integration between the meta-language and object language. As discussed in the related work section, C++'s standard template library is notationally simpler to use, in part because of such integration. A multi-level language such as MetaML, in which both levels are the same, also achieves such integration, but it does not strike us as an ideal setting for a general component framework, for reasons we have stated earlier. On the other hand, the "Turing tarpit" looms here: the combination of two entirely different, and independently complex, languages may push the entire package beyond the realm of practical usability. Integrating the two levels could go a considerable distance toward alleviating this problem. It would also allow us to address a problem that we have not mentioned: capture of variables. In Scheme, this problem has led to the development of "hygienic macros" [3]; since we have a similar combination of features — open terms and higher-order functions — we may be able to benefit from this technology.

Acknowledgements

Uday Reddy and An Le provided useful feedback on an earlier draft of this paper. We also appreciate the help of Joel Jones, whose compilation expertise helped us implement the prototype. The anonymous SAIG referees made many useful suggestions, for which we are most grateful.

References

1. Don Batory, Bernie Lofaso, and Yannis Smaragdakis.
   JTS: Tools for implementing domain-specific languages.
   In *Fifth Intl. Conf. on Software Reuse*, June 1998.
2. A. Bawden.
   Quasiquotation in lisp.
   In *In Proceedings of the ACM SIGPLAN Symposium on Partial Evaluation and Semantics-Based Program Manipulation (PEPM-99)*, pages 18–42, January 22–23 1999.
3. William Clinger and Jonathan Rees.
   Macros that work.
   In *Proc. of the Conf. on Principles of Programming Languages (POPL)*, pages 155–160, 1991.
4. Krzysztof Czarnecki and Ulrich W. Eisenecker.
   Synthesizing objects.
   In Rachid Guerraoui, editor, *13th European Conference on Object-Oriented Programming (ECOOP '99)*, pages 18–42, June 1999.
5. Krzysztof Czarnecki and Ulrich W. Eisenecker.
   Static metaprogramming in C++.
   In *Generative Programming: Methods, Techniques, and Applications*, chapter 8, pages 251–279. Addison-Wesley, 2000.

6. Dawson Engler.
   Incorporating applications semantics and control into compilation.
   In *Proceedings of the Conference on Domain-Specific Languages*,
   Santa Barbara, California, USA, October 15–17 1997.
7. Dawson R. Engler, Wilson C. Hsieh, and M. Frans Kaashoek.
   'C: A language for high-level, efficient, and machine-independent
   dynaic code generation.
   In *Conference Record of POPL '96: The* 23rd *ACM
   SIGPLAN-SIGACT Symposium on Principles of Programming Languages*, pages
   131–144, St. Petersburg Beach, Florida, 21–24 January 1996.
8. J. Hummel, A. Azevedo, D. Kolson, and A. Nicolau.
   Annotating the java byte codes in support of optimization.
   In *ACM 1997 Workshop on Java for Science and Engineering
   Computation*, June 1997.
9. Sun Microsystems Incorporated.
   The java hotspot performance engine architecture: A white paper about
   sun's second generation performance technology.
   Technical report, April 1999.
10. J. Jones and S. Kamin.
    Annotating java class files with virtual registers for performance.
    Concurrency: Practice and Experience, to appear.
11. Sam Kamin, Miranda Callahan, and Lars Clausen.
    Lightweight and generative components I: Source-level components.
    In *First International Symposium on Generative and
    Component-Based Software Engineering (GCSE'99)*, September 28–30 1999.
12. Gregor Kiczales, John Lamping, Anurag Mendhekar, Chris Maeda, Cristina Videira
    Lopes, Jean-Marc Loingtier, and John Irwin.
    Aspect-oriented programming.
    In *Proc. European Conference on Object-Oriented Programming
    (ECOOP)*, volume LNCS 1241. Springer-Verlag, June 1997.
13. David R. Musser and Atul Saini.
    *STL Tutorial and Reference Guide: C++ Programming with the
    Standard Template Library*.
    Addison-Wesley Professional Computing Series, 1996.
14. Charles Simonyi.
    The death of computer languages, the birth of intentional
    programming.
    In *NATO Science Committee Conference*, 1995.
15. Marty Sirkin, Don Batory, and Vivek Singhal.
    Software components in a data structure precompiler.
    In *Intl. Conf. on Software Eng.*, pages 437–446, 1993.
16. Walid Taha and Tim Sheard.
    Multi-stage programming with explicit annotations.
    In *Proceedings of the ACM SIGPLAN Symposium on Partial
    Evaluation and Semantics-Based Program Manipulation (PEPM-97)*, volume 32,
    12 of *ACM SIGPLAN Notices*, pages 203–217, New York, June 12–13 1997.
    ACM Press.
17. Todd Veldhuizen.
    Using C++ template metaprograms.
    C++ Report, 7(4):36–43, May 1995.

Appendix

This appendix contains the code for the caching example discussed in section 3.2.
We give the client first, followed by two caching components. Each component
creates a class called `cacheComponent` which contains two methods, `cacher` and
`setupcache`. Each of these methods has a single integer argument and returns
the Fibonacci number of that argument; the difference is that `setupcache` initializes the cache before calling `cacher`. For our experiments, we timed a single
call to `setupcache`, with various arguments. `quickCacheComponent` is the component that uses the simple 10–element cache. `moduloCacheComponent` uses the
2–element cache. The timings shown in the second and third columns of the table
in section 3.2 were obtained from running (`theClient quickCacheComponent`)
and (`theClient moduloCacheComponent`), respectively.

```
fun fibmaker thename =
 <<if (x < 3)
     return x;
   else
     return ('Method(thename) (x-1) + 'Method(thename) (x-2)); >>;

fun theClient theComponent =
    let val code = load (theComponent fibmaker)
    in (seq code <<cacheComponent.setupcache(5);>>)
    end;

fun quickCacheComponent thecode =
   <<class cacheComponent {
       static int cachesize;
       static int[] ncache;

       private static int original (int x) {
           'Stt(thecode "cacher")
       }

       private static int cacher (int x) {
         if ((x < cachesize) && (ncache[x] != -1))
           return ncache[x];
         else {
             int newres;
             newres = original (x);
             if (x < cachesize)
               ncache[x] = newres;
             return newres;
         }
       }

       public static int setupcache (int x) {
         int i = 0;
         cachesize = 10;
```

```
        ncache = new int[cachesize];
        while (i < cachesize) {
          ncache[i] = -1;
          i++;
        }
        return cacher (x);
      }
  }>>;

fun moduloCacheComponent thecode =
  <<class cacheComponent {
      static int cachesize;
      static int[] cachekeys;
      static int[] cachevalues;

      private static int original (int x) {
        `Stt(thecode "cacher")
      }

      private static int cacher (int x) {
        if (cachekeys[x%cachesize] == x)
          return cachevalues[x%cachesize];
        else {
          int newres;
          newres = original (x);
          cachekeys[x%cachesize] = x;
          cachevalues[x%cachesize] = newres;
          return newres;
        }
      }

      public static int setupcache (int x) {
        int i = 0;
        cachesize = 2;
        cachekeys = new int[cachesize];
        cachevalues = new int[cachesize];
        while (i < cachesize) {
          cachekeys[i] = -1;
          i++;
        }
        return cacher (x);
      }
  }>>;
```

Fragmental Specialization

Simon Helsen and Peter Thiemann

Universität Freiburg, Institut für Informatik
Georges-Köhler-Allee, D-79110 Freiburg, Germany
{helsen,thiemann}@informatik.uni-freiburg.de

Abstract. Traditional offline program specialization relies on staging of a computation into two levels, static and dynamic. We present a generalization thereof where the static input data of one level is split up in a potentially unknown number of separate fragments. These fragments arrive in an unspecified order and are specialized as they arrive. Potential applications of the technique include separate compilation via specialization, efficient implementation of reflective languages, and just-in-time compilation.

We have implemented our new specialization technique in the PGG specialization system [27] for Scheme. We have proved correctness for a first-order fragment.

1 Introduction

Partial evaluation [15,5] is an established technique for speeding up a program by specializing it with respect to known parts of its input. One particularly attractive application of partial evaluation is compilation [8,4,16,22,21]. Compilation is achieved by specializing an interpretive definition of a programming language with respect to a program.

While this scheme is flawless in theory and workable in practice, it always requires the whole program to be present. Hence, it is not applicable to separate compilation. In contrast, real compilers can compile one module at a time. They rely on a linker to combine the compiled modules later on.

Unfortunately, traditional partial evaluators cannot handle this task satisfactorily. Only the work of Heldal and Hughes [12,13] seriously tackles separate compilation of modular programs by partial evaluation. Their approach requires a complete redesign of the analysis and specialization phase. In consequence, their technique is difficult to understand and lacks a correctness proof.

In specialization terms, separate compilation amounts to repeatedly specializing an interpreter with respect to different compilation units (modules). The combination of the resulting specialized program fragments to a meaningful whole is left to a linker. Abstracting from the problem of separate compilation, the specializer should process the same program repeatedly with respect to different fragments of the static input. The specialized program is the combination of the resulting specialized program fragments. We make the static input fragments available via an index and use a special `access` construct to map an index to its corresponding fragment. Hence, the name *fragmental specialization*.

W. Taha (Ed.): SAIG 2000, LNCS 1924, pp. 51–71, 2000.

Fragmental specialization applies to the problem of separate compilation. In this context, the meaning of `access` is quite intuitive. It maps a module name (the index) to its program text (the data fragment), so it corresponds to loading the compilation unit or its interface description. An interpreter must `access` the program text of a compilation unit before it can start executing that code.

What is the meaning of `access` at specialization time? The main difference to the standard semantics, is that only *one* fragment of the indexed set is available to a run of the specializer. Furthermore, there is no control over the order in which the fragments of the indexed set are presented to the specializer.

Consider again separate compilation. Suppose that the specializer specializes an interpreter with respect to a module M (in other words, it compiles module M). If, during that specialization, the `access` construct requests the same module, M, it means that the interpreter is processing a *local* procedure call and compilation/specialization simply proceeds by generating that call. If `access` requests a different module, M', the interpreter is processing a non-local procedure call and then there are two possibilities. If the specializer has processed M' before, it generates a backwards call to the corresponding entry point of M'. In other words, the non-local procedure call is automatically linked to a previously compiled module. Otherwise, if M' is still to be processed, the specializer generates a forward call in the compiled code of M. At the same time, it makes a note of which parts of M' are to be processed when it is presented to the specializer. This technique is tantamount to back-patching, the difference is that the first *reference* determines the target address.

Specialization with respect to an indexed set of static input fragments blends well with standard partial evaluation technology. An extension of the specializer's memoization mechanism (a caching scheme which enables the specializer to share specialized code and to generate mutually recursive procedures, thus improving termination of specialization) is sufficient to implement it. The `access` construct is built into the specializer and controls the extended memoization mechanism to obtain the effect outlined above.

Contribution. We have specified specialization with respect to an indexed set of static input fragments. It is implemented in the PGG system [27], an offline partial evaluator for Scheme [17]. Our technique can be used

- to compile modules in an arbitrary order;
- to compile mutually recursive modules; and
- to compile programs comprised of an *a priori* unknown number of modules, enabling dynamic loading of modules.

All these points improve on the results of Heldal and Hughes [12,13].

We provide a correctness proof of the specializer consisting of the standard type soundness result for the (type-based) binding-time analysis and a proof that specialization preserves the semantics. The proof is formalized for a first-order fragment of the language but the techniques carry over to the full language. The particular difficulty of this proof lies in the necessity to formalize the memoization mechanism of a specializer and prove its correctness. This has not been done before in the literature.

Overview. Section 2 introduces the basics of offline partial evaluation. Section 3 discusses separate compilation of modular programs, the main application of our specialization framework. Section 4 sets up the theoretical background for a first-order functional language. It culminates in a correctness proof. Section 5 discusses implementation issues Finally, we discuss related work and conclude.

The examples in Section 3 require some knowledge of Scheme.

2   Offline Partial Evaluation

Offline partial evaluation [15,5] is a specialization technique that guides its specialization-time computation with the annotations generated by a *binding-time analysis*. The annotations are S for constructs that process *static* data, which is available at specialization time, and D for constructs that depend on *dynamic* data, which is only available at run-time. Specialization boils down to interpreting the annotated program, evaluating the static constructs and generating code for the dynamic ones. Since specialization performs reductions under dynamic control (it processes the body of a dynamic lambda abstraction and it processes both branches of a conditional if the condition is dynamic), specialization may not terminate even though the original program always terminates. To remedy this behavior and to allow for multiple specialized variants of the same source text, offline partial evaluators usually implement *function memoization* [15,25], a caching scheme which enables the specializer to share specialized code and to generate mutually recursive procedures (polyvariant program point specialization). It also improves termination of specialization.

3   Separate Compilation of Modular Programs

A simple framework for separate compilation for untyped languages considers a modular program as a set of program fragments, indexed by module names. Every program fragment defines names and references names. Every fragment *exports* some defined names, which are visible to other fragments, and every fragment may *import* some names from other fragments. Separate compilation means to compile single program fragments in isolation so that we obtain an executable after combining (i.e., linking) the compiled program fragments.

In the rest of this section, we demonstrate how specialization of an interpreter using our approach achieves separate compilation in this sense. In particular, we define a tiny language and show two example interpreters for it that achieve compilation via specialization. All specialized code in this section is generated with the PGG specialization system for Scheme [27] and the source files are provided with the distribution. In our approach, the binding-time properties of the interpreter determine to what extent separate compilation is possible and the two examples demonstrate the main possibilities.

Syntax of the register machine language:

$$module ::= (block^+)$$
$$block \quad ::= (label \ . \ instr^*)$$
$$instr \quad ::= (\texttt{Incr} \ reg) \mid (\texttt{Decr} \ reg) \mid (\texttt{Jz} \ reg \ label) \mid (\texttt{Jump} \ label)$$

Example program:

```
mod1 : ((add . ((jz 1 copy)        mod2 : ((copy . ((jz 2 test)
                (decr 1)                           (incr 1)
                (incr 0)                           (decr 2)
                (jump add)))                       (jump copy)))
        (finis . ()))                     (test . ((jz 1 finis)
                                                   (jump add))))
```

Fig. 1. The Register Machine Language

A Source Language and Its Interpreter. Figure 1 defines the syntax of a register-machine language ([12,13]) together with an example program. A module is a non-empty sequence of blocks. A block is a sequence of instructions starting with a label. An instruction either increments a register, decrements a register, performs a conditional jump to a label if some register is zero, or it performs an unconditional jump to a label. A target label is either local or implicitly imported from a different module. All defined labels are implicitly exported. This mechanism is similar to the rudimentary support for separate compilation in assemblers.

The example contains two modules, *mod1* and *mod2*, with mutual references to each other. In particular, label `copy` is referenced in *mod1* and defined in *mod2*, whereas `finis` and `add` are defined in *mod1* and referenced in *mod2*.

An interpreter defines the semantics of the language. Its first part (Fig. 2) deals with syntax dispatch and the execution of the arithmetic instructions. The other part is the jump processor, which may be replaced.

In Fig. 2, function (`exec jump instrs regs`) takes three parameters: a function to process jumps, `jump`, a list of instructions to execute, `instrs`, and a list of register values, `regs`. To process a `Jump` instruction, `exec` calls (`jump label regs`), where `label` is the target label and `regs` is the list of registers.

Besides standard Scheme lists, the code uses a user-defined datatype `list` with some utility functions. This datatype enables partially static treatment in the specializer, in particular, arity raising the elements of the list of registers. The function `::` is the `list` constructor, `hd` and `tl` are the corresponding selectors (head and tail). The function `split` takes a number i and a list l. It splits the list into a prefix of length i and the rest of the list. The result is a pair of lists (also a partially static user-defined datatype) and `fst` and `snd` select the components of this pair. The `concat` function concatenates its list arguments.

The following two subsections concentrate on the `jump` processor. We exhibit two variants that implement different behavior.

```
(define (exec jump instrs regs)
  (let loop ((instrs instrs) (regs regs))
    (if (null? instrs)
        (hd regs)
        (let ((instr (car instrs)) (instrs (cdr instrs)))
          (case (car instr)
            ((Incr) (let* ((regno (cadr instr))
                           (xxx (split regno regs))
                           (regs1 (fst xxx))
                           (regs2 (snd xxx))
                           (reg (hd regs2)))
                      (loop instrs
                            (concat regs1 (:: (+ reg 1) (tl regs2))))))
            ((Decr) (let* ((regno (cadr instr))
                           (xxx (split regno regs))
                           (regs1 (fst xxx))
                           (regs2 (snd xxx))
                           (reg (hd regs2)))
                      (loop instrs
                            (concat regs1 (:: (- reg 1) (tl regs2))))))
            ((Jz) (let* ((regno (cadr instr))
                         (label (caddr instr))
                         (xxx (split regno regs))
                         (reg (hd (snd xxx))))
                    (if (zero? reg)
                        (jump label regs)
                        (loop instrs regs))))
            ((Jump) (let* ((label (cadr instr)))
                      (jump label regs)))
            (else (error "Illegal Instruction")))))))
```

Fig. 2. Dispatch and Arithmetic Part of the Interpreter

Static Module Structure. The first approach relies on making as much information static as possible. A separate export declaration associates each globally visible label with the module in which it is defined. Each label that is not mentioned in the global declaration is considered local. Here is such a declaration:

```
((add . mod1) (finis . mod1) (copy . mod2)))
```

Since it is unknown which of the exported procedures of a program gets called, the main function of the interpreter has a name parameter with binding time dynamic. The interpreter tests the supplied name against the list of exported names to obtain the name of the module containing name's definition. At specialization time, these tests create a dispatch to all functions declared in the list. This technique coincides with a standard binding-time improving transformation ("The Trick" [15]).

```
(define (jump exported-names modname)
  (lambda (name args)
    (let* ((is-exported (assoc name exported-names))
           (name+mod (or is-exported (cons name modname))))
      (access (cdr name+mod)
        (lambda (this-modname this-mod)
          (let ((found (assoc name this-mod)))
            (if found
                (exec (jump exported-names this-modname) (cdr found) args)
                (error "Undefined name"))))))))

(define (main exported-names name nargs initial-args)
  (let ((args (clone nargs initial-args)))
    (let loop ((exports exported-names))
      (if (null? exports)
          (dyn-error "Unknown name")
          (let ((export (car exports)))
            (if (eqv? name (car export))
                ((jump exported-names (cdr export)) (car export) args)
                (loop (cdr exports))))))))
```

Fig. 3. Jump Processor with Declarations

Figure 3 implements such a `jump` processor. The `main` procedure first copies the dynamic argument list into a partially-static list of register values of predetermined length, `nargs`. The `loop` procedure dispatches over the `exported-names`, an association list mapping a label to its defining module. Once the corresponding module is found, it calls `jump` on the static version of the name.

In `jump`, the parameters `exported-names`, `modname`, and `name` are all static. It first constructs the fully qualified name, `name+mod`, of the entry point. Then it loads the corresponding module and searches for the name locally. If successful, this search binds `found` to a pair of the `name` and the code referenced by it. Finally, it calls `exec` to run the code.

The procedure (`access` *index process*), used to load the module's text, is built into the specializer. Its first parameter, *index*, is an index value (the name of a module) and its second parameter, *process*, is a procedure with two parameters. Once the indexed value is successfully accessed, *process* is called with the index value as the first parameter and the indexed value as the second parameter.

Each call to `access` builds a memoization point. Since all procedure calls, including local ones, are processed through the `jump` function, each block in the source program gives rise to a procedure in the specialized program. The only concession towards specialization in this code is the repeated lookup of the initial entry point in the export declaration.

Compiled code from the initial specialization run

```
(define (main-1 x-2 x-1)
  (let*
      ((mlet-3 (car x-1))     (mlet-4 (cdr x-1))
       (mlet-5 (car mlet-4)) (mlet-6 (cdr mlet-4))
       (mlet-7 (car mlet-6)) (mlet-8 (cdr mlet-6)))
    (case x-2
      ((add)    (jump-2 mlet-3 mlet-5 mlet-7))
      ((finis) (jump-3 mlet-3 mlet-5 mlet-7))
      ((copy)   (jump-4 mlet-3 mlet-5 mlet-7))
      (else     (error "Unknown name")))))
```

Compiled code for *mod1*

```
(define (jump-2 mlet-3 mlet-2 mlet-1)
  (if (zero? mlet-2)
      (jump-4 mlet-3 mlet-2 mlet-1)
      (jump-2 (+ mlet-3 1) (- mlet-2 1) mlet-1)))
(define (jump-3 mlet-3 mlet-2 mlet-1) mlet-3)
```

Compiled code for *mod2*

```
(define (jump-5 mlet-3 mlet-2 mlet-1)
  (if (zero? mlet-2)
      (jump-3 mlet-3 mlet-2 mlet-1)
      (jump-2 mlet-3 mlet-2 mlet-1)))
(define (jump-4 mlet-3 mlet-2 mlet-1)
  (if (zero? mlet-1)
      (jump-5 mlet-3 mlet-2 mlet-1)
      (jump-4 mlet-3 (+ mlet-2 1) (- mlet-1 1)))))
```

Fig. 4. Compiled Code for Static Module Structure

Compilation with this interpreter yields satisfactory results. The specializer compiles modules in any order. It compiles all exported functions in every module, so that mutual recursion is possible. Each module is compiled at most once and the compiled code looks quite natural.

Figure 4 shows compiled code for the register-machine program from Figure 1. The parameter, x-2, of the specialized main-1 procedure is the entry label and the parameter, x-1, contains the argument list. Arity raising of the argument list with respect to three registers yields the three parameters, mlet-3, mlet-5, and mlet-7, to the specialized variants of the jump function. The (case x-2 ...) construct implements the required dispatch.

The dispatch code seems inefficient but it executes only once, when the compiled program starts. All other calls, intra-module as well as cross-module ones, are compiled as direct jumps.

```
(define (jump mod+name args)
  (access (car mod+name)
    (lambda (this-modname this-mod)
      (let ((found (assoc (cdr mod+name) this-mod)))
        (if found
            (exec jump (cdr found) args)
            (error "Undefined name"))))))

(define (jump-initial modulename name args)
  (access modulename
    (lambda (mod-name mod-body)
      (let loop ((names (map (lambda (block) (car block)) mod-body)))
        (if (null? names) (dyn-error "unknown name")
            (let ((this-name (car names)))
              (if (eqv? name this-name)
                  (jump (cons mod-name this-name) args)
                  (loop (cdr names)))))))))

(define (main modulename name nargs initial-args)
  (let ((args (clone nargs initial-args)))
    (jump-initial modulename name args)))
```

Fig. 5. Jump Processor without Declarations

Dynamic Module Structure. The only inconvenience of the previous interpreter is the specification of the association of labels to modules before a compilation can start. While this is not unreasonable in ordinary software development, it becomes problematic if this association is not statically known. For example, a program might compute the name of a module or it might receive it over the network. At this point, another feature of (access *index process*) comes to bear. Previously, the *index* value was static but the specializer can deal with a dynamic *index* value, too. In the latter case, the specializer processes *any* index and corresponding fragment and calls the *process* function with that index value and the indexed fragment, which at that point become statically known to the specializer. In addition, the specializer reinstalls an identical dynamic access construct to wait for further indexes. This re-installation generates code that dispatches on the index value at run-time.

Figure 5 shows an implementation of the jump processor, which requires that all non-local calls must use qualified names of the form (*module . label*). The main function calls jump-initial with all arguments dynamic. The loop function implements The Trick over the unknown name by scanning the labels from the current module. Thus, in the call to jump only args is dynamic.

The example source (see Fig. 1) changes accordingly: *mod1* calls (mod2 . copy) instead of copy and so on. Figure 6 shows the compiled code after these changes. The startup function initializes the register list and calls

The startup function

```
(define (main-1 x-3 x-2 x-1)
  (let* ((mlet-4 (car x-1))
         (mlet-5 (cdr x-1))
         (mlet-6 (car mlet-5))
         (mlet-7 (cdr mlet-5))
         (mlet-8 (car mlet-7))
         (mlet-9 (cdr mlet-7)))
    (jump-initial-2 x-3 x-2 mlet-4 mlet-6 mlet-8)))
```

Compiled code for *mod1*

```
(define (jump-3 mlet-3 mlet-2 mlet-1)
  (if (zero? mlet-2)
      (jump-6 mlet-3 mlet-2 mlet-1)
      (jump-3 (+ mlet-3 1) (- mlet-2 1) mlet-1)))
(define (jump-4 mlet-3 mlet-2 mlet-1) mlet-3)
(define (jump-initial-2 x-5 x-4 mlet-3 mlet-2 mlet-1)
  (if (eq? 'mod1 x-5)
      (case x-4
        ((add) (jump-3 mlet-3 mlet-2 mlet-1))
        ((finis) (jump-4 mlet-3 mlet-2 mlet-1))
        (else (error "unknown name")))
      (jump-initial-5 x-5 x-4 mlet-3 mlet-2 mlet-1)))
```

Compiled code for *mod2*

```
(define (jump-6 mlet-3 mlet-2 mlet-1)
  (if (zero? mlet-1)
      (jump-7 mlet-3 mlet-2 mlet-1)
      (jump-6 mlet-3 (+ mlet-2 1) (- mlet-1 1))))
(define (jump-7 mlet-3 mlet-2 mlet-1)
  (if (zero? mlet-2)
      (jump-4 mlet-3 mlet-2 mlet-1)
      (jump-3 mlet-3 mlet-2 mlet-1)))
(define (jump-initial-5 x-5 x-4 mlet-3 mlet-2 mlet-1)
  (if (eq? 'mod2 x-5)
      (case x-4
        ((copy) (jump-6 mlet-3 mlet-2 mlet-1))
        ((test) (jump-7 mlet-3 mlet-2 mlet-1))
        (else (error "unknown name")))
      (jump-initial-8 x-5 x-4 mlet-3 mlet-2 mlet-1)))
```

Compiled code for the empty module

```
(define (jump-initial-8 x-5 x-4 mlet-3 mlet-2 mlet-1)
  (error "invalid index"))
```

Fig. 6. Compiled Code for Dynamic Module Structure

`jump-initial-2`. The dispatch is now distributed over the modules since the existence of a function name is only known upon arrival of a module. This also explains the code for the empty module, which is produced when no more modules arrive. As before, the run-time dispatch happens only once.

4   Theoretical Background

For clarity, the specification of the specialization and the statement and proof of its correctness deal with a first-order functional Mini-language. We use, $\overline{x}$, for the sequence, $x_1, \ldots, x_n$, and similar shorthands apply to other entities.

A Simple First-Order Language. Figure 7 presents the first-order language. A program is a list of definitions followed by an expression. A definition is a triple of a function name, a list of formal parameters, and an expression. Expressions can be variables, constants, conditionals, primitive operations, and function calls. Function calls are special. Their first parameter always accesses the underlying indexed value.

The semantics is standard [18], except for the partial function ω. It is the index function for the underlying indexed value. It is a parameter of the program semantics $\mathcal{P}[\![]\!]$ and is fed into the first parameter of every function. The result of a function call cannot be defined unless the indexing function ω is defined at v_0. In that case, the actual parameter is the *indexed value*, that is $\omega(v_0)$.

In the equations, *let* $x_\perp = v$ *in* v' stands for *case* v *of* $\perp \to \perp \mid x_\perp \to v'$.

A Two-Level First-Order Language. Figures 8 and 9 specify syntax and semantics of a two-level variant of the first-order language. The grammar specifies the additional items with respect to Fig. 7. The interesting aspect is in the treatment of function calls in the specialized program. The result, *Val*, of specializing an expression is a (lifted) base value, if the expression is static, or a (lifted) pair of an expression and a set H. The set H models the *pending list*, which collects generated function calls that still need to be processed by the specializer. If the specialization of an expression returns the pair (r, η) then the specializer must provide specialized function definitions as prescribed by η. The final result of specialization is a specialized program π and a residual expression, r.

In the equations, underlining indicates primitive operations that generate code. For example, $\underline{b}$ is a constant expression with $\mathcal{C}[\![\underline{b}]\!] = b$. To avoid formalizing the generation of names for specialized variants of functions, we assume that there is an injective function $\lceil \cdot \rceil$ that maps a function name and a list of (static) base values to a function name. Since the language is first-order and deals only with base values, the original names can be reused without conflict.

To simplify the specification further, function arguments are grouped by their binding time. The parameters 1 through k are static, whereas the parameters $k + 1$ through $k + u$ are dynamic. The special indexing parameter can be static or dynamic. It determines the binding time of the `access` construct.

Syntactic domains

$$
\begin{aligned}
Ident \ni x & \quad \text{denumerable set of identifiers} \\
Const \ni c & \quad \text{denumerable set of constant symbols} \\
Op \ni o & \quad \text{denumerable set of operator symbols} \\
Fname \ni f & \quad \text{denumerable set of function symbols} \\
Prog \ni p & ::= d; \ldots d; e \\
Def \ni d & ::= f(x, \ldots, x) = e \\
Exp \ni e & ::= x \mid c \mid \text{if } e\ e\ e \mid o(e \ldots e) \mid \text{access } f(e \ldots e)
\end{aligned}
$$

Semantic domains

$$
\begin{aligned}
b \in Base &= \text{set of base values, as discrete CPO} \\
\psi \in \Psi &= Ident \rightarrow Base \\
\varphi \in \Phi &= Ident \rightarrow Base^{n+1} \rightarrow Base_\perp \\
\omega \in \Omega &= Base \hookrightarrow Base
\end{aligned}
$$

Ω is the pointed CPO of partial functions.

Semantic functions

$$
\begin{aligned}
\mathcal{C}[\![\,]\!] &: Const \rightarrow Base & \text{unspecified} \\
\mathcal{O}[\![\,]\!] &: Op \rightarrow Base^n \rightarrow Base & \text{unspecified} \\
\mathcal{E}[\![\,]\!] &: Exp \rightarrow \Psi \rightarrow \Phi \rightarrow Base_\perp \\
\mathcal{P}[\![\,]\!] &: Prog \rightarrow \Psi \rightarrow \Omega \rightarrow Base_\perp
\end{aligned}
$$

Semantic equations

$$
\begin{aligned}
\mathcal{E}[\![x]\!]\psi\varphi &= (\psi(x))_\perp \\
\mathcal{E}[\![c]\!]\psi\varphi &= \mathcal{C}[\![c]\!]_\perp \\
\mathcal{E}[\![\text{if } e_1\ e_2\ e_3]\!]\psi\varphi &= \text{let } b_\perp = \mathcal{E}[\![e_1]\!]\psi\varphi \text{ in} \\
& \quad \text{if } b \text{ then } \mathcal{E}[\![e_2]\!]\psi\varphi \text{ else } \mathcal{E}[\![e_3]\!]\psi\varphi \\
\mathcal{E}[\![o(e_1 \ldots e_n)]\!]\psi\varphi &= \text{let } b_{1\perp} = \mathcal{E}[\![e_1]\!]\psi\varphi \text{ in} \\
& \quad \ldots \\
& \quad \text{let } b_{n\perp} = \mathcal{E}[\![e_n]\!]\psi\varphi \text{ in} \\
& \quad (\mathcal{O}[\![o]\!](b_1, \ldots, b_n))_\perp \\
\mathcal{E}[\![\text{access } f(e_0 \ldots e_n)]\!]\psi\varphi &= \text{let } b_{0\perp} = \mathcal{E}[\![e_0]\!]\psi\varphi \text{ in} \\
& \quad \ldots \\
& \quad \text{let } b_{n\perp} = \mathcal{E}[\![e_n]\!]\psi\varphi \text{ in} \\
& \quad \varphi(f)(b_0, \ldots, b_n)
\end{aligned}
$$

Semantics of a program

$$
\begin{aligned}
\mathcal{P}[\![d_1; \ldots; d_k; e]\!]\psi\omega &= \\
\mathcal{E}[\![e]\!]\psi(\text{fix } \lambda\varphi.[f \mapsto \lambda v_0, \overline{v}.\text{if } & v_0 \in dom(\omega) \text{ then } \mathcal{E}[\![e]\!][x_0 \mapsto \omega(v_0), \overline{x} \mapsto \overline{v}]\varphi \text{ else } \perp \\
\mid f(x_0, \overline{x}) = e & \in \{d_1, \ldots, d_k\}])
\end{aligned}
$$

Fig. 7. A First-Order Language and Its Semantics

Syntactic domains (additions)

$$2Prog \ni p' ::= d'; \ldots d'; e'$$
$$2Def \ni d' ::= f(x, \ldots, x) = e'$$
$$2Exp \ni e' ::= x \mid c \mid \texttt{lift}\ e' \mid \texttt{if}^\beta\ e'\ e'\ e' \mid o^\beta(e' \ldots e') \mid \texttt{access}\ f^\beta(e' \ldots e')$$
$$BTime \ni \beta ::= S \mid D \quad \text{where } S < D$$

Semantic domains

$$
\begin{aligned}
b \in Base &= \text{set of base values, as discrete CPO} \\
r \in RExp &\quad \text{residual expressions (see Fig. 11)} \\
RDef &\quad \text{residual definition (see Fig. 11)} \\
v \in Val &= Base \cup RExp \times H \\
\psi' \in \Psi' &= Ident \to Val \\
\eta \in H &= Set(Fname \times Base^{k+1}) \\
\pi \in \Pi &= Set(RDef) \\
\omega \in \Omega &= Base \hookrightarrow Base
\end{aligned}
$$

The sets H and Π are CPOs under the subset ordering.

Semantic functions

$$
\begin{aligned}
\mathcal{C}[\![\,]\!] &: Const \to Base & \text{unspecified} \\
\mathcal{O}[\![\,]\!] &: Op \to Base^n \to Base & \text{unspecified} \\
\mathcal{S}[\![\,]\!] &: 2Exp \to \Psi' \to Val_\bot \\
\mathcal{T}[\![\,]\!] &: 2Prog \to \Psi' \to \Omega \to (\Pi \times RExp)_\bot
\end{aligned}
$$

Fig. 8. Two-Level First-Order Language, Syntax, and Semantics, Part 1

Specialization is also standard up to the collection of the H component from dynamic results. Most static constructs are omitted since their specialization is identical to the standard semantics (Fig. 7). The interesting bit is the definition of the two versions of

$$\texttt{access}\ f^\beta(e'_0 e'_1 \ldots e'_k e'_{k+1} \ldots e'_{k+u})$$

Regardless of β, the specializer specializes all the parameter expressions, expecting results of the specified binding times. If e'_0 is static with value b_0, the specializer generates a function call to $\lceil f, b_0, b_1, \ldots, b_k \rceil$ where $b_1, \ldots, b_k$ are the values of the static parameters. The H component of the result is set up to contain the tuple $\lceil f, b_0, b_1, \ldots, b_k \rceil$. The fixpoint in function $\mathcal{T}[\![\,]\!]$ picks up this tuple and generates the corresponding specialized function, but only if the indexed value is available.

If e'_0 is dynamic, the specializer also generates a residual function call, but to $\lceil f, *, b_1, \ldots, b_k \rceil$, and notes this in the H component of the result. The symbol $*$ is a special, otherwise unused, base value, and is taken to stand for *any* module. The *letrec* in $\mathcal{T}[\![\,]\!]$ picks up this tuple. It generates a specialized function, which is defined by pattern matching on the index parameter. In contrast to the previous case, it does not pick up one static value for b_0 but it picks up *all possible* static

Semantic equations

$$\mathcal{S}[\![x]\!]\psi' = \psi(x)_\perp$$

$$\mathcal{S}[\![c]\!]\psi' = (\mathcal{C}[\![c]\!], [])_\perp$$

$$\mathcal{S}[\![\mathtt{lift}\ e']\!]\psi' = let\ b_\perp = \mathcal{S}[\![e']\!]\psi'\ in\ (\underline{b}, [])_\perp$$

$$\mathcal{S}[\![\mathtt{if}^D\ e'_1\ e'_2\ e'_3]\!]\psi' = let\ (r_1, \eta_1)_\perp = \mathcal{S}[\![e'_1]\!]\psi'\ in$$
$$let\ (r_2, \eta_2)_\perp = \mathcal{S}[\![e'_2]\!]\psi'\ in$$
$$let\ (r_3, \eta_3)_\perp = \mathcal{S}[\![e'_3]\!]\psi'\ in$$
$$(\underline{\mathtt{if}}\ r_1\ r_2\ r_3, \eta_1 \cup \eta_2 \cup \eta_3)_\perp$$

$$\mathcal{S}[\![o^D(e'_1 \ldots e'_n)]\!]\psi' = let\ (r_1, \eta_1)_\perp = \mathcal{S}[\![e'_1]\!]\psi'\ in$$
$$\ldots$$
$$let\ (r_n, \eta_n)_\perp = \mathcal{S}[\![e'_n]\!]\psi'\ in$$
$$(\underline{o}(r_1, \ldots, r_n), \eta_1 \cup \ldots \cup \eta_n)_\perp$$

$$\mathcal{S}[\![\mathtt{access}\ f^S(e'_0, e'_1 \ldots e'_{k+u})]\!]\psi' = let\ b_{0\perp} = \mathcal{S}[\![e'_0]\!]\psi'\ in$$
$$\ldots$$
$$let\ b_{k\perp} = \mathcal{S}[\![e'_k]\!]\psi'\ in$$
$$let\ (r_1, \eta_1)_\perp = \mathcal{S}[\![e'_{k+1}]\!]\psi'\ in$$
$$\ldots$$
$$let\ (r_u, \eta_u)_\perp = \mathcal{S}[\![e'_{k+u}]\!]\psi'\ in$$
$$(\underline{\lceil f, b_0, \ldots, b_k \rceil}(r_1, \ldots, r_u),$$
$$\eta_1 \cup \ldots \cup \eta_u \cup \{\lceil f, b_0, \ldots, b_k \rceil\})_\perp$$

$$\mathcal{S}[\![\mathtt{access}\ f^D(e'_0, e'_1 \ldots e'_{k+u})]\!]\psi' = let\ (r_0, \eta_0)_\perp = \mathcal{S}[\![e'_0]\!]\psi'\ in$$
$$let\ b_{1\perp} = \mathcal{S}[\![e'_1]\!]\psi'\ in$$
$$\ldots$$
$$let\ b_{k\perp} = \mathcal{S}[\![e'_k]\!]\psi'\ in$$
$$let\ (r_1, \eta_1)_\perp = \mathcal{S}[\![e'_{k+1}]\!]\psi'\ in$$
$$\ldots$$
$$let\ (r_u, \eta_u)_\perp = \mathcal{S}[\![e'_{k+u}]\!]\psi'\ in$$
$$(\underline{\lceil f, *, b_1, \ldots, b_k \rceil}(r_0, r_1, \ldots, r_u),$$
$$\eta_1 \cup \ldots \cup \eta_u \cup \{\lceil f, *, b_1, \ldots, b_k \rceil\})_\perp$$

Semantics of specialization
Let $d'_i \equiv f_i(x_{(i,0)}, \overline{x}_i) = e'_i$, for $1 \le i \le k$.

$$\mathcal{T}[\![d'_1; \ldots; d'_k; e']\!]\psi'\omega$$
$$= let\ (r_0, \eta_0)_\perp = \mathcal{S}[\![e']\!]\psi'\ in$$
$$letrec\ (\pi, \eta) =$$
$$let\ X = \{(buildDef\{\lceil f_i, b_0, \ldots, b_k \rceil(x_{(i,k+1)}, \ldots, x_{(i,k+u)}) = r\}, \eta'')$$
$$\mid \lceil f_i, b_0, \ldots, b_k \rceil \in \eta \cup \eta_0,\ b_0 \in dom(\omega),$$
$$(r, \eta'')_\perp = \mathcal{S}[\![e'_i]\!][x_{(i,0)} \mapsto \omega(b_0), x_{(i,1)} \mapsto b_1, \ldots, x_{(i,k)} \mapsto b_k,$$
$$x_{(i,k+1)} \mapsto (x_{(i,k+1)}, []), \ldots, x_{(i,k+u)} \mapsto (x_{(i,k+u)}, [])]\}$$
$$\cup \{(buildDef\{\lceil f_i, *, b_1, \ldots, b_k \rceil(b_0, x_{(i,k+1)}, \ldots, x_{(i,k+u)}) = r\}, \eta'')$$
$$\mid \lceil f_i, *, b_1, \ldots, b_k \rceil \in \eta \cup \eta_0,\ b_0 \in dom(\omega),$$
$$(r, \eta')_\perp = \mathcal{S}[\![e'_i]\!][x_{(i,0)} \mapsto \omega(b_0), x_{(i,1)} \mapsto b_1, \ldots, x_{(i,k)} \mapsto b_k,$$
$$x_{(i,k+1)} \mapsto (x_{(i,k+1)}, []), \ldots, x_{(i,k+u)} \mapsto (x_{(i,k+u)}, [])]\}$$
$$in\ (Set(d' \mid (d', \eta'') \in X), \bigcup Set(\eta'' \mid (d', \eta'') \in X))$$

Fig. 9. Two-Level First-Order Language, Syntax, and Semantics, Part 2

values for $b_0 \in dom(\omega)$ at once. This behavior will turn out to be crucial in the proof of semantics preservation.

Specialization of fragments can be understood as repeating $\mathcal{T}[\![p']\!]\psi'\omega$ with ω drawn from an increasing sequence in Ω, as more and more indexed values are presented to the specializer. The implementation reflects this behaviour by increasing the memoization cache, but it only generates new code.

Annotated Types

$$\begin{aligned}
&\text{Function Types} &&\sigma ::= \rho \times \ldots \times \rho \to \rho \\
&\text{Annotated Types} &&\rho ::= (\tau; \beta) \qquad \tau ::= \mathbf{base} \\[6pt]
&\text{Function Environments} &&\Delta ::= \emptyset \mid \Delta[f : \sigma] \\
&\text{Variable Environments} &&\Gamma ::= \emptyset \mid \Gamma[x : \rho]
\end{aligned}$$

Typing rules

$$(var)\frac{\Gamma(x) = \rho}{\Delta, \Gamma \vdash x : \rho} \qquad (const)\frac{}{\Delta, \Gamma \vdash c : (\mathbf{base}; S)} \qquad (lift)\frac{\Delta, \Gamma \vdash e' : (\mathbf{base}; S)}{\Delta, \Gamma \vdash \mathbf{lift}\ e' : (\mathbf{base}; D)}$$

$$(if)\frac{\Delta, \Gamma \vdash e'_1 : (\mathbf{base}; \beta) \quad \Delta, \Gamma \vdash e'_2 : (\tau; \beta') \quad \Delta, \Gamma \vdash e'_3 : (\tau; \beta') \quad \beta \leq \beta'}{\Delta, \Gamma \vdash \mathbf{if}^\beta\ e'_1\ e'_2\ e'_3 : (\tau; \beta')}$$

$$(prim)\frac{\Delta, \Gamma \vdash e'_1 : (\mathbf{base}; \beta) \quad \ldots \quad \Delta, \Gamma \vdash e'_n : (\mathbf{base}; \beta)}{\Delta, \Gamma \vdash o^\beta(e'_1 \ldots e'_n) : (\mathbf{base}; \beta)}$$

$$(call\text{-}access)\frac{\Delta(f) = \rho_1 \times \ldots \times \rho_n \to (\tau; D) \quad \Delta, \Gamma \vdash e'_0 : (\mathbf{base}; \beta)}{\quad (\forall 1 \leq i \leq k)\ \Delta, \Gamma \vdash e'_i : (\tau_i; S) \quad (\forall 1 \leq i \leq u)\ \Delta, \Gamma \vdash e'_{k+i} : (\tau_{k+i}; D)}{\Delta, \Gamma \vdash \mathbf{access}\ f^\beta(e'_0 e'_1 \ldots e'_k e'_{k+1} \ldots e'_{k+u}) : (\tau; D)}$$

$$(def)\frac{\Delta(f) = \rho_1 \times \ldots \times \rho_n \to (\tau; D) \quad \Delta, [x_i : \rho_i] \vdash e' : (\tau; D)}{\Delta \vdash_d f(x_1 \ldots x_n) = e'}$$

$$(prog)\frac{\Delta \vdash_d d'_1 \quad \ldots \quad \Delta \vdash_d d'_m \quad \Delta, \Gamma \vdash e' : (\tau; D)}{\Delta, \Gamma \vdash_p d'_1; \ldots d'_m; e'}$$

Fig. 10. Binding-Time Analysis for the First-Order Language

Binding-Time Analysis. Figure 10 presents the rules for binding-time analysis for the two-level language. Besides function types for top-level functions, the language has binding-time annotated types $(\mathbf{base}; \beta)$. Function and variable environments are standard. There are typing judgments for expressions $(\Delta, \Gamma \vdash e' : \rho$: function environment Δ and variable environment Γ entails that e' has annotated type ρ), definitions $(\Delta \vdash_d d')$ and programs $(\Delta, \Gamma \vdash_p p')$ with the usual meanings. The binding-time rules are standard [15,26], but the rule for

Syntactic domains

$$RExp \ni r \quad ::= x \mid c \mid \text{if } r\ r\ r \mid o(r \ldots r) \mid f(r \ldots r)$$
$$RDef \ni d'' ::= f(x, \ldots, x) = r$$
$$RProg \ni p'' ::= (\Pi; r)$$

Semantic domains

$$\varphi' \in \Phi' = Ident \to Base^* \to Base_\perp$$

Semantic functions

$$\mathcal{E}'[\![\,]\!] : RExp \to \Psi \to \Phi' \to Base_\perp$$
$$\mathcal{P}'[\![\,]\!] : RProg \to \Psi \to Base_\perp$$

Semantic equations

$$\mathcal{E}'[\![f(r_1 \ldots r_n)]\!]\psi\varphi' = \text{let } b_{1\perp} = \mathcal{E}'[\![r_1]\!]\psi\varphi' \text{ in } \ldots$$
$$\text{let } b_{n\perp} = \mathcal{E}'[\![r_n]\!]\psi\varphi' \text{ in } \varphi'(f)(b_1, \ldots, b_n)$$

Semantics of a program

$$\mathcal{P}'[\![(\pi; r)]\!]\psi = \mathcal{E}'[\![r]\!]\psi(\text{fix } \lambda\varphi'.[\ f \mapsto \lambda\overline{v}.\mathcal{E}[\![r]\!][\overline{x} \mapsto \overline{v}]\varphi' \mid f(\overline{x}) = r \in \pi] \cup$$
$$[\ g \mapsto \lambda v_0\overline{v}.\text{if } v_0 = b_1 \text{ then } \mathcal{E}[\![r_1]\!][\overline{x} \mapsto \overline{v}]\varphi' \text{ else } \ldots$$
$$\text{else if } v_0 = b_n \text{ then } \mathcal{E}[\![r_n]\!][\overline{x} \mapsto \overline{v}]\varphi' \text{ else } \perp$$
$$\mid g(b_1\overline{x}) = r_1, \ldots, g(b_n\overline{x}) = r_n \in \pi])$$

Fig. 11. Syntax and Semantics of the Target Language

`access` needs some attention. The binding-time of the call to f depends solely on the binding-time of the index e'_0. The first k parameters are static and the remaining are dynamic. The result of specializing a call to f, and the result type of its definition, are dynamic since the specializer never unfolds calls.

The Target Language. The target language (Fig. 11) differs from the source language in that it has ordinary functions instead of `access` procedures. The semantic equations for $\mathcal{E}'[\![\,]\!]$ are identical to the ones for $\mathcal{E}[\![\,]\!]$ up to the rule for function call. There are two kinds of function definitions. The g-style definitions perform a pattern match on a base value in the first argument. They originate from the specialization of an `access` call with a dynamic index parameter. The remaining f-style definitions are standard. They originate from the specialization of an `access` call with a static index parameter.

Correctness. The correctness of specialization has two facets. The first facet is a type preservation result for the binding-time analysis. We need a few auxiliary definitions.

Definition 1. Let $\psi \in \Psi$ and $\psi'' \in \Psi'$.

- $Val^S = Base$ and $Val^D = RExp \times H$;
- $\Gamma \models \psi'$ iff, for all $x : (\tau; \beta) \in \Gamma$, $\psi'(x) \in Val^\beta$;

- $\Gamma \models \psi \sim \psi'$ iff, $\Gamma \models \psi'$, $dom(\psi) = dom(\psi')$, and for all $x : (\tau; \beta) \in \Gamma$, if $\beta = S$ then $\psi'(x) = \psi(x)$ and if $\beta = D$ then $\psi'(x) = (x, [])$.

Theorem 1. (Type Preservation)
Suppose $\Delta, \Gamma \vdash_p p'$ *and* $\Gamma \models \psi'$. *Then* $\mathcal{T}[\![p']\!]\psi'\omega \in Val^D{}_\perp$.

The proof of this theorem rests on the following lemma for expressions, which is standard and straightforward to prove. Specialization of an expression always terminates because there is no call unfolding.

Lemma 1. *Suppose* $\Delta, \Gamma \vdash e' : (\tau; \beta)$ *and* $\Gamma \models \psi'$.
*   Then* $\mathcal{S}[\![e']\!]\psi' \in Val^\beta{}_\perp \setminus \{\perp\}$.

Given type preservation, we can show semantics preservation. The function $|\cdot|$ is the erasure function that maps two-level entities (expressions, definitions, programs, types, etc) to the underlying standard entities. It erases all annotations and `lift` constructs.

Theorem 2. (Semantics Preservation) *Let* p' *be an annotated program with* $\Delta, \Gamma \vdash_p p'$. *Let* $\psi \in \Psi$ *and* $\psi' \in \Psi'$ *so that* $\Gamma \models \psi \sim \psi'$.
*   If* $\mathcal{P}[\![|p'|]\!]\psi\omega = v$ *and* $\mathcal{T}[\![p']\!]\psi'\omega = (\pi, r)_\perp$ *then* $\mathcal{P}'[\![\pi; r]\!]\psi = v$.

Proving this theorem requires a lemma that states the appropriate result for expressions. The lemma is proved by induction on the two-level expression e'.

Lemma 2. *Let* e' *be an annotated expression with* $\Delta, \Gamma \vdash e' : \rho$. *Let* $\psi \in \Psi$ *and* $\psi' \in \Psi'$ *so that* $\Gamma \models \psi \sim \psi'$. *Let* $\varphi \in \Phi$.
*   Suppose* $\mathcal{E}[\![|e'|]\!]\psi\varphi\omega = y$ *and* $\mathcal{S}[\![e']\!]\psi' = v'_\perp$.

- *If* $v' = (r, \eta)$ *and for all* $\varphi' \in \Phi'$ *such that, for all* $\lceil f, b_0, \ldots, b_k \rceil \in \eta$ *and* $b_{k+1}, \ldots, b_{k+u} \in Base^*$, *it holds that*

$$\varphi(f)(b_0, \ldots, b_{k+u}) = \varphi'(\lceil f, b_0, \ldots, b_k \rceil)(b_{k+1}, \ldots, b_{k+u})$$

and, for all $\lceil f, *, b_1, \ldots, b_k \rceil \in \eta$ *and* $b_0, b_{k+1}, \ldots, b_{k+u} \in Base^*$, *it holds that*

$$\varphi(f)(b_0, \ldots, b_{k+u}) = \varphi'(\lceil f, *, b_1, \ldots, b_k \rceil)(b_0, b_{k+1}, \ldots, b_{k+u})$$

*   then* $\mathcal{E}'[\![r]\!]\psi\varphi' = y$.
- *If* $v' = b$ *then* $y = b_\perp$.

The proof of the main theorem proceeds by fixpoint induction.

5   Implementation

We have implemented specialization with respect to an indexed set of static values in the latest release of the PGG specialization system for Scheme [27]. In the implementation, a lot of the code for dealing with `access` can be shared with the standard memoization code. Type signatures, a standard feature of PGG, are used internally to impose the proper types on the arguments of access.

Furthermore, the implementation can process the fragments of static input in two modes. Either there is a separate session with the specializer for each group of fragments as it arrives, or all fragments arrive during a single session. To optimize the latter case, the implementation additionally puts a function value in every entry of the memoization table. This function is the second parameter of the access construct. It takes the index and the corresponding value as parameters and delivers the specialized body of the function determined by the entry.

The access construct is implemented in terms of another primitive, _access, which behaves non-deterministically under the standard semantics. It is simpler to implement because –when its first argument is dynamic– it always grabs the next indexed value that arrives and calls the *process* procedure with the static index and the value. It is easy to implement the better behaved access in terms of _access with a macro definition.

```
(define-syntax access
  (syntax-rules ()
    ((access index f)
     (let ((dyn-index index))
       (letrec
         ((jump
            (lambda ()
              (_access
               dyn-index
               (lambda (static-index value)
                 (if (null? value)
                     (dyn-error "invalid index")
                     (if (eq? dyn-index static-index)
                         (f static-index value)
                         (jump)))))))))
         (jump))))))
```

The macro implements "The Trick" over the indexes. It cannot be implemented as a function with PGG's monovariant analyses because every use of access might have a different type and different binding times.

6   Related Work

Heldal and Hughes [12,13] have developed a partial evaluator specifically tailored towards compiling modular languages via specialization. While they develop much of the technology from scratch, we reuse standard solutions from an existing specializer as much as possible. Their framework requires that module dependencies be acyclic, whereas our approach does not place such restrictions: as demonstrated in Section 3, the specializer compiles mutually dependent modules in arbitrary order. Their partial evaluator employs a third binding time, *late static*, to generate a dispatch function in an interface file. In our approach, the memoization cache plays this role. We substitute a lookup in the memoization cache for executing their late static code from the interface file. The memoization cache can be kept in memory between specializations or it can be dumped to a file and resurrected when specialization continues. Otherwise, our approach reuses existing specialization techniques.

One could argue that a dynamic `access` is late static, but we actually obtain *late staticness* by having `access` itself static (it is specialized away) while its first argument, the index, is dynamic.

The third binding time in Heldal and Hughes's specializer can be used to transmit additional "link-time" data between modules. It is not clear how to transmit such data in our approach. However, if module signatures contain type information on imports and exports it is possible to encode type information so that type-safe linking is ensured.

Sundaresh and Hudak [23,24] describe a framework to construct *incremental programs*. Such programs can update the result of a computation efficiently if only a small part of the input changes. They obtain this effect by fixing a decomposition of the input, specializing the program with respect to each part of the input separately, and combining the results with a special linking combinator. Although this technique shares some similarities with ours, there are two fundamental differences. First, the input is split up in a fixed number of parts which have a fixed position relative to each other. In contrast, our approach allows an unbounded number of parts to be specialized separately and in any order. Second, Sundaresh's and Hudak's system is biased towards incremental changes of individual parts. Specialization of every part happens in isolation and the linking combinator recombines the specialized parts to one monolithic program. In our approach the result is a list of compiled parts and we cannot specialize in complete isolation.

A quite different problem is the specialization of modular programs as considered by Dussart et al. [6]. It considers a *subject program* divided into modules, and the authors argue that polymorphic binding-time analysis combined with the cogen approach to program specialization is the right tool for this endeavor. In contrast, we consider applications where the *static data is divided* into several parts. As an application we consider the *compilation of modular programs* by repeated specialization of the same interpreter with respect to one module at a time.

Glück and Jørgensen [9,10,11] have studied multi-level specialization. It can deal with any finite number of specialization stages. Every specialization round, one level is specialized away to produce a newly annotated program. In our work, we only maintain two binding times and all fragments have the same binding time. It might be possible to differentiate between flavors of staticness, e.g., "static now" and "static after access", as a further refinement. Moreover, in multi-level specialization, the number of stages is fixed before specialization starts. In contrast, the number of fragments in our approach need not be known *a priori*.

7   Conclusion

We have presented specialization with respect to an indexed set of static input fragments. It is sufficiently expressive to perform separate compilation for simple modular languages via specialization of an interpreter. Our technique has been integrated with the PGG specialization system and it opens interesting new applications. Our correctness proof is interesting in its own right because it formalizes the function memoization mechanism, which is usually left out of formal treatments.

In combination with a specializer that delivers directly executable specialized code [22], our technique can be used for just-in-time compilation of mobile code. In this scenario, modules in a higher-level language arrive, for example, from the network. Upon arrival, they trigger their own compilation, that is, specialization of the language's interpreter with respect to the module's text. The compiled code is directly linked with the rest of the program and thus immediately executable. This work is currently in progress.

Acknowledgments. We thank Olivier Danvy, John Hughes, Michael Sperber and the anonymous referees for their helpful comments on earlier drafts of this paper.

References

1. Kenichi Asai, Satoshi Matsuoka, and Akinori Yonezawa. Duplication and partial evaluation — for a better understanding of reflective languages. *Lisp and Symbolic Computation*, 9(2/3):203–241, May/June 1996.
2. Luca Cardelli. Program fragments, linking, and modularization. In Neil D. Jones, editor, *Proc. 24th Annual ACM Symposium on Principles of Programming Languages*, pages 266–277, Paris, France, January 1997. ACM Press.
3. Charles Consel. Polyvariant binding-time analysis for applicative languages. In David Schmidt, editor, *Proc. ACM SIGPLAN Symposium on Partial Evaluation and Semantics-Based Program Manipulation PEPM '93*, pages 66–77, Copenhagen, Denmark, June 1993. ACM Press.
4. Charles Consel and Olivier Danvy. Static and dynamic semantics processing. In POPL1991 [20], pages 14–24.
5. Charles Consel and Olivier Danvy. Tutorial notes on partial evaluation. In *Proc. 20th Annual ACM Symposium on Principles of Programming Languages*, pages 493–501, Charleston, South Carolina, January 1993. ACM Press.
6. Dirk Dussart, Rogardt Heldal, and John Hughes. Module-sensitive program specialisation. In PLDI1997 [19], pages 206–214.
7. Dirk Dussart, Fritz Henglein, and Christian Mossin. Polymorphic recursion and subtype qualifications: Polymorphic binding-time analysis in polynomial time. In Alan Mycroft, editor, *Proc. International Static Analysis Symposium, SAS'95*, volume 983 of *Lecture Notes in Computer Science*, pages 118–136, Glasgow, Scotland, September 1995. Springer-Verlag.
8. Yoshihiko Futamura. Partial evaluation of computation process — an approach to a compiler-compiler. *Systems, Computers, Controls*, 2(5):45–50, 1971.

9. Robert Glück and Jesper Jørgensen. Efficient multi-level generating extensions for program specialization. In Doaitse Swierstra and Manuel Hermenegildo, editors, *International Symposium on Programming Languages, Implementations, Logics and Programs (PLILP '95)*, volume 982 of *Lecture Notes in Computer Science*, pages 259–278, Utrecht, The Netherlands, September 1995. Springer-Verlag.

10. Robert Glück and Jesper Jørgensen. Fast multi-level binding-time analysis for multiple program specialization. In *PSI-96: Andrei Ershov Second International Memorial Conference, Perspectives of System Informatics*, volume 1181 of *Lecture Notes in Computer Science*, Novosibirsk, Russia, June 1996. Springer-Verlag.

11. Robert Glück and Jesper Jørgensen. An automatic program generator for multi-level specialization. *Lisp and Symbolic Computation*, 10(2):113–158, July 1997.

12. Rogardt Heldal and John Hughes. Partial evaluation and separate compilation. In Charles Consel, editor, *Proc. ACM SIGPLAN Symposium on Partial Evaluation and Semantics-Based Program Manipulation PEPM '97*, pages 1–11, Amsterdam, The Netherlands, June 1997. ACM Press.

13. Rogardt Heldal and John Hughes. Extending a partial evaluator which supports separate compilation. *Theoretical Computer Science*, to appear.

14. Fritz Henglein and Christian Mossin. Polymorphic binding-time analysis. In Donald Sannella, editor, *Proceedings of European Symposium on Programming*, volume 788 of *Lecture Notes in Computer Science*, pages 287–301. Springer-Verlag, April 1994.

15. Neil D. Jones, Carsten K. Gomard, and Peter Sestoft. *Partial Evaluation and Automatic Program Generation*. Prentice-Hall, 1993.

16. Jesper Jørgensen. Generating a compiler for a lazy language by partial evaluation. In *Nineteenth Annual ACM SIGACT-SIGPLAN Symposium on Principles of Programming Languages. Albuquerque, New Mexico*, pages 258–268, Albuquerque, New Mexico, January 1992. ACM Press.

17. Richard Kelsey, William Clinger, and Jonathan Rees. Revised[5] report on the algorithmic language Scheme. *Higher-Order and Symbolic Computation*, 11(1):7–105, 1998. Also appears in ACM SIGPLAN Notices 33(9), September 1998. Available electronically as http://www.neci.nj.nec.com/homepages/kelsey/r5rs.ps.gz.

18. Peter D. Mosses. *Denotational Semantics*, volume B of *Handbook of Theoretical Computer Science*, chapter 11. Elsevier Science Publishers, Amsterdam, 1990.

19. *Proc. of the ACM SIGPLAN '97 Conference on Programming Language Design and Implementation*, Las Vegas, NV, USA, June 1997. ACM Press.

20. *18th Annual ACM Symposium on Principles of Programming Languages*, Orlando, Florida, January 1991. ACM Press.

21. Michael Sperber and Peter Thiemann. Realistic compilation by partial evaluation. In *Proc. of the ACM SIGPLAN '96 Conference on Programming Language Design and Implementation*, pages 206–214, Philadelphia, PA, USA, May 1996. ACM Press.

22. Michael Sperber and Peter Thiemann. Two for the price of one: Composing partial evaluation and compilation. In PLDI1997 [19], pages 215–225.

23. Raman S. Sundaresh. Building incremental programs using partial evaluation. In Paul Hudak and Neil D. Jones, editors, *Proc. ACM SIGPLAN Symposium on Partial Evaluation and Semantics-Based Program Manipulation PEPM '91*, pages 83–93, New Haven, CT, June 1991. ACM. SIGPLAN Notices 26(9).

24. Raman S. Sundaresh and Paul Hudak. Incremental computation via partial evaluation. In POPL1991 [20], pages 1–13.

25. Peter Thiemann. Implementing memoization for partial evaluation. In Herbert Kuchen and Doaitse Swierstra, editors, *International Symposium on Programming Languages, Implementations, Logics and Programs (PLILP '96)*, volume 1140 of *Lecture Notes in Computer Science*, pages 198–212, Aachen, Germany, September 1996. Springer-Verlag.

26. Peter Thiemann. A unified framework for binding-time analysis. In Michel Bidoit and Max Dauchet, editors, *TAPSOFT '97: Theory and Practice of Software Development*, volume 1214 of *Lecture Notes in Computer Science*, pages 742–756, Lille, France, April 1997. Springer-Verlag.

27. Peter Thiemann. *The PGG System—User Manual*. Universität Freiburg, Freiburg, Germany, March 2000. Available from
http://www.informatik.uni-freiburg.de/proglang/software/pgg/.

A New Termination Approach for Specialization

Litong Song and Yoshihiko Futamura

Department of Information and Computer Science, Waseda University, Okubo 3-4-1
Shinjuku-ku, Tokyo 169-8555, Japan
{slt,futamura}@futamura.info.waseda.ac.jp

Abstract. Well-quasi orderings, and particularly homeomorphic embedding, recently became popular to ensure the termination of program specialization and transformation techniques. In this paper, we present a termination approach called recursive condition approach to ensure the termination of online specializers. Just like some traditional approaches, recursive condition approach is also based on well-quasi orderings using homeomorphic embedding. However, instead of using the arguments of functions, the conditions invoking recursive calls are used. Because the recursive condition approach exploits the recursive conditions which, to some extent, contain some semantic information of original programs, we believe this approach is more adequate and can produce more efficient residual programs than traditional approaches using well-quasi orderings/homeomorphic embedding. Furthermore, we present an approach (called combined approach) that combines the advantages of the recursive condition approach and the traditional approach.

1 Introduction

Partial evaluation is a program transformation technique which, given a program and parts of its arguments, produces a residual program w.r.t. those known arguments. Partial evaluation is widely used not only as a general optimization tool but also as generator for programs such as compiler and parser. However, in general, the termination of partial evaluation is undecidable. Therefore, any termination condition, which guarantees termination of partial evaluation, sometimes loses chances for specialization which leads to less efficient residual programs.

Partial evaluation can be classified as offline and online ones. In offline partial evaluators, a static analysis called binding-time analysis (BTA) is first made to a given program and parts of its arguments, and then the program is specialized. At specialization time, if a new function call (at least an argument is bounded to a new static value) is met, it will be specialized. Although BTA plays an important role in ensuring the termination of specialization, it does not always ensure the termination. Existing offline evaluators such as Similix[2], Tempo[4] and Cmix[1] do not automatically ensure the termination of specialization. In online partial evaluators, a given program is directly specialized without any static analysis, so the specialization of the program is more prone to non-termination. Most online partial evaluators (e.g., [3, 9, 15, 17, 21, 25, 26, 27]) have adopted some termination criterions to avoid infinite specialization.

W.Taha (Ed.): SAIG 2000, LNCS 1924, pp. 72-91, 2000.
© Springer-Verlag Berlin Heidelberg 2000

As a traditional way, "bound approach is to simply impose an arbitrary bound. Such a bound is of course not motivated by any property, structural or otherwise, of the program under consideration. Therefore, it will typically lead to either too little or too much specialization" [14].

Another traditional way is to adopt well-founded orderings (wfo) (e.g., [3, 17, 21, 22, 27]). Recently, well-quasi orderings (wqo), and particularly homeomorphic embedding, became popular to ensure the termination of program specialization and transformation techniques (e.g., [9, 15, 23, 25, 26]). Moreover, [14] has demonstrated that, in the case of dynamic techniques such as partial evaluation and partial deduction, the approaches based on well-quasi orderings are more powerful (powerful in the sense of admitting more terminating computations) than those based on well-founded orderings. Note, in general, a termination condition admitting more terminating computations will provide more chances for optimizations and is therefore often viewed to be more powerful, though too many computations may lead to inefficiency of code space.

We have noticed that, almost all the traditional approaches, which are based on well-founded orderings and well-quasi orderings, essentially use only the arguments of programs to decide when to terminate. In detail, whether a specialization is allowed to continue depends if the sequence of recursive calls appearing in the specialization is monotonic w.r.t. well-founded orderings, or quasi-monotonic w.r.t. well-quasi orderings. We think that the reason for using arguments is that in programming languages with pattern matching (e.g. Prolog) the head of a function (or predicate) indicates the termination condition of the function (or predicate). In this paper, we will call the way of using arguments as *argument approach*.

Although the argument approach is useful for ensuring the termination of partial evaluation, in many cases it easily loses chances of optimizing programs. On the one hand, when a given program is written in some programming language without pattern matching (e.g., Common Lisp or C), the arguments of the program often fail in telling us any termination information about the program. On the other hand, argument approach also exposes its limitations in dealing with numerals. This is because, more often than not, the numeral arguments of programs can not reflect any property, structural or otherwise, of the programs. Therefore, argument approach often leads to either too much or too little specialization. Let us look at the following trivial example:

$$p(x, y) \equiv \underline{if}\ x \leq -100\ \underline{then}\ x$$
$$\underline{else}\ \underline{if}\ x > 100\ \underline{then}\ y\ \underline{else}\ p(x+1, y-1)$$

When $x=0$ and y is unknown, $p(0, y)$ will be specialized and the sequence of function calls appearing in specializing $p(x, y)$ will be $p(0, y)$, $p(1, y-1)$, ..., $p(10, y-10)$, ... Because "$p(0, y)$" is embedded in "$p(10, y-10)$", the sequence above is not quasi-monotonic w.r.t homemorphic embedding relation. According to argument approach, the specialization above has to terminate at recursive call $p(10, y-10)$. In fact, if we make the specialization continue until termination condition $x>100$ is satisfied, then a very efficient residual program $y-101$ can be obtained.

If y is known and x is unknown, argument approach leads easily to too many computations and the corresponding residual program, which is hardly more efficient than the original program, takes too much code space. Of course, if there are some complicated expressions w.r.t. y in the original program, this specialization may be worthwhile. Actually, whether a specialization is worthwhile or not is also an undecidable issue. Nevertheless, any termination approach had better to be more reasonably flexible and generous so as to provide more optimization chance. As to too many computations and the corresponding residual program with low space efficiency, to some extent, they can be solved by post-processing and man-machine interaction. The recursive program above is essentially equivalent to the following non-recursive program:

$$opt\_p(x, y) \equiv \underline{if}\ x \leq -100\ \underline{then}\ x$$
$$\underline{else}\ \underline{if}\ x > 100\ \underline{then}\ y\ \underline{else}\ y + x - 101$$

To the best of our knowledge, the transformation from p to opt_p can be achieved only by GPC [6] since GPC is equipped with a theorem proving system. In this paper, we assume that the partial evaluators we use do not include theorem proving systems.

The termination of recursive programs is decided by the recursive conditions of these programs, so we should try to seek some useful information about termination from the recursive conditions. Based on homeomorphic embedding, in this paper we present a new termination approach (called recursive condition approach) of ensuring the termination of online partial evaluation. Instead of using arguments, recursive condition approach pays attention to the constraints invoking recursive calls. Relatively, recursive condition approach is more sensitive to the termination information of programs, so it is more reasonable and can produce more efficient residual programs. Furthermore, we also present a more powerful and practical approach (called combined approach) by combining argument approach and recursive condition approach in the sense of homeomorphic embedding.

2   Well-Quasi Ordering and Homeomorphic Embedding

Well-quasi orderings, in particular, homeomorphic embedding is usually used to prove or ensure the termination of term rewriting systems [5, 19], partial evaluation [9, 24, 25, 26] and partial deduction [3, 15]. Formally, well-quasi orderings can be defined as follows.

Definition 1 (quasi order). *A quasi order $\preceq$ on a set S is a reflexive and transitive binary relation on $S \times S$.*

Definition 2 (quasi-monotonic). *Let $\preceq$ be a quasi order on S. A sequence of elements $s_1, s_2, \ldots$ in S is called* quasi-monotonic *w.r.t. $\preceq$ if there are no $1 \leq i < j$ such that $s_i \preceq s_j$.*

Definition 3 (well-quasi order, well-quasi ordered set). *Let $\preceq$ be a quasi order on S. Then $\preceq$ is called a* well-quasi order (wqo) *on S, and S is called a* well-quasi ordered set *under $\preceq$ if there is no infinite quasi-monotonic sequence in S w.r.t. $\preceq$.*

An interesting and useful wqo is homeomorphic embedding [10, 13].

Definition 4 (homeomorphic embedding relation). *Let $\preccurlyeq$ be a quasi order on S_1 and $S_2=\{a_1a_2...a_n|\ a_i{\in}S_1,\ 1{\leq}n\}$. The* homeomorphic embedding relation $\preccurlyeq_{emb}$ *on $S_2{\times}S_2$ is defined as:*

$$a_1a_2...a_n \preccurlyeq_{emb} b_1b_2...b_m\ iff\ \forall j_{(1 \leq j \leq n)}.(a_j \preccurlyeq b_{i_j})$$

where, $1{\leq}i_1{<}i_2...{<}i_n{\leq}m$.

Theorem 1. *If $\preccurlyeq$ is a wqo on S_1, then homeomorphic embedding relation $\preccurlyeq_{emb}$ is a wqo on S_2.*

Definition 5 (cardinal product quasi order). *Let $\preccurlyeq_1, ..., \preccurlyeq_n$ be quasi orders on S_1, ..., S_n respectively and $S^n=\{(a_1, a_2, ..., a_n)|\ a_i{\in}S_i, 1{\leq}i{\leq}n\}$. Cardinal product quasi order $\preccurlyeq^n$ on S^n is defined as:*

$$(a_1, a_2, ..., a_n) \preccurlyeq^n (b_1, b_2, ..., b_n)\ iff\ \forall i_{(1 \leq i \leq n)}.(a_i \preccurlyeq_i b_i)$$

Theorem 2. *If $\preccurlyeq_1, ..., \preccurlyeq_n$ are wqo's on $S_1, ..., S_n$ respectively, cardinal product quasi order $\preccurlyeq^n$ is a wqo on S^n.*

For the proof of Theorem 1 and Theorem 2 refer to [10, 13]. Furthermore, cardinal product quasi order can be extended as follows:

Definition 6 (heterogeneous cardinal product quasi order). *Let $\preccurlyeq^1, ..., \preccurlyeq^n$ be quasi orders on $S^1, ..., S^n$ respectively. Heterogeneous cardinal product quasi order $\precsim^n$ on $\bigcup_{i=1}^{n}S^i$ is defined as:*

$$(a_1, a_2, ..., a_m) \precsim^n (b_1, b_2, ..., b_m)\ iff\ 1{\leq}m{\leq}n{\wedge}(a_1, a_2, ..., a_m) \preccurlyeq^m (b_1, b_2, ..., b_m)$$

Lemma 1. *If $\preccurlyeq^1, ..., \preccurlyeq^n$ are wqo's on $S^1, ..., S^n$ respectively, the heterogeneous cardinal product quasi order $\precsim^n$ is a wqo on $\bigcup_{i=1}^{n}S^i$.*

The proof of Lemma 1 is easy, so we omit it here.

3   A Functional Programming Language

Before introducing the recursive condition approach, it is necessary to fix the programming language used in this paper. Here, we exploit McCarthy's conditional [16] to define recursive programs. We assume all programs are free of side effects.

Definition 7 (recursive program). *Any recursive program $f(X)$, which contains no calls to other non-primitive recursive programs, is defined as:*

$$f(X){\equiv}[\ {\neg}b(X){\rightarrow}a(X);\ b(X){\rightarrow}E;\ ]$$

where
1. *X may be a list of variables $[x_1, ..., x_n]$.*
2. *a does not contain any free call to f.*
3. *E may be any one of the following 3 expressions:*
    (i) $f(X, f(d_1(X)), ..., f(d_n(X)))$, where $d_i(1{\leq}i{\leq}n)$ may be (i) or (ii).

(ii) $g(X, f(d_1(X)), ..., f(d_n(X)))$, *where g may be any primitive function or any non-recursive function.*

(iii) $[\ \neg b(X) \rightarrow E_1;\ b(X) \rightarrow E_2;\ ]$.

4. *b does not contain any free f and is a conjunctive normal form $o_1 \wedge ... \wedge o_m$, where o_i is a disjunctive normal form of binary relation expression in the form of $e_1 \oplus e_2$ or $\neg(e_1 \oplus e_2)$, $\oplus \in \{=, <, >, \neq, \leq, \geq, \subset, \supset, \subseteq, \supseteq\}$.*

Note any n-ary relation expression $\otimes(e_1,...,e_n)$ can be transformed into a binary relation expression (e.g., $\otimes(e_1,...,e_n)$ is equivalent to $\otimes(e_1,...,e_n)$=true).

Semantics is call-by-value. Values of variables can be Int, Float, Char, Bool, List and String. In this program, the branch containing "$a(X)$" is always terminating, while E may contain recursive calls.

4   Recursive Condition and Condition Index

We have mentioned recursive condition approach exploits the recursive conditions of recursive programs. How to extract termination information from recursive conditions is therefore a key point. The extracted information, to some extent, should reflect termination tendency of programs. In general, the extracted information and the mapping function from recursive conditions to this information can be defined as follows:

Definition 8 (condition index function, condition index) *Let B be a set of condition expressions, S be a well-quasi ordered set under a wqo. We call the mapping $M_S: B \rightarrow S$ as a* condition index function *on S, and, for any condition expression b, we call $M_S(b)$ as the* condition index *in S of b.*

The condition index functions used in this paper are defined in the following sections.

4.1   Condition Index Function for Binary Relation Expression

Assume f is a recursive program and b is a recursive condition of f. In case of b being a binary relation expression (e.g., $e_1 \oplus e_2$), with the iteration of f, if the "distance" of e_1 and e_2 becomes smaller and smaller, and finally e_1 becomes equal to e_2, then the computation of f will terminate naturally. This is because:

1. In case of $\oplus$ being anti-reflexive (e.g., $<$), when e_1 becomes equal to e_2 then $e_1 \oplus e_2$ is obviously not satisfied and so the computation of f terminates.
2. In case of $\oplus$ being reflexive (e.g., $\leq$), when e_1 becomes equal to e_2, then $e_1 \oplus e_2$ is satisfied and so the computation of f continues. However, according to the assumption that the "distance" of e_1 and e_2 becomes smaller and smaller with the iteration of f, the computation of f must terminate in the next iteration. Otherwise, in the next iteration, both $e_1=e_2$ and $e_1 \neq e_2$ will be in contraction with the assumption above.

As a sufficient termination condition, the "distance" of e_1 and e_2 becomes smaller and smaller with the iteration of f, is natural and effective in practice. Therefore, we define condition index by using the "distance" of e_1 and e_2. Before giving the definition of condition index function for binary relation expression, it is necessary to introduce a notion as follows.

Definition 9 (number of uncommon elements). *Let L be a list, in case L=[] or unknown, len(L)≡0; in case L=[H | T], len(L)≡1+len(T). For any lists L_1 and L_2, if the length of the longest common static subsequence of L_1 and L_2 is k, then the value of len(L_1)+len(L_2)-2k is called the* number of uncommon elements *of L_1 and L_2.*

For example, let L_1=[a, b, c, b, d | T], L_2=[b, d, c, a | T] and T=unknown. The length of the longest common static subsequence (b, c) of L_1 and L_2 is 2, so the number of uncommon elements is 5+4-2×2=5.

Let α={'+', '-', '.', '0', '1', '2', '3', '4', '5', '6', '7', '8', '9', 'U'}, the condition index function $\Re$ for binary relation expression is defined as follows:

Definition 10 (condition index function for binary relation expression). $\Re$: *Binary relation expression→α*. For any binary relation expression r ($e_1 \oplus e_2$ or ¬($e_1 \oplus e_2$)),*

$$\Re(r) \equiv \begin{cases} \text{"U"} & if\ (e_1,e_2 \in Int \cup Float \cup Char \cup Bool) \wedge (e_1\ or\ e_2\ is\ unknown) \\ t(e_1 - e_2) & if\ e_i \in Int \cup Float \\ t(ord(e_1) - ord(e_2)) & if\ e_i \in Char \cup Bool \\ t(p(lst(e_1), lst(e_2))) & if\ e_i \in String \\ t(p(e_1, e_2)) & if\ e_i \in List \end{cases}$$

where, t(v) denotes the string notation of integer or float v, lst(s) denotes the list notation of string s, p(l_1,l_2) denotes the number of uncommon elements of list l_1 and l_2, and ord(c) denotes the ordinal number (e.g., ASCII code for Char) of Char or Bool c.

For example, $\Re(10>1)$="+9", $\Re([a, a, b] \neq [])$="+3", $\Re(x>1)$="U".

Definition 11 (homeomorphic embedding relation $\preccurlyeq_{emb}$). Homeomorphic embedding relation $\preccurlyeq_{emb}$ on $\alpha^* \times \alpha^*$ *is defined as:*

$$a_1 a_2 ... a_n \preccurlyeq_{emb} b_1 b_2 ... b_m\ iff\ \forall j_{(1 \leq j \leq n)} \exists i_{(1 \leq i_j \leq m)}.(a_j = b_{i_j})$$

For example, "-1" $\preccurlyeq_{emb}$ "-10", "+31" $\preccurlyeq_{emb}$ "+351".
Because α contains a finite number of elements, quasi order = is a wqo on α. According to Theorem 1, $\preccurlyeq_{emb}$ is a wqo on α^*.

4.2   Condition Index Function for Disjunctive Normal Form

In case of recursive condition *b* being a disjunctive normal form $r_1 \vee ... \vee r_n$, the corresponding condition index is defined as a cardinal product of the condition indices for binary relation expressions r_1, ..., r_n.

Definition 12 (condition index function for disjunctive normal form). $\Re_o$: *Disjunctive normal form→$\bigcup_{n=1}^{N}(\alpha^*)^n$. For any disjunctive normal form o ($r_1 \vee ... \vee r_n$, $1 \leq n \leq N$),*

$$\Re_o(o) \equiv (\Re(r_1), ..., \Re(r_n))$$

For example, $\Re_o(10>0\vee9<2)=($ "+10", "U" $)$, $\Re_o(x_1>x_2\vee0<10)=($ "U", "−10" $)$.

Definition 13 (quasi order $\precsim_o$). *Quasi order* $\precsim_o$ *on* $\bigcup_{n=1}^{N}(\alpha*)^n$ *is defined as:*

$$(a_1, ..., a_n)\precsim_o(b_1, ..., b_n) \text{ iff } \forall i_{(1\leq i\leq N)}.(a_i\preccurlyeq_{emb}b_i)$$

For example, ("-10", "-11") $\precsim_o($ "U", "+10"), ("0", "U") $\precsim_o($ "-10", "U").

Because $\preccurlyeq_{emb}$ is a wqo on $\alpha*$, according to Lemma 1, $\precsim_o$ is a wqo on $\bigcup_{n=1}^{N}(\alpha*)^n$.

4.3   Condition Index Function for Conjunctive Normal Form

In case of recursive condition b being a conjunctive normal form $o_1\wedge...\wedge o_m$, the corresponding condition index is defined as a cardinal product of the condition indices for disjunctive normal forms $o_1, ..., o_m$.

Definition 14 (condition index function for conjunctive normal form). $\Re_b$: *Conjunctive normal form* $\rightarrow \bigcup_{m=1}^{N}(\bigcup_{n=1}^{N}(\alpha*)^n)^m$. *For any conjunctive normal form b $(o_1\wedge...\wedge o_m, 1\leq m\leq N)$,*

$$\Re_b(b)\equiv(\Re_o(o_1), ..., \Re_o(o_m))$$

For example, $\Re_b(1>0\wedge9<20)=(($ "+1"), ("-11")), $\Re_b(x_1>x_2\wedge2<9)=(($ "U"), ("-7")).

Definition 15 (quasi order $\precsim_b$). *Quasi order* $\precsim_b$ *on* $\bigcup_{m=1}^{N}(\bigcup_{n=1}^{N}(\alpha*)^n)^m$ *is defined as:*

$$(a_1, ..., a_m)\precsim_b(b_1, ..., b_m) \text{ iff } \forall i_{(1\leq m\leq N)}.(a_i\precsim_o b_i)$$

For example, (("0"), ("-1")) $\precsim_b(($ "1"), ("0")), (("U"), ("0")) $\precsim_b(($ "U"), ("10")).

Because $\precsim_o$ is a wqo on $\bigcup_{n=1}^{N}(\alpha*)^n$, according to Lemma 1, $\precsim_b$ is a wqo on $\bigcup_{m=1}^{N}(\bigcup_{n=1}^{N}(\alpha*)^n)^m$.

4.4   Branch-Sensitive Condition Index Function

Usually, a recursive program contains multiple branches, some of which contain recursive calls and some of which do not. Let f be a recursive program containing n branches, and the branch conditions corresponding to these branches be $b_1, ..., b_n$ respectively. Moreover, let $f(e_1)\xrightarrow{b_{i1}}f(e_2)\xrightarrow{b_{i2}}...f(e_k)\xrightarrow{b_{ij}}...$ ($j\geq1$ and $ij\geq1$) be a sequence of recursive calls appearing in the specialization of f, according to recursive condition approach, we will check if sequence $\Re_b(b_{i1}), \Re_b(b_{i2}), ..., \Re_b(b_{ij}), ...$ is quasi-monotonic w.r.t. $\precsim_b$ to decide if the computation of this sequence terminates or not. However, for any two different branch conditions b_i and b_j, it is unreasonable and undesirable to compare $\Re_b(b_i)$ and $\Re_b(b_j)$ in the sense of $\precsim_b$. That is to say, we hope to use a kind of branch-sensitive condition index. This can be achieved by easily attaching a unique number to the every branch condition above. The branch-sensitive condition index function and the corresponding well-quasi order can be defined as follows:

Definition 16 (branch-sensitive condition index function). $\Re_1$: *Conjunctive normal form*$\rightarrow$*Int*$\times\bigcup_{m=1}^{N}(\bigcup_{n=1}^{N}(\alpha*)^n)^m$. *For any conjunctive normal form* b_i,

$$\Re_1(b_i)\equiv(i, \Re_b(b_i))$$

Definition 17 (quasi order $\precsim_1$). Quasi order $\precsim_1$ *on* $Int\times\bigcup_{m=1}^{N}(\bigcup_{n=1}^{N}(\alpha*)^n)^m$ *is defined as*:

$$(a_1, a_2)\precsim_1(b_1, b_2) \text{ iff } a_1=b_1\wedge a_2\precsim_b b_2$$

For any two different branch conditions b_i and b_j, because $i\neq j$, $\Re_1(b_i)\not\precsim_1\Re_1(b_i)$ holds. Moreover, because the number of branch conditions is finite, quasi order = is a wqo on the set of these numbers. According to Lemma 1, quasi order $\precsim_1$ is a wqo on Int $\times$ $\bigcup_{m=1}^{N}(\bigcup_{n=1}^{N}(\alpha*)^n)^m$.

5   Recursive-Calling Tree and Termination of Specialization

Usually, discussing termination certainly touches upon some kind of tree (e.g., GPC-tree [6], SLDNF-tree [15]), which indicates the process of a computation, specialization or transformation. In this paper, we also introduce a tree called recursive-calling tree to discuss termination of specialization. For any specialization, there is a corresponding recursive-calling tree, which takes every recursive call appearing in the specialization as a node. Therefore, the termination of a specialization is equivalent to the finiteness of the corresponding recursive-calling tree.

5.1   Recursive-Calling Tree

Before formally defining recursive-calling tree, we must first introduce two notions.

Definition 18 (generalization). *If* $f(k_1, \ldots, k_m, u_{m+1}, \ldots, u_n)$ *is a function call to recursive function* $f(x_1, \ldots, x_n)$, *and* $k_1, \ldots, k_m$ *are known actual arguments and* $u_{m+1}, \ldots, u_n$ *are unknown actual arguments, then* $f(k_1, \ldots, k_m, x_{m+1}, \ldots, x_n)$ *is called the generalization of* $f(k_1, \ldots, k_m, u_{m+1}, \ldots, u_n)$.

Definition 19 (partial residual expression). *For any binary relation expression* $e_1\oplus e_2$ *(or* $\neg(e_1\oplus e_2)$), *if both* e_1 *and* e_2 *are residual expressions after specialized, then the binary relation expression above is called* partial residual expression. *Moreover; if all the binary relation expressions* $r_1, \ldots, r_n$ *are partial residual expressions then disjunctive normal form* $r_1\vee\ldots\vee r_n$ *is called* partial residual expression; *if all the disjunctive normal forms* $o_1, \ldots, o_n$ *are partial residual expressions then conjunctive normal form* $o_1\wedge\ldots\wedge o_n$ *is called* partial residual expression.

Partial residual expressions will be used to derive condition indices.

Recursive-calling tree (RCT) is a kind of tree structure, which is similar to GPC-tree [6] except that not only branch conditions but also the semantic order of recursive calls are considered in. Syntactically RCT consists of three parts:

- Root : the initial function call.
- Node: a recursive call, or an expression (leave node).
- Edge: an arrow labeled with a partial residual expression, or a line labeled with "gen" (generalization).

Semantically, RCT is constructed as Figure 1 and Figure 2.

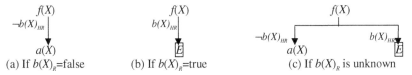

Fig. 1. RCT construction of a call $f(X)$ to function f defined in Definition 7, where $b(X)_{HR}$ and $b(X)_R$ are partial residual expression and residual expression of $b(X)$, respectively.

In Figure 1, the block node $\boxed{E}$ indicates this node needs to be constructed further. This construction of $\boxed{E}$ is defined as Figure 2.

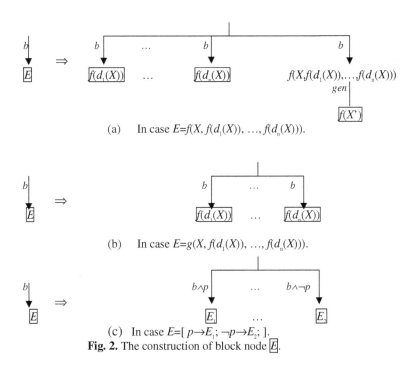

(a)   In case $E=f(X, f(d_1(X)), …, f(d_n(X)))$.

(b)   In case $E=g(X, f(d_1(X)), …, f(d_n(X)))$.

(c)   In case $E=[\, p{\rightarrow}E_1;\; \neg p{\rightarrow}E_2;\,]$.

Fig. 2. The construction of block node $\boxed{E}$.

5.2   Termination of Specialization

According to the description in Section 5.1, a specialization corresponds to a RCT where any recursive call appearing in this specialization corresponds to a node of this RCT, and an edge links up the node and its a successor. In constructing a RCT, if the sequence of condition indices on a path, which starts from the root and ends at a leave node, is not quasi-monotonic w.r.t. a predefined wqo then the construction of this path will terminate. Additionally, the construction of a path must also terminate when: (i) the dangling leave node of this path is not a recursive call; (ii) the dangling leave node of this path is exactly same as an ancestor node (*Termination-on-the-Second-Call* [6]). The two additional termination criterions are widely used in partial evaluation.

Obviously, the termination of a specialization is equivalent to the finiteness of the corresponding RCT.

Definition 20 (well-quasi ordered RCT). *A RCT is called* well-quasi ordered *if the sequence of the condition indices on every path of the RCT is quasi-monotonic w.r.t. a predefined wqo.*

Theorem 3. *A RCT is finite if it is well-quasi ordered* (For the proof see Appendix).

6   Examples

In this section, we use some examples to demonstrate the advantages and weaknesses of recursive condition approach.

Example 1 (McCarthy's 91-function). $f(n) \equiv [\ n > 100 \rightarrow n-10;\ n \leq 100 \rightarrow f(f(n+11));\ ]$

If $f(98)$ be a function call to f, RCT of $f(98)$ will be as Figure 3.

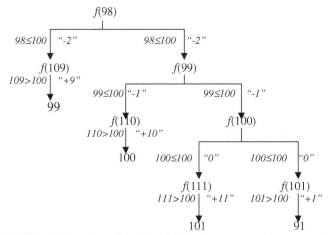

Fig. 3. RCT of $f(98)$, where the left and right of any arrow edge are partial residual expression and condition index respectively (the condition index function used here is $\Re$).

In Figure 3, the sequence of the condition indices on any path is quasi-monotonic w.r.t. $\preccurlyeq_{emb}$, so the computation of $f(98)$ will continue until the final result 91 is obtained. In fact, for any static argument n, the computation of $f(n)$ will continue until a correct result is obtained (Proof refers to Appendix). Contrarily, the computation based on argument approach leads easily to too early termination so that a final value can not be obtained. For example, if $f(1)$ is a function call to f, because $f(1)=f(f(12))$ and "$f(1)$" $\preccurlyeq_{emb}$ "$f(12)$", the computation of $f(12)$ has to terminate undesirably.

Example 3 (Pattern Matcher). Let M be a pattern matcher, i.e.

$M(p, t, w)\equiv[\ p=[]\rightarrow$true;

$\qquad p\neq[]\rightarrow[\ t=[]\rightarrow$false;

$\qquad\qquad t\neq[]\rightarrow[\ car(p)=car(t)\rightarrow M(cdr(p), cdr(t), w++[car(p)]);$

$\qquad\qquad\qquad car(p)\neq car(t)\rightarrow[\ w=[]\rightarrow M(p, cdr(t), []);$

$\qquad\qquad\qquad\qquad w\neq[]\rightarrow M(w++p, cdr(w)++t, []);\ ]\ ]\ ]\ ]$

where $x++y=append(x, y)$, p and t stand for *pattern* and *text* respectively.

Let $p=[A, A, B]$, $w=[]$, then RCT of $M([A, A, B], t, [])$ will be as Figure 4.

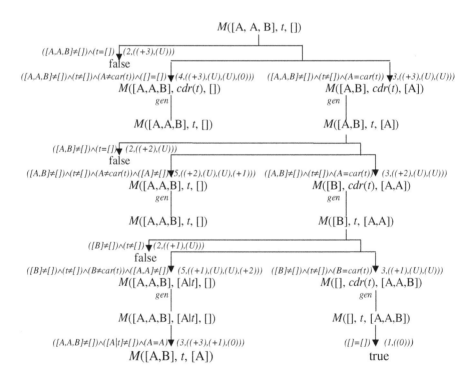

Fig. 4. RCT of $M([A, A, B], t, [])$, where condition index function $\Re_1$ is used. Note the five branch conditions $p=[]$, $p\neq[]\wedge t=[]$, $p\neq[]\wedge t\neq[]\wedge car(p)=car(t)$, $p\neq[]\wedge t\neq[]\wedge car(p)\neq car(t)\wedge w=[]$ and $p\neq[]\wedge t\neq[]\wedge car(p)\neq car(t)\wedge w\neq[]$ are numbered 1, 2, 3, 4 and 5 respectively.

In Figure 4, the sequence of the condition indices on any path is quasi-monotonic w.r.t. $\precsim_1$, so residual program is as follows:

$M_{AAB}(t)\equiv[\ t=[]\rightarrow\text{false};\ t\neq[]\rightarrow[\ A\neq car(t)\rightarrow M_{AAB}(cdr(t));\ A=car(t)\rightarrow M_{AB}(cdr(t));\ ]]$
$M_{AB}(t)\equiv[\ t=[]\rightarrow\text{false};\ t\neq[]\rightarrow[\ A\neq car(t)\rightarrow M_{AAB}(t);\ A=car(t)\rightarrow M_{B}(cdr(t));\ ]]$
$M_{B}(t)\equiv[\ t=[]\rightarrow\text{false};\ t\neq[]\rightarrow[\ B\neq car(t)\rightarrow M_{AB}(t);\ B=car(t)\rightarrow\text{true};\ ]]$

Because $M([A, A, B], t, [])\precsim_{emb}M([A, A, B], [A\mid t], [])$, according to argument approach, the specialization of $M([A, A, B], [A\mid t], [])$ terminates, and the residual program is as follows:

$M_{AAB}(t)\equiv[\ t=[]\rightarrow\text{false};\ t\neq[]\rightarrow[\ A\neq car(t)\rightarrow M_{AAB}(cdr(t));\ A=car(t)\rightarrow M_{AB}(cdr(t));\ ]]$
$M_{AB}(t)\equiv[\ t=[]\rightarrow\text{false};\ t\neq[]\rightarrow[\ A\neq car(t)\rightarrow M_{AAB}(t);\ A=car(t)\rightarrow M_{B}(cdr(t));\ ]]$
$M_{B}(t)\equiv[\ t=[]\rightarrow\text{false};\ t\neq[]\rightarrow[\ B\neq car(t)\rightarrow M_{AAB}([A\mid t]);\ B=car(t)\rightarrow\text{true};\ ]]$

Between the two residual programs, the former is more efficient, because recursive call $M_{AAB}([A\mid t])$ is not computed in the latter.

In many cases, recursive condition approach shows its superiority to argument approach, but in some cases, recursive condition approach also leads to inefficient residual programs because of premature early termination.

Example 3. Let g be a recursive function defined as:

$g(m, n)\equiv[\ mod(m, n)\neq0\rightarrow1;\ mod(m, n)=0\rightarrow g(m/n, n+1)+1;\ ]$

where $m, n\in$ Int.

When both m and n are known, if recursive condition $mod(m, n)=0$ is satisfied, the corresponding condition index is always equal to (("0")). This will make the computation of $g(m, n)$ terminate too early than desirable. Contrarily, argument approach can solve the problem very well since the value of m is descendant in computation.

7   Discussion

To achieve a better comprehension to recursive condition approach, in this section we make an intuitive comparison between recursive condition approach and traditional argument approach.

Recursive condition approach

While specializing a recursive program, recursive condition approach first extracts some information (in the form of a cardinal product of a cardinal product of numeral strings or "U") from the recursive conditions that turn to be true or unknown. Afterwards, in the sense of corresponding recursive-calling tree, if the sequence of the condition indices on a computing path is not quasi-monotonic w.r.t. a predefined wqo, then the dangling leave of this path will be forcedly suspended, else the dangling leave can be specialized further.

According to the definitions of condition indices and the corresponding wqo's, the quasi-monotonicity of condition indices, to some extent, can imply or reflect the natural termination tendency of recursive programs. Therefore, we believe recursive condition approach is a natural and promising termination approach.

Argument approach

While specializing a recursive program, argument approach pays attention to the actual arguments of the program. In the sense of RCT, if the sequence of the actual arguments appearing in a computing path is not quasi-monotonic w.r.t. a predefined wqo, then the dangling leave of this path will be forcedly suspended, else the dangling leave can be specialized further.

In essence, the effectiveness of argument approach depends on the dynamic fluctuating tendency of the actual arguments appearing in specialization. When a recursive function (or predicate) is written in a programming language (e.g. Prolog) with pattern matching, the recursive condition of the function (or predicate) is usually implied in the head of the function. In this case, the patterns of actual arguments often become smaller and smaller with the iteration of this function (or predicate), and this is a typical characteristic of those recursive functions (or predicates). Therefore, argument approach often demonstrates its powerfulness. However, for those recursive functions not written in programming languages with pattern matching, we have no way to find any positive relation between the actual arguments and the termination tendencies of recursive functions. In this case, argument approach often leads to blind specialization and inefficient residual programs (because of too early or too late termination).

In this paper, for the convenience of discussion, we only use recursive programs whose recursive conditions are obviously written. Actually, recursive condition approach applies also to those recursive programs whose recursive conditions are not written obviously, if we adopt some ways of recognizing recursive conditions. For example, function $append(x, y)$ can be written as follows:

$$append([], y) \equiv y$$
$$append([H \mid T], y) \equiv cons(H, append(T, y))$$

According to the definition above, we can easily get to know that the termination condition and recursive condition of $append(x, y)$ are $x=[]$ and $x \neq []$ respectively. In general, for any recursive call appearing in a function definition, the corresponding recursive condition should be the conjunctive form of, the condition (written obviously in program) of the branch where the recursive call locates, and the equalities or inequalities about some arguments and their patterns written obviously in program.

In this paper, as a compared object, argument approach implies the naive and basic argument approach. An extended version of argument approach is presented in [15], which uses not only arguments but also characteristic tree. Although this termination approach strengthens the powerfulness (e.g., Example 2 can be solved very well) of argument approach, essentially it is still a variant of argument approach. Contrarily, recursive condition approach can also use characteristic tree in the same way as [15], and the recursive condition approach extended in this way will be certainly powerful than the original one.

8 Combined Approach

Any termination approach may lead to too little or too much specialization for efficiency concerns. However, preventing too little specialization is the crux of the matter. We have noticed both the recursive condition approach and the argument approach are the termination approaches based on homeomorphic embedding. This provides us with a condition of easily combining the two approaches. In detail, for any recursive program $f(X)$ and its a recursive condition $b(X)$, we can redefine the old condition index $Ms(b(X))$ as a new one in the form of $(X, Ms(b(X)))$.

Definition 21 (new condition index function $\Re_2$). $\Re_2$: *Conjunctive normal form* $\rightarrow \alpha^*$
$\times (Int \times \bigcup_{m=1}^{N} (\bigcup_{n=1}^{N} (\alpha^*)^n)^m)$, *for any conjunctive normal form* $b(X)$,

$$\Re_2(b(X)) \equiv (X, \Re_1(b(X)))$$

Definition 22 (quasi order $\lesssim_2$). Quasi order $\lesssim_2$ *on* $\alpha^* \times (Int \times \bigcup_{m=1}^{N} (\bigcup_{n=1}^{N} (\alpha^*)^n)^m)$
is defined as:

$$(a_1, a_2) \lesssim_2 (b_1, b_2) \text{ iff } a_1 \trianglelefteq b_1 \wedge a_2 \lesssim_1 b_2$$

Here, homeomorphic embedding relation $\trianglelefteq$ (cf., [9, 14, 15, 24, 25, 26]) is defined inductively as:

1. $X \trianglelefteq Y$ *for all variables X, Y*
2. $s \trianglelefteq f(t_1, \ldots, t_n)$ *if* $s \trianglelefteq t_i$ *for some i*
3. $f(s_1, \ldots, s_n) \trianglelefteq f(t_1, \ldots, t_n)$ *if* $\forall i_{(1 \leq i \leq n)}.(s_i \trianglelefteq t_i)$

Moreover, we suppose alphabet α represents the set of all the possible characters used in the programming language defined in Definition 7. If α is a set of a finite number of elements, $\trianglelefteq$ is a wqo and then $\lesssim_2$ is also a wqo. Obviously, the combined approach will admit much more computations than recursive condition approach and argument approach.

Although there is no way to quantitatively compare the powerfulness of the argument approach, the recursive condition approach and the combined approach, we can give an intuitive comparison by using Figure 5.

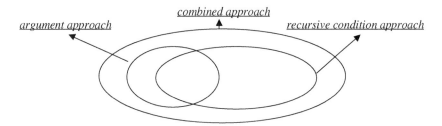

Fig. 5. An intuitive comparison of the argument approach, the recursive condition approach and the combined approach, where any ellipse indicates the set of the specialization that can be sufficiently fulfilled by using the corresponding approach.

We have checked many examples by using the three approaches above. Due to limited space, by using ten examples, we give a comparison table of the three approaches.

Table 1. A comparison of A, R and C, where A: argument approach, R: recursive condition approach, C: combined approach, $\geq$: more powerful than, $=$: as powerful as, ∇: incompariable.

Original programs	Static inputs	Comparison		
Example 1	n	$R \geq A$	$C \geq A$	$C = R$
71-function	n	$R \geq A$	$C \geq A$	$C = R$
Hailstorm function	n	$R \nabla A$	$C \geq A$	$C \geq R$
Example 2	p and t	$R = A$	$C = A$	$C = R$
	p	$R \geq A$	$C \geq A$	$C = R$
	t	$R = A$	$C = A$	$C = R$
Ackermann function	m and n	$R = A$	$C = A$	$C = R$
	m or n	$R = A$	$C = A$	$C = R$
Example 3	m and n	$R \leq A$	$C = A$	$C \geq R$
	m	$R = A$	$C = A$	$C = R$
	n	$R \leq A$	$C = A$	$C \geq R$
Mergesort function	x	$R = A$	$C = A$	$C = R$
C1 function	x and y and z	$R \geq A$	$C \geq A$	$C = R$
	x and y	$R \geq A$	$C \geq A$	$C = R$
	y and z	$R \geq A$	$C \geq A$	$C = R$
	x and z	$R \leq A$	$C = A$	$C \geq R$
	x or y or z	$R \leq A$	$C = A$	$C \geq R$
C2 function	x and y and z	$R = A$	$C = A$	$C = R$
	x and y	$R = A$	$C = A$	$C = R$
	y and z	$R = A$	$C = A$	$C = R$
	x and z	$R \leq A$	$C = A$	$C \geq R$
	x or y or z	$R \leq A$	$C = A$	$C \geq R$
Takeuchi's Tak function	x and y and z	$R \nabla A$	$C \geq A$	$C \geq R$
	x and y	$R \nabla A$	$C \geq A$	$C \geq R$
	y and z	$R \nabla A$	$C \geq A$	$C \geq R$
	x and z	$R \nabla A$	$C \geq A$	$C \geq R$
	x or y or z	$R \leq A$	$C = A$	$C \geq R$

Here, *71*-function, *Hailstorm* function, *Ackermann* function, *Mergesort* function, *C1* function, *C2* function and *Takeuchi's Tak* function are shown in Appendix.

9   Conclusion and Future Work

In this paper, we presented a new termination approach of ensuring the termination of specialization. This new approach is a technique based on well-quasi orderings (particularly, homeomorphic embedding). Compared with traditional techniques, the new approach is natural and effective, since it exploits some semantic information contained in recursive conditions of recursive programs. To some extent, this semantic information implies the termination tendency of recursive programs, and therefore this makes the new approach be sensitive to the termination semantics of recursive programs. Moreover, the new termination approach is independent of any programming language.

Furthermore, for powerfulness and practicability concerns, we propose a more powerful termination approach by combining recursive condition approach and traditional argument approach. If recursive condition approach is viewed to be recursive condition sensitive and argument approach is viewed to be argument sensitive, then the combined approach can be viewed to be sensitive to both recursive conditions and arguments. In specialization, only when the sequence of the cardinal products of condition index and arguments is not quasi-monotonic w.r.t. a well-quasi order on the set of the cardinal products above, specialization terminates. To the best of our knowledge, the combined approach is the most powerful one of all the existing techniques based on homeomorphic embedding.

Just as mentioned in [14], for some applications, the argument approach based on homeomorphic embedding relation remains too restrictive and in particular it does not always deal satisfactorily with fluctuating structure. The use of characteristic trees remedies this problem to some extent [15]. Nevertheless, the use of characteristic trees can not be regarded to be an essential remedy to this kind of technique, since it can also be combined with recursive condition approach. The use of characteristic trees is actually a powerful technique, a new recursive condition approach combined with characteristic trees will be a future work of this paper.

Moreover, for recursive condition approach, the binary relation expression contained in recursive conditions is a key point. When a recursive condition is only a binary relation expression and the expression is an equality, according Definition 10, as long as the expression is satisfied, the corresponding condition index will always be equal to "0" or "U" so that specialization may terminate too early (e.g., Example 3). Although it is rare in practice to use a single equality as recursive condition, finding a clever and effective way to deal with equality will be another future work.

Acknowledgment

We would like to thank Robert Glück for his useful comments and discussions.

References

1. Andersen L.O. Program analysis and specialization for the C programming language, *Ph.D. thesis*, DIKU, University of Copenhagen (1994).
2. Bondorf A., Danvy O. Automatic autoprojection of recursive equations with global variables and abstract data types, *Science of Computer Programming*, Vol. 16, pp 151-195 (1991).
3. Bruynooghe M., De Schreye D., Martens B. A general criterion for avoiding infinite unfolding during partial deduction. *New Generation Computing*, 11(1): pp47-79 (1992).
4. Consel C. et al. A uniform approach for compile-time and run-time specialization. In: Danvy O., Glück R., Thiemann P. (eds.), *Partial Evaluation. Proceedings. LNCS*, Vol. 1110, pp54-72, Springer-Verlag (1996).

5.   Dershowitz N. Termination of rewriting. *Journal of Symbolic Computation*, 3:69-116 (1987).
6.   Futamura Y., Nogi K., Takano A., Essence of generalized partial computation. *Theoretical Computer Science* 90, pp61-79 (1991).
7.   Futamura Y., Konishi Z, Implementation of experimental system for automatic program transformation based on generalized partial computation, to appear in *Computer Software*.
8.   Futamura Y., Song L., Konishi Z. Control structures and termination conditions for generalized partial computation (GPC), *The 15th National Conference of Computer Software Society of Japan*, D5-1, pp313~316, 9,1998)
9.   Glück R., Sørensen M. H. A roadmap to supercompilation. In Danvy O., Glück R., Thiemann P., editors. *Proceedings of the 1996 Dagstuhl Seminar on Partial Evaluation*, *LNCS* 1110, pp137-160, Springer-Verlag (1996).
10. Higman G. Ordering by divisibility in abstract algebras. *Proceedings of the London Mathematical Society*, 2: pp326-336 (1952).
11. Kenneth Kunen. Handbook of mathematical logic. pp371-401, Editted by Jon Brawise, North-Holland.
12. Knuth D. E., Morris J. H., Pratt V. R. Fast pattern matching in strings. *SIAM Journal on Computing*, 6(2): pp323-350 (1977).
13. Kruskal J. B. Well-quasi ordering, the tree theorem, and Vazsonyi's conjecture. *Transactions of the American Mathematical Society*, 95: pp210-225 (1960).
14. Leuschel M. On the power of homeomorphic embedding for online termination, *SAS'98*, pp230-245 (1998).
15. Leuschel M., Martens B., De Schreye D. Controlling generalization and polyvariance in partial deduction of normal logic programs, *TOPLAS*, 20(1), pp209-258 (1998).
16. McCarthy J. Recursive functions of symbolic expressions and their computation by machine. *Communications of the ACM* 3(4): 184-195 (1960).
17. Martens B., De Schreye D. Automatic finite unfolding using well-founded measures. *The Journal of Logic Programming*, 28(2): pp89-146 (1996).
18. Meyer U. Techniques for partial evalutaion of imperative languages, *PEPM'91*, pp94-105 (1991).
19. Middeldorp A., Zantema H. Simple termination of rewrite systems. *Theoretical Computer Science*, 175(1): pp127-158 (1997).
20. Nash-Williams, C. St. J. A. On well-quasi-ordering finite trees, *Proc. Cambridge Philos. Soc.* 59(4) pp833-835 (1963).
21. Ruf E. Topics in online partial evaluation. Ph.D thesis, Standford University (1993).
22. Sahlin D. Mixtus: An automatic partial evaluator for full Prolog. *New Generation Computing*, 12(1): pp7-51 (1993).
23. Song L., Futamura Y. A termination function of recursive programs and its application to partial evaluation, *The 56th National Conference of Information Processing Society of Japan*, 3E-4, pp312-313, 3,1998.
24. Sørensen M. H., Glück R. An algorithm of generalization in positive super-compilation. In J.W.Lloyd, editor, *Proceedings ILOS'95*, pp465-479, Portland, USA (1995).
25. Sørensen M. H., Glück R., Jones N. D. A positive supercompiler. In: *Journal of Functional Programming*, 6(6): pp811-838 (1996).
26. Turchin V. F. The concept of a supercompiler. *TOPLAS*, 8(3): pp292-325 (1986).
27. Weise D., Conybeare R., Ruf E., Seligman S. Automatic online partial evaluation. In *Proceeding of the Conference on Functional Programming Languages and Computer Architectures*, *LNCS* 523, pp165-191, Harvard University, Springer-Verlag (1991).

Appendices

The proof of Theorem 3:

Proof: According to the definition of RCT, for any RCT t, Nodes(t) consists of recursive calling nodes and value nodes (leave nodes), Edges(t) consists of the arrows labeled with partial residual expressions and the lines labeled with "gen". Moreover, the number of son nodes of any recursive calling node is at most equal to, the number of all the branches containing no recursive calls, and the number of all the recursive calls appearing in program definition. Therefore, t must be a tree structure owning finite number of branches. Furthermore, for any path starting from Root(t) and ending up at a leave node, except the edge ending up at the leave node, the sequence of the condition indices on the path must be quasi-monotonic w.r.t. a predefined wqo. Therefore, any path must be finitely long. According to [11], in any infinite tree of containing a finite number of branches, there must be a path of infinite length. By reduction to absurdity, t must be a finite tree structure. (QED)

The proof that, based on recursive condition approach, the computation of 91 function will not terminate until a final result (a positive integer) is evaluated:

According to $f(n)\equiv$if $n>100$ then $n-10$ else 91, we exploit structure inductive method to prove the proposition above. Here, we distinguish between two phases to prove that some property $P(n)$ holds for any integer n.

For any integer k ($k\leq100$),
1. in case of $n>k$, $P(n)$ holds.
2. in case of $n\leq k$, if $P(n+11)$ holds then $P(n)$ also holds.

Firstly, let us prove the following proposition, where $k=78$.

Proposition. If $n\leq89$, then the actual argument of any recursive call appearing in the computation of $f(n)$ must be greater than n.

Proof: Because $n+11\leq100$, according to the definition of f, $f(n)=f(f(n+11))=f(91)$. Obviously, while computing $f(n)$, $f(n+11)$ must be computed first and then $f(91)$ is computed. All the recursive calls appearing in the computation of $f(91)$ are as follows:

$$f(91)=f(f(102))=f(92)=\ldots=f(101)=91$$

Obviously, the actual argument of any recursive call is greater than 91. Furthermore, we test and verify that the actual argument of any recursive call appearing in the computation of $f(n+11)$ is greater than n.
1. in case of $n>78$, i.e. $79\leq n\leq89$, all the recursive calls appearing in the computation of $f(n+11)$ are as follows:

$$f(n+11)=f(f(n+22))=f(n+12)=\ldots=f(101)=91$$

Obviously, any actual argument above is greater than $n+11$.
2. in case of $n\leq78$, because $n+11\leq89$, according to the assumption that the actual argument of any recursive call appearing in the computation of $f(n+11)$ is greater than $n+11$, these actual arguments are of course greater than n.

(QED)

Secondly, let $k=89$ and prove the following theorem:

Theorem. Based on recursive condition approach, any computation of 91 function will not terminate until a final result (a positive integer) is evaluated.

Proof:
1. in case of $n>100$, it is obvious that the computation of $f(n)$ will terminate at once.

2. in case of $90 \leq n \leq 100$, if we try to compute $f(90)$, ..., $f(100)$, we can find the computations of the eleven calls above will continue until 91 is evaluated.
3. in case of $n \leq 89$, assume the computation of $f(n+11)$ continues until a positive integer is evaluated. In RCT($f(n)$), root $f(n)$ should have two son: node $f(n+11)$ and node $f(91)$, and the condition index of recursive condition $n \leq 100$ should be $((t(n-100)))$. According to structure inductive method, in RCT($f(n+11)$), except the edges ending up at leave nodes, the sequence of the condition indices on any computing path should be quasi-monotonic w.r.t. $\lesssim_b$. Furthermore, in RCT(f(91)), except the edges ending up at leave nodes, the sequence of the condition indices on any computing path is quasi-monotonic w.r.t. $\lesssim_b$. On the one hand, because $n-100<0$, in the sense of homeomorphic embedding, it is impossible that there is some relation between $((t(n-100)))$ and any condition index capitalized with symbol '+' appearing in the descendant nodes of $f(n)$. On the other hand, if the condition index of a descendant node (e.g., $f(n')$) of $f(n)$ is capitalized with symbol '-', according to the proposition above, $n'>n$ holds and so $n'-100>n-100$ holds.

Therefore, it is impossible for $t(n-100) \preccurlyeq_{emb} t(n'-100)$, and the computation of 91 function will not terminate until a positive integer is evaluated. (QED)

The definitions of function *71*, *Hailstorm*, *Ackermann*, *Mergesort*, *C1*, *C2* and *Takeuchi's Tak*.

$f71(n) \equiv [n>70 \rightarrow n; n \leq 70 \rightarrow f(f(n+11);]$
where $n \in$ Int.

$Hailstrom(n) \equiv [n=1 \rightarrow 1;$
$\qquad n \neq 1 \rightarrow [odd(n) \rightarrow Hailstorm(3n+1);$
$\qquad\qquad \neg odd(n) \rightarrow Hailstorm(n/2);]]$
where $n \in$ Int and $n \geq 0$.

$Ack(m, n) \equiv [m=0 \rightarrow n+1;$
$\qquad m \neq 0 \rightarrow [n=0 \rightarrow Ack(m-1, 1);$
$\qquad\qquad n \neq 0 \rightarrow Ack(m-1, Ack(m, n-1));]]$
where $m, n \in$ Int and $m, n \geq 0$.

$Mergesort(x) \equiv [x=[] \rightarrow [];$
$\qquad x \neq [] \rightarrow [cdr(x)=[] \rightarrow car(x);$
$\qquad\qquad cdr(x) \neq [] \rightarrow$ let $(x_1, x_2)=Split(x)$
$\qquad\qquad\qquad$ in $Merge(Mergesort(x_1), Mergesort(x_2));]]$

$Split(x) \equiv [x=[] \rightarrow [];$
$\qquad x \neq [] \rightarrow$ let $(y_1, y_2)=Split(cdr(x))$ in $([car(x) | y_2], y_1);]$

$Merge(x, y) \equiv [x=[] \rightarrow y;$
$\qquad x \neq [] \rightarrow [y=[] \rightarrow x;$
$\qquad\qquad y \neq [] \rightarrow [car(x) \leq car(y) \rightarrow Merge(cdr(x), y);$
$\qquad\qquad\qquad car(x)>car(y) \rightarrow Merge(x, cdr(y));]]]$

$C1(x, y, z) \equiv [x=y \rightarrow [y=z \rightarrow [];$
$\qquad\qquad\qquad y \neq z \rightarrow [z \mid C1(x, y, z+1)];]$
$\qquad\qquad x \neq y \rightarrow [x \mid C1(x+1, y, z)];]$

where, $x, y, z \in$ Int, $x, y, z \geq 0$ and $y \geq x, z$.

$C2(x, y, z) \equiv [x=y \rightarrow [y=z \rightarrow [];$
$\qquad\qquad\qquad y \neq z \rightarrow [z \mid C2(x, y, z-1)];]$
$\qquad\qquad x \neq y \rightarrow [x \mid C2(x-1, y, z)];]$

where, $x, y, z \in$ Int, $x, y, z \geq 0$ and $y \leq x, z$.

$Tak(x, y, z) \equiv [x \leq y \rightarrow y;$
$\qquad\qquad x > y \rightarrow Tak(Tak(x-1, y, z), Tak(y-1, z, x), Tak(z-1, x, y));]$

where, $x, y, z \in$ Int.

Multi-stage Imperative Languages:
A Conservative Extension Result

Cristiano Calcagno[1] and Eugenio Moggi[1*]

DISI, Univ. di Genova, Genova, Italy
{calcagno,moggi}@disi.unige.it

Abstract. This paper extends the recent work [CMT00] on the opera-tional semantics and type system for a core language, called M $\dot{\mathrm{n}}\dot{\mathrm{M}}$ L$_{\mathrm{ref}}^{\mathrm{BN}}$, which exploits the notion of *closed type* (see also [MTBS99]) to safely combine imperative and multi-stage programming. The main novelties are the identification of a larger set of closed types and the addition of a binder for useless variables. The resulting language is a conservative extension of M $\dot{\mathrm{n}}\dot{\mathrm{M}}$ L$_{\mathrm{ref}}$, a simple imperative subset of SML.

1 Introduction

This paper extends recent work [CMT00] on the operational semantics and type system for a core language, called MiniML$_{\mathrm{ref}}^{\mathrm{BN}}$, which exploits the notion of *closed type* (see also [MTBS99]) to safely combining imperative and multi-stage pro-gramming. One would expect that the addition of staging constructs to an im-perative language should not prevent writing programs like those in normal im-perative languages. In fact, a practical multi-stage programming language like MetaML [Met00] is designed to be *a conservative extension* of a standard pro-gramming language, like SML, for good pragmatic reasons: to gain acceptance from an existing user community, and to confine the challenges for new users to the staging constructs only.

Unfortunately, MiniML$_{\mathrm{ref}}^{\mathrm{BN}}$ fails to be a conservative extension of a simple im-perative language like MiniML$_{\mathrm{ref}}$ (i.e. MiniML with ML-style references), because certain well-typed programs in MiniML$_{\mathrm{ref}}$ fail to be well-typed in MiniML$_{\mathrm{ref}}^{\mathrm{BN}}$. Technically, the problem is that the *closed types* of MiniML$_{\mathrm{ref}}^{\mathrm{BN}}$ are not closed under function types (and that locations may store only values of closed types). The best one can do is to define a translation _* from MiniML$_{\mathrm{ref}}$ to MiniML$_{\mathrm{ref}}^{\mathrm{BN}}$ respecting typing and operational semantics. The translation uses the closed type constructor [_] and closedness annotations, in particular the translation of a functional type is $(t_1 \to t_2)* \stackrel{\Delta}{=} [t_1* \to t_2*]$, which records that a functional type in the source language is a *closed functional type* in the target language.

From a language design perspective the main contribution of this paper is a core language, called MiniML$_{\mathrm{ref}}^{\mathrm{meta}}$, which extends *conservatively* the simple im-perative language MiniML$_{\mathrm{ref}}$ with the staging constructs of MetaML (and a few

---

[*] Research partially supported by MURST and ESPRIT WG APPSEM.

W. Taha (Ed.): SAIG 2000, LNCS 1924, pp. 92–107, 2000.

other features related to closed types). A safe combination of imperative and multi-stage programming in $\mathsf{MiniML}_{\mathsf{ref}}^{\mathsf{meta}}$ is enforced through the use of closed types, as done in [CMT00] for $\mathsf{MiniML}_{\mathsf{ref}}^{\mathsf{BN}}$.

Technically, the main novelty over [CMT00] is the identification of a larger set of closed types, which includes functional types of the form $t \to c$ where c is a closed type. The closed types of $\mathsf{MiniML}_{\mathsf{ref}}^{\mathsf{BN}}$ enjoy the following property: values of closed types are closed, i.e. have no free variables. The closed types of $\mathsf{MiniML}_{\mathsf{ref}}^{\mathsf{meta}}$ enjoy a weaker property (which is the best one can hope for functional types): the free variables in values of closed types are *useless*, i.e. during evaluation they will never be evaluated (at level 0).

Examples. The restriction of storable values to closed types is motivated by the following MetaML session:

```
-| val a = ref <1>;
val a = ... : ref <int>
-| val b = <fn x => ~(a:=<x>; <2>)>;
val b = <fn x => 2> : <int -> int>
-| val c = !a;
val c = <x> : <int>
```

In evaluating the second declaration, the variable x goes outside the scope of the binding lambda, and the result of the third line is wrong, since x is not bound in the environment, even though the session is well-typed according to naive extensions of previously proposed type systems for MetaML. This form of **scope extrusion** is specific to multi-level and multi-stage languages, and it does *not* arise in traditional programming languages, where evaluation is generally restricted to closed terms. The problem lies in the *run-time interaction between free variables and references*. In the type system we propose the above session is not well-typed: a:=<x> cannot be typed, because <x> is not of a closed type.

$\mathsf{MiniML}_{\mathsf{ref}}^{\mathsf{meta}}$ allows among the closed types some functional types, while in $\mathsf{MiniML}_{\mathsf{ref}}^{\mathsf{BN}}$ functional types are never closed. The following interactive session, is typable in $\mathsf{MiniML}_{\mathsf{ref}}^{\mathsf{meta}}$ but not in $\mathsf{MiniML}_{\mathsf{ref}}^{\mathsf{BN}}$.

```
-| val l = ref(fn x => x+1);
val l = (ref fn ...) : (int -> int) ref
-| <fn x => ~(l := (fn y => ((fn z => y+1) <x>)); <x+1>)>;
val it = <(fn x => x+1)> : <int -> int>
```

The first line creates a reference to functions from integers to integers; and the second assigns the function fn y => ((fn z => y+1) <x>) to it. As a result, the variable x escapes from its binder and leaks into the store. However, this cannot be observed because the variable is "useless": if we supply an argument to the stored function, the inner application will be evaluated, discarding the term <x>. The operational semantics presented here solves the problem with a binder for useless variables, introduced before storing a term.

Relation to MiniML$_\mathsf{ref}^\mathsf{BN}$. There is a significant overlap between MiniML$_\mathsf{ref}^\mathsf{meta}$ and MiniML$_\mathsf{ref}^\mathsf{BN}$. We refer to [CMT00] for a broader discussion of related work [DP96,Dav96,TS97,TBS98,MTBS99,BMTS99,Tah99,TS00]. For those familiar with MiniML$_\mathsf{ref}^\mathsf{BN}$ (recalled in Appendix A) we summarize the differences:

- MiniML$_\mathsf{ref}^\mathsf{meta}$ has no closedness annotation $[e]$, and the closed type constructor $[\_]$ cannot be applied to a closed type c. These are *cosmetic* changes, motivated by the following remarks in [CMT00]: closedness annotations play no role in the operational semantics, and a closed type c is *semantically* isomorphic to $[c]$ via the mapping $x \mapsto [x]$. When closedness annotations are removed, the isomorphism becomes an identity, thus the syntax for MiniML$_\mathsf{ref}^\mathsf{meta}$ types *forbids* $[c]$, since it is *equal* to c.
- MiniML$_\mathsf{ref}^\mathsf{meta}$ has a let-binder $(\mathsf{let}_c x = e_1 \text{ in } e_2)$ corresponding to $(\mathsf{let}\,[x\!:\!c] = [e_1] \text{ in } e_2)$ of MiniML$_\mathsf{ref}^\mathsf{BN}$, for variables of closed type.
- MiniML$_\mathsf{ref}^\mathsf{meta}$ has a larger set of closed types, in particular a functional type $t \to c$ is closed whenever c is closed. This property is essential to prove that every well-formed MiniML$_\mathsf{ref}$ program is also well-formed in MiniML$_\mathsf{ref}^\mathsf{meta}$.
- MiniML$_\mathsf{ref}^\mathsf{meta}$ has a new binder $\bullet e$, called Bullet, which binds all the free variables in e. When all the free variables in e are *useless*, $\bullet e$ and e are *semantically* equivalent. Bullet is used in the operational semantics to prevent scope extrusion (for this purpose it replaces the constant fault of [CMT00]), and to annotate terms whose free variables are useless.

  In an implementation, Bullet should help improve efficiency, since one knows that $\mathrm{FV}(\bullet e) = \emptyset$ without examining the whole of e. For instance, the function $\bullet \lambda x.e$ does not depend on the environment, only on the argument. Our operational semantics is too abstract to support claims about efficiency, but we expect that a reformulation in terms of weak explicit substitution ([LM99,B97]) could make such claims precise.

  In general, checking whether a variable is useless requires a static analysis (preferably of the whole program, see [WS99]). The MiniML$_\mathsf{ref}^\mathsf{meta}$ type system has a simple rule to infer $\bullet e\!:\!c^n$, namely $e\!:\!c^n$ when all the free variables in e have level $> n$. This rule makes sense only in the context of multi-level languages, but it infers $\bullet(!\,l\,\langle x \rangle)\!:\!c^n$, where l is a location of closed type $\langle t \rangle \to c$, which is beyond conventional analyses.

Structure of the Paper. Section 2 introduces MiniML$_\mathsf{ref}$, which is MiniML of [CDDK86] with ML-style references. Section 3 introduces MiniML$_\mathsf{ref}^\mathsf{meta}$, which extends MiniML$_\mathsf{ref}$ with

- The three staging constructs of MetaML [TS97,TBS98,Met00]: Brackets $\langle e \rangle$, Escape ~e and Run run e.
- A let-binder $(\mathsf{let}_c x = e_1 \text{ in } e_2)$ for variables of closed type.
- A binder $\bullet e$, called Bullet, of all the free variables in a term e of closed type.

We also prove type safety along the lines of [CMT00]. Section 4 shows that MiniML$_\mathsf{ref}^\mathsf{meta}$ is a conservative extension of MiniML$_\mathsf{ref}$. Section 5 discusses improvements to the type system through the addition of sub-typing, alternatives to Bullet, and variation to the syntax and operational semantics of MiniML$_\mathsf{ref}^\mathsf{meta}$.

2   MiniML_ref

This section describes the syntax, type system and operational semantics of MiniML_ref, an extension of MiniML ([CDDK86]) with ML-style references. Types t are defined as

$$t \in \mathsf{T} ::= \mathsf{nat} \mid \mathsf{ref}\, t \mid t_1 \rightarrow t_2$$

The sets of MiniML_ref terms and values are parametric in an infinite set of variables $x \in \mathsf{X}$ and an infinite set of locations $l \in \mathsf{L}$

$$e \in \mathsf{E} ::= x \mid \lambda x.e \mid e_1 e_2 \mid \mathsf{fix}\, x.e \mid \mathsf{z} \mid \mathsf{s}\, e \mid (\mathsf{case}\, e\, \mathsf{of}\, \mathsf{z} \rightarrow e_1 \mid \mathsf{s}\, x \rightarrow e_2) \mid$$
$$\qquad \mathsf{ref}\, e \mid\, !\, e \mid e_1 := e_2 \mid l$$
$$v \in \mathsf{V} ::= \lambda x.e \mid \mathsf{z} \mid \mathsf{s}\, v \mid l$$

The first line lists the MiniML terms: variables, abstraction, application, fix-point for recursive definitions, zero, successor, and case-analysis on natural numbers. The second line lists the three SML operations on references, and constants l for locations. These constants are not allowed in user-defined programs, but they are instrumental to the operational semantics of MiniML_ref.

Note 1. We will use the following notation and terminology

- Term equivalence, written $\equiv$, is α-conversion. $\mathrm{FV}(e)$ is the set of variables free in e. E_0 indicates the set of terms without free variables. Substitution of e_1 for x in e_2 (modulo $\equiv$) is written $e_2[x := e_1]$.
- m, n range over the set N of natural numbers. Furthermore, $m \in \mathsf{N}$ is identified with the set $\{i \in \mathsf{N} \mid i < m\}$ of its predecessors.
- $f \colon A \overset{fin}{\rightarrow} B$ means that f is a partial function from A to B with a finite domain, written $dom(f)$.
- $\Sigma \colon \mathsf{L} \overset{fin}{\rightarrow} \mathsf{T}$ is a *signature* (for locations only), written $\{l_i \colon \mathsf{ref}\, t_i \mid i \in m\}$.
- $\Gamma \colon \mathsf{X} \overset{fin}{\rightarrow} \mathsf{T}$ is a type assignment, written $\{x_i \colon t_i \mid i \in m\}$.
- $\mu \in \mathsf{S} \overset{\Delta}{=} \mathsf{L} \overset{fin}{\rightarrow} \mathsf{V}_0$ is a store, where V_0 is the set of closed values.
- $\Sigma, l \colon \mathsf{ref}\, t$, $\Gamma, x \colon t$ and $\mu\{l = v\}$ denote extension/update of a signature, assignment and store respectively.

Type System. The type system of MiniML_ref is given in Figure 1, and it enjoys the following basic properties:

Lemma 1 (Weakening).

1. $\Sigma; \Gamma \vdash e \colon t_2$ *and* x *fresh imply* $\Sigma; \Gamma, x \colon t_1 \vdash e \colon t_2$
2. $\Sigma; \Gamma \vdash e \colon t_2$ *and* l *fresh imply* $\Sigma, l \colon \mathsf{ref}\, t_1; \Gamma \vdash e \colon t_2$

Lemma 2 (Substitution).
$\Sigma; \Gamma \vdash e_1 \colon t_1$ *and* $\Sigma; \Gamma, x \colon t_1 \vdash e_2 \colon t_2$ *imply* $\Sigma; \Gamma \vdash e_2[x := e_1] \colon t_2$

We say that a store μ is well-formed for Σ (and write $\Sigma \models \mu$) $\overset{\Delta}{\Longleftrightarrow}$

$$dom(\Sigma) = dom(\mu) \text{ and } \Sigma \vdash v \colon t \text{ whenever } \mu(l) = v \text{ and } \Sigma(l) = \mathsf{ref}\, t.$$

$$\frac{\Gamma(x) = t}{\Sigma; \Gamma \vdash x : t} \qquad \frac{\Sigma; \Gamma, x : t_1 \vdash e : t_2}{\Sigma; \Gamma \vdash \lambda x.e : t_1 \to t_2} \qquad \frac{\Sigma; \Gamma \vdash e_1 : t_1 \to t_2 \quad \Sigma; \Gamma \vdash e_2 : t_1}{\Sigma; \Gamma \vdash e_1 e_2 : t_2}$$

$$\frac{\Sigma; \Gamma, x : t \vdash e : t}{\Sigma; \Gamma \vdash \blacksquare x x.e : t} \qquad \frac{}{\Sigma; \Gamma \vdash z : \mathsf{nat}} \qquad \frac{\Sigma; \Gamma \vdash e : \mathsf{nat}}{\Sigma; \Gamma \vdash \mathsf{s} e : \mathsf{nat}}$$

$$\frac{\Sigma; \Gamma \vdash e : \mathsf{nat} \quad \Sigma; \Gamma \vdash e_1 : t \quad \Sigma; \Gamma, x : \mathsf{nat} \vdash e_2 : t}{\Sigma; \Gamma \vdash (\mathsf{case}\, e\, \mathsf{of}\, z \to e_1 \mid \mathsf{s}\, x \to e_2) : t} \qquad \frac{\Sigma; \Gamma \vdash e : t}{\Sigma; \Gamma \vdash \mathsf{ref}\, e : \mathsf{ref}\, t}$$

$$\frac{\Sigma; \Gamma \vdash e : \mathsf{ref}\, t}{\Sigma; \Gamma \vdash !\, e : t} \qquad \frac{\Sigma; \Gamma \vdash e_1 : \mathsf{ref}\, t \quad \Sigma; \Gamma \vdash e_2 : t}{\Sigma; \Gamma \vdash e_1 := e_2 : \mathsf{ref}\, t} \qquad \frac{\Sigma(l) = \mathsf{ref}\, t}{\Sigma; \Gamma \vdash l : \mathsf{ref}\, t}$$

Fig. 1. Type System for MiniML$_{\mathsf{ref}}$

Operational Semantics. The operational semantics of MiniML$_{\mathsf{ref}}$ is given in Figure 2. The semantics is non-deterministic because of the rule for evaluating ref e. Evaluation of a term $e \in \mathsf{E}_0$ with an initial store μ_0 can lead to

- a *result* v and a new store μ_1, when we can derive $\mu_0, e \hookrightarrow \mu_1, v$, or
- a *run-time error*, when we can derive $\mu_0, e \hookrightarrow \mathsf{err}$.

Evaluation of a term may also lead to divergence, although a big-step operational semantics can express this third possibility only indirectly. One would have to adopt a reduction semantics (as advocated by [WF94]) to achieve a more accurate classification of the possible computations. In our setting, Type Safety means that evaluation of a well-typed program cannot lead to a run-time error, namely

Theorem 1 (Safety). $\mu_0, e \hookrightarrow d$ *and* $\Sigma_0 \models \mu_0$ *and* $\Sigma_0 \vdash e : t$ *imply that there exist* μ_1 *and* v *and* Σ_1 *such that* $d \equiv (\mu_1, v)$ *and* $\Sigma_0, \Sigma_1 \models \mu_1$ *and* $\Sigma_0, \Sigma_1 \vdash v : t$.

3   MiniML$_{\mathsf{ref}}^{\mathsf{meta}}$

This section describes the syntax, type system and operational semantics of MiniML$_{\mathsf{ref}}^{\mathsf{meta}}$, and establishes Type Safety. Types t, closed types c and open types o are defined as

$$t \in \mathsf{T} ::= c \mid o$$
$$c \in \mathsf{C} ::= \mathsf{nat} \mid t_1 \to c_2 \mid [o] \mid \mathsf{ref}\, c$$
$$o \in \mathsf{O} ::= t_1 \to o_2 \mid \langle t \rangle$$

Intuitively, a term can be assigned a closed type c only when its free variables are *useless*. The set of MiniML$_{\mathsf{ref}}^{\mathsf{meta}}$ terms is parametric in an infinite set of variables $x \in \mathsf{X}$ and an infinite set of locations $l \in \mathsf{L}$

$$e \in \mathsf{E} ::= x \mid \lambda x.e \mid e_1 e_2 \mid \mathsf{fix}\, x.e \mid \mathsf{z} \mid \mathsf{s}\, e \mid (\mathsf{case}\, e\, \mathsf{of}\, \mathsf{z} \to e_1 \mid \mathsf{s}\, x \to e_2) \mid$$
$$\langle e \rangle \mid {}^{\sim} e \mid \mathsf{run}\, e \mid (\mathsf{let}_c x = e_1 \,\mathsf{in}\, e_2) \mid \bullet e \mid$$
$$\mathsf{ref}\, e \mid !\, e \mid e_1 := e_2 \mid l$$

$$\mu_0, \lambda x.e \hookrightarrow \mu_0, \lambda x.e \qquad \frac{\mu_0, e_1 \hookrightarrow \mu_1, \lambda x.e \quad \mu_1, e_2 \hookrightarrow \mu_2, v_2 \quad \mu_2, e[x:=v_2] \hookrightarrow \mu_3, v}{\mu_0, e_1 e_2 \hookrightarrow \mu_3, v}$$

$$\frac{\mu_0, e_1 \hookrightarrow \mu_1, v \not\equiv \lambda x.e}{\mu_0, e_1 e_2 \hookrightarrow err} \qquad \frac{\mu_0, e[x:= \blacksquare x x.e] \hookrightarrow \mu_1, v}{\mu_0, \blacksquare x x.e \hookrightarrow \mu_1, v} \qquad \mu_0, z \hookrightarrow \mu_0, z$$

$$\frac{\mu_0, e \hookrightarrow \mu_1, v}{\mu_0, se \hookrightarrow \mu_1, sv} \qquad \frac{\mu_0, e \hookrightarrow \mu_1, z \quad \mu_1, e_1 \hookrightarrow \mu_2, v}{\mu_0, (\text{case } e \text{ of } z \to e_1 \mid s x \to e_2) \hookrightarrow \mu_2, v}$$

$$\frac{\mu_0, e \hookrightarrow \mu_1, v \not\equiv z \mid se'}{\mu_0, (\text{case } e \text{ of } z \to e_1 \mid s x \to e_2) \hookrightarrow err} \qquad \frac{\mu_0, e \hookrightarrow \mu_1, sv \quad \mu_1, e_2[x:=v] \hookrightarrow \mu_2, v_2}{\mu_0, (\text{case } e \text{ of } z \to e_1 \mid s x \to e_2) \hookrightarrow \mu_2, v_2}$$

$$\frac{\mu_0, e \hookrightarrow \mu_1, v \quad l \notin dom(\mu_1)}{\mu_0, \text{ref } e \hookrightarrow \mu_1\{l = v\}, l} \qquad \frac{\mu_0, e \hookrightarrow \mu_1, l \quad \mu_1(l) \equiv v}{\mu_0, !e \hookrightarrow \mu_1, v}$$

$$\frac{\mu_0, e \hookrightarrow \mu_1, v \not\equiv l \in dom(\mu_1)}{\mu_0, !e \hookrightarrow err} \qquad \frac{\mu_0, e_1 \hookrightarrow \mu_1, l \quad \mu_1, e_2 \hookrightarrow \mu_2, v}{\mu_0, e_1 := e_2 \hookrightarrow \mu_2\{l = v\}, l}$$

$$\frac{\mu_0, e_1 \hookrightarrow \mu_1, v \not\equiv l \in dom(\mu_1)}{\mu_0, e_1 := e_2 \hookrightarrow err} \qquad \mu_0, l \hookrightarrow \mu_0, l$$

The rules for error propagation follow the ML-convention, i.e. for every normal evaluation rule $\dfrac{\{\mu_i, e_i \hookrightarrow \mu_{i+1}, v_i \mid i \in n\}}{\mu_0, e \hookrightarrow \mu_n, v}$ and every $m \in n$ one should add an error propagation rule $\dfrac{\{\mu_i, e_i \hookrightarrow \mu_{i+1}, v_i \mid i \in m\} \quad \mu_m, e_m \hookrightarrow err}{\mu_0, e \hookrightarrow err}$.

Fig. 2. Operational Semantics for MiniML$_{\text{ref}}$

The second line lists the three multi-stage constructs of MetaML [TS97]: *Brackets* $\langle e \rangle$ and *Escape* $\~{}e$ are for building and splicing code, and *Run* is for executing code. The second line lists also a let-binder $(\text{let}_c x = e_1 \text{ in } e_2)$ for variables of closed type, and a binder *Bullet* $\bullet e$, which binds all the free variables of e, hence $FV(\bullet e) = \emptyset$, and $(\bullet e)[x := e_1] \equiv \bullet e$.

Note 2. We will use the following notation and terminology (see also Note 1)

- w ranges over terms not of the form $\bullet e$, while $\circ w$ can be either w of $\bullet w$.
- $\Sigma: L \overset{fin}{\to} T$ is a *signature* (for locations only), written $\{l_i : \text{ref } c_i \mid i \in m\}$.
- $\Delta: X \overset{fin}{\to} (C \times N)$ and $\Gamma: X \overset{fin}{\to} (T \times N)$ are type-and-level assignments, written $\{x_i : c_i^{n_i} \mid i \in m\}$ and $\{x_i : t_i^{n_i} \mid i \in m\}$ respectively.
  We use the following operations on type-and-level assignments:
  $\{x_i : t_i^{n_i} \mid i \in m\}^{+n} \overset{\Delta}{=} \{x_i : t_i^{n_i+n} \mid i \in m\}$ adds n to the level of the x_i;
  $\{x_i : t_i^{n_i} \mid i \in m\}^{\leq n} \overset{\Delta}{=} \{x_i : t_i^{n_i} \mid n_i \leq n \wedge i \in m\}$ removes the x_i with level $> n$.
- $\Gamma, x : t^n$ and $\Delta, x : c^n$ denote the extension of type-and-level assignments.

Remark 1. The new binder Bullet $\bullet e$ serves many purposes, which the constant fault of [CMT00] can fulfill only in part (e.g. fault is not typable). Intuitively, $\bullet e$ is like a closure (e, ρ), where ρ is the environment (explicit substitution) mapping all variables to fault, and in addition it records that e should have a closed type.

$$\frac{}{\Sigma; \Delta; \Gamma \vdash x : t^n} \ (\Delta, \Gamma)(x) = t^n \qquad \frac{\Sigma; \Delta; \Gamma, x : t_1^n \vdash e : t_2^n}{\Sigma; \Delta; \Gamma \vdash \lambda x.e : t_1 \to t_2^n}$$

$$\frac{\Sigma; \Delta; \Gamma \vdash e_1 : t_1 \to t_2^n \quad \Sigma; \Delta; \Gamma \vdash e_2 : t_1^n}{\Sigma; \Delta; \Gamma \vdash e_1 e_2 : t_2^n} \qquad \frac{\Sigma; \Delta; \Gamma, x : t^n \vdash e : t^n}{\Sigma; \Delta; \Gamma \vdash \mathbf{fix}\, x.e : t^n} \qquad \frac{}{\Sigma; \Delta; \Gamma \vdash \mathtt{z} : \mathtt{nat}^n}$$

$$\frac{\Sigma; \Delta; \Gamma \vdash e : \mathtt{nat}^n}{\Sigma; \Delta; \Gamma \vdash \mathtt{s}\,e : \mathtt{nat}^n} \qquad \frac{\Sigma; \Delta; \Gamma \vdash e : \mathtt{nat}^n \quad \Sigma; \Delta; \Gamma \vdash e_1 : t^n \quad \Sigma; \Delta; \Gamma, x : \mathtt{nat}^n \vdash e_2 : t^n}{\Sigma; \Delta; \Gamma \vdash (\mathtt{case}\, e \,\mathtt{of}\, \mathtt{z} \to e_1 \mid \mathtt{s}\,x \to e_2) : t^n}$$

$$\frac{\Sigma; \Delta; \Gamma \vdash e : c^n}{\Sigma; \Delta; \Gamma \vdash \mathtt{ref}\,e : \mathtt{ref}\,c^n} \qquad \frac{\Sigma; \Delta; \Gamma \vdash e : \mathtt{ref}\,c^n}{\Sigma; \Delta; \Gamma \vdash !e : c^n} \qquad \frac{\Sigma; \Delta; \Gamma \vdash e_1 : \mathtt{ref}\,c^n \quad \Sigma; \Delta; \Gamma \vdash e_2 : c^n}{\Sigma; \Delta; \Gamma \vdash e_1 := e_2 : \mathtt{ref}\,c^n}$$

$$\frac{}{\Sigma; \Delta; \Gamma \vdash l : \mathtt{ref}\,c^n} \ \Sigma(l) = \mathtt{ref}\,c \qquad \frac{\Sigma; \Delta; \Gamma \vdash e : t^{n+1}}{\Sigma; \Delta; \Gamma \vdash \langle e \rangle : \langle t \rangle^n} \qquad \frac{\Sigma; \Delta; \Gamma \vdash e : \langle t \rangle^n}{\Sigma; \Delta; \Gamma \vdash \tilde{\ }e : t^{n+1}}$$

$$\frac{\Sigma; \Delta; \Gamma \vdash e : [\langle t \rangle]^n}{\Sigma; \Delta; \Gamma \vdash \mathtt{run}\,e : t^n} \qquad \frac{\Sigma; \Delta^{\le n}; \emptyset \vdash e : o^n}{\Sigma; \Delta; \Gamma \vdash e : [o]^n} \qquad \frac{\Sigma; \Delta; \Gamma \vdash e : [o]^n}{\Sigma; \Delta; \Gamma \vdash e : o^n}$$

$$\frac{\Sigma; \Delta; \Gamma \vdash e_1 : c^n \quad \Sigma; \Delta, x : c^n; \Gamma \vdash e_2 : t^n}{\Sigma; \Delta; \Gamma \vdash (\mathtt{let}_c\, x = e_1 \,\mathtt{in}\, e_2) : t^n} \qquad \frac{\Sigma; \Delta_1^{+(n+1)}; \Gamma_1^{+(n+1)} \vdash e : c^n}{\Sigma; \Delta; \Gamma \vdash \bullet e : c^n}$$

Fig. 3. Type System for $\mathsf{MiniML}_{\mathsf{ref}}^{\mathsf{meta}}$

The typing rule for Bullet, in combination with Type Safety (Theorem 2), formalizes the property that in a term of closed type (at level n) all the free variables (at level $> n$) are *useless*. In fact, during evaluation a variable bound by Bullet (unlike variables captured by other binders) cannot get instantiated, thus its occurrences must disappear before reaching level 0 (otherwise they will cause a run-time error).

The operational semantics of Figure 2 uses Bullet to prevent scope extrusion when a location l is initialized or assigned. In fact, what gets stored in l is the closed value $\bullet w$, instead of the value w. Therefore, if a free variable in w was is the scope of an enclosing binder, e.g. x in $\langle \lambda x.\tilde{\ }(l := w; \langle x \rangle) \rangle$, it is caught by Bullet, instead of becoming free.

Unlike locations (which exist only at execution time) and fault (which is not typable), Bullet could be used in user-defined programs to record that a term has a closed type. The operational semantics uses such information when evaluating an application (if $\lambda x.e$ has a closed type, then e must have a closed type) and a let-binder (the let must bind x to a term of closed type) for capturing free variables. For instance, during evaluation of $\bullet(\lambda x.e)\, v$ the free variables of v get captured in $\bullet(e[x := v])$.

3.1 Type System

Figure 3 gives the type system of $\mathsf{MiniML}_{\mathsf{ref}}^{\mathsf{meta}}$. A typing judgement has the form $\Sigma; \Delta; \Gamma \vdash e : t^n$, read "$e$ has type t and level n under the assignment $\Sigma; \Delta; \Gamma$". Σ gives the type of locations which can be used in e, Δ and Γ (must have disjoint domains and) give the type and level of variables which may occur free in e.

Remark 2. All typing rules, except the last four, are borrowed from [CMT00]. The introduction and elimination rules for $[o]$ say that $[o]$ is a sub-type of o. The rule for $(\text{let}_c x = e_1 \text{ in } e_2)$ incorporates the typing rule (close*) of [CMT00]. The rule for $\bullet e$ says that Bullet binds all the free variables in e. One can think of $\bullet e$ as the closure (e, ρ), where ρ is the environment (explicit substitution) mapping all variables to fault.

The type system enjoys the following basic properties (see also [CMT00]):

Lemma 3 (Weakening).

1. $\Sigma; \Delta; \Gamma \vdash e : t_2^n$ *and* x *fresh imply* $\Sigma; \Delta; \Gamma, x : t_1^m \vdash e : t_2^n$
2. $\Sigma; \Delta; \Gamma \vdash e : t_2^n$ *and* x *fresh imply* $\Sigma; \Delta, x : c^m; \Gamma \vdash e : t_2^n$
3. $\Sigma; \Delta; \Gamma \vdash e : t_2^n$ *and* l *fresh imply* $\Sigma, l : \text{ref } c_1; \Delta; \Gamma \vdash e : t_2^n$

Lemma 4 (Substitution).

1. $\Sigma; \Delta; \Gamma \vdash e_1 : t_1^m$ *and* $\Sigma; \Delta; \Gamma, x : t_1^m \vdash e_2 : t_2^n$ *imply* $\Sigma; \Delta; \Gamma \vdash e_2[x := e_1] : t_2^n$
2. $\Sigma; \Delta^{\leq m}; \emptyset \vdash e_1 : c^m$ *and* $\Sigma; \Delta, x : c^m; \Gamma \vdash e_2 : t_2^n$ *imply* $\Sigma; \Delta; \Gamma \vdash e_2[x := e_1] : t_2^n$

3.2   Operational Semantics

The operational semantics of $\text{MiniML}_{\text{ref}}^{\text{meta}}$ is given in Figure 4. The rules derive evaluation judgements of the form $\mu, e \xrightarrow{n} d$, where $\mu \in S$ is a *value store* (see below). In the rules v ranges over terms, but *a posteriori* one can show that v ranges over *values at level* n (see below). We will show that evaluation of a well-typed program cannot lead to a run-time error (Theorem 2).

Definition 1. *The set* $V^n \subset E$ *of values at level* n *is defined by the BNF*

$$v^n \in V^n ::= w^n \mid \bullet w^n$$
$$w^0 \in W^0 ::= \lambda x.e \mid z \mid s\, v^0 \mid \langle v^1 \rangle \mid l$$
$$\begin{aligned} w^{n+1} \in W^{n+1} ::= \ & x \mid \lambda x.v^{n+1} \mid v_1^{n+1} v_2^{n+1} \mid \text{fix } x.v^{n+1} \mid z \mid s\, v^{n+1} \mid \\ & (\text{case } v^{n+1} \text{ of } z \to v_1^{n+1} \mid s\, x \to v_2^{n+1}) \mid \langle v^{n+2} \rangle \mid \text{run } v^{n+1} \mid \\ & (\text{let}_c x = v_1^{n+1} \text{ in } v_2^{n+1}) \mid \\ & \text{ref } v^{n+1} \mid !\, v^{n+1} \mid v_1^{n+1} := v_2^{n+1} \mid l \end{aligned}$$
$$w^{n+2} \in W^{n+2}+ = {}^{\sim}v^{n+1}$$

$\mu \in S \overset{\Delta}{=} L \overset{fin}{\to} V_0^0$ *is a* **value store**, *where* V_0^0 *is the set of closed values at level* 0. *We write* $\Sigma \models \mu \overset{\Delta}{\Longleftrightarrow} dom(\Sigma) = dom(\mu)$ *and* $\Sigma; \emptyset \vdash v : c^0$ *whenever* $\mu(l) = v$ *and* $\Sigma(l) = \text{ref } c$.

The following result establishes basic facts about the operational semantics, similar to those established for $\text{MiniML}_{\text{ref}}^{\text{BN}}$ (see [CMT00]).

Lemma 5 (Values). $\mu_0, e \xrightarrow{n} \mu_1, v$ *and* μ_0 *is value store imply* μ_1 *is a value store,* $dom(\mu_0) \subseteq dom(\mu_1)$, $v \in V^n$ *and* $\text{FV}(v) \subseteq \text{FV}(e)$.

In the rules below $\circ w$ is a meta-expression ranging over terms of the form w and $\bullet w$.

Normal Evaluation

$$\mu_0, \lambda x.e \stackrel{0}{\hookrightarrow} \mu_0, \lambda x.e \qquad \frac{\mu_0, e_1 \stackrel{0}{\hookrightarrow} \mu_1, \lambda x.e \quad \mu_1, e_2 \stackrel{0}{\hookrightarrow} \mu_2, v_2 \quad \mu_2, e[x := v_2] \stackrel{0}{\hookrightarrow} \mu_3, v}{\mu_0, e_1 e_2 \stackrel{0}{\hookrightarrow} \mu_3, v}$$

$$\mu_0, x \stackrel{0}{\hookrightarrow} \text{err} \qquad \frac{\mu_0, e_1 \stackrel{0}{\hookrightarrow} \mu_1, \bullet\lambda x.e \quad \mu_1, e_2 \stackrel{0}{\hookrightarrow} \mu_2, v_2 \quad \mu_2, \bullet(e[x := v_2]) \stackrel{0}{\hookrightarrow} \mu_3, v}{\mu_0, e_1 e_2 \stackrel{0}{\hookrightarrow} \mu_3, v}$$

$$\frac{\mu_0, e_1 \stackrel{0}{\hookrightarrow} \mu_1, v \not\equiv \circ\lambda x.e}{\mu_0, e_1 e_2 \stackrel{0}{\hookrightarrow} \text{err}} \qquad \frac{\mu_0, e[x := \square x x.e] \stackrel{0}{\hookrightarrow} \mu_1, v}{\mu_0, \square x x.e \stackrel{0}{\hookrightarrow} \mu_1, v} \qquad \mu_0, z \stackrel{0}{\hookrightarrow} \mu_0, z$$

$$\frac{\mu_0, e \stackrel{0}{\hookrightarrow} \mu_1, v}{\mu_0, se \stackrel{0}{\hookrightarrow} \mu_1, sv} \qquad \frac{\mu_0, e \stackrel{0}{\hookrightarrow} \mu_1, \circ z \quad \mu_1, e_1 \stackrel{0}{\hookrightarrow} \mu_2, v_1}{\mu_0, (\text{case } e \text{ of } z \to e_1 \mid sx \to e_2) \stackrel{0}{\hookrightarrow} \mu_2, v_1}$$

$$\frac{\mu_0, e \stackrel{0}{\hookrightarrow} \mu_1, v \not\equiv \circ z \mid \circ sv}{\mu_0, (\text{case } e \text{ of } z \to e_1 \mid sx \to e_2) \stackrel{0}{\hookrightarrow} \text{err}} \qquad \frac{\mu_0, e \stackrel{0}{\hookrightarrow} \mu_1, \circ sv \quad \mu_1, e_2[x := \circ v] \stackrel{0}{\hookrightarrow} \mu_2, v_2}{\mu_0, (\text{case } e \text{ of } z \to e_1 \mid sx \to e_2) \stackrel{0}{\hookrightarrow} \mu_2, v_2}$$

$$\frac{\mu_0, e \stackrel{0}{\hookrightarrow} \mu_1, \circ w}{\mu_0, \text{ref } e \stackrel{0}{\hookrightarrow} \mu_1\{l = \bullet w\}, l} l \notin dom(\mu_1) \qquad \frac{\mu_0, e \stackrel{0}{\hookrightarrow} \mu_1, \circ l}{\mu_0, !e \stackrel{0}{\hookrightarrow} \mu_1, v} \mu_1(l) \equiv v$$

$$\frac{\mu_0, e \stackrel{0}{\hookrightarrow} \mu_1, \circ w}{\mu_0, !e \stackrel{0}{\hookrightarrow} \text{err}} w \notin dom(\mu_1) \qquad \frac{\mu_0, e_1 \stackrel{0}{\hookrightarrow} \mu_1, \circ l \quad \mu_1, e_2 \stackrel{0}{\hookrightarrow} \mu_2, \circ w}{\mu_0, e_1 := e_2 \stackrel{0}{\hookrightarrow} \mu_2\{l = \bullet w\}, l} l \in dom(\mu_1)$$

$$\frac{\mu_0, e_1 \stackrel{0}{\hookrightarrow} \mu_1, \circ w}{\mu_0, e_1 := e_2 \stackrel{0}{\hookrightarrow} \text{err}} w \notin dom(\mu_1) \qquad \mu_0, l \stackrel{0}{\hookrightarrow} \mu_0, l \qquad \frac{\mu_0, e \stackrel{1}{\hookrightarrow} \mu_1, v}{\mu_0, \langle e \rangle \stackrel{0}{\hookrightarrow} \mu_1, \langle v \rangle}$$

$$\frac{\mu_0, e \stackrel{1}{\hookrightarrow} \mu_1, v}{\mu_0, \tilde{\ } e \stackrel{0}{\hookrightarrow} \text{err}} \qquad \frac{\mu_0, e \stackrel{0}{\hookrightarrow} \mu_1, \circ\langle v \rangle \quad \mu_1, \bullet v \stackrel{0}{\hookrightarrow} \mu_2, v_0}{\mu_0, \text{run } e \stackrel{0}{\hookrightarrow} \mu_2, v_0} \qquad \frac{\mu_0, e \stackrel{0}{\hookrightarrow} \mu_1, v \not\equiv \circ\langle e' \rangle}{\mu_0, \text{run } e \stackrel{0}{\hookrightarrow} \text{err}}$$

$$\frac{\mu_0, e_1 \stackrel{0}{\hookrightarrow} \mu_1, \circ w \quad \mu_1, e_2[x := \bullet w] \stackrel{0}{\hookrightarrow} \mu_2, v_2}{\mu_0, (\text{let}_c x = e_1 \text{ in } e_2) \stackrel{0}{\hookrightarrow} \mu_2, v_2} \qquad \frac{\mu_0, e \stackrel{n}{\hookrightarrow} \mu_1, \circ w}{\mu_0, \bullet e \stackrel{n}{\hookrightarrow} \mu_1, \bullet w}$$

Symbolic Evaluation

$$\mu_0, x \stackrel{n+1}{\hookrightarrow} \mu_0, x \qquad \frac{\mu_0, e \stackrel{n+2}{\hookrightarrow} \mu_1, v}{\mu_0, \langle e \rangle \stackrel{n+1}{\hookrightarrow} \mu_1, \langle v \rangle} \qquad \frac{\mu_0, e \stackrel{0}{\hookrightarrow} \mu_1, \langle v \rangle}{\mu_0, \tilde{\ } e \stackrel{1}{\hookrightarrow} \mu_1, v} \qquad \frac{\mu_0, e \stackrel{0}{\hookrightarrow} \mu_1, \bullet\langle \circ w \rangle}{\mu_0, \tilde{\ } e \stackrel{1}{\hookrightarrow} \mu_1, \bullet w}$$

$$\frac{\mu_0, e \stackrel{0}{\hookrightarrow} \mu_1, v \not\equiv \circ\langle e' \rangle}{\mu_0, \tilde{\ } e \stackrel{1}{\hookrightarrow} \text{err}} \qquad \frac{\mu_0, e \stackrel{n+1}{\hookrightarrow} \mu_1, v}{\mu_0, \tilde{\ } e \stackrel{n+2}{\hookrightarrow} \mu_1, \tilde{\ } v}$$

In all other cases symbolic evaluation is applied to the immediate sub-terms from left to right without changing level.

Error Propagation

The rules for error propagation follow the ML-convention (see Figure 2).

Fig. 4. Operational Semantics for $\text{MiniML}^{\text{meta}}_{\text{ref}}$

Proof. By induction on the derivation of the evaluation judgement $\mu_0, e \overset{n}{\hookrightarrow} \mu_1, v$. Notice that in the rules evaluating ref e and $e_1 := e_2$ it is important that we store $\bullet w$, since w may have free variables.

The following lemma is used to prove type safety in the case for evaluating run e at level 0. The result holds also for closed types of the form nat and ref c.

Lemma 6 (Closedness). *If* $\Sigma; \Delta^{+1}; \Gamma^{+1} \vdash \circ w^0 : [o]^0$, *then* $\mathrm{FV}(w^0) = \emptyset$.

Proof. By induction on the derivation of $\Sigma; \Delta^{+1}; \Gamma^{+1} \vdash \circ w^0 : [o]^0$.

Evaluation of run e at level 0 requires to view a value v at level 1 as a term to be evaluated at level 0. The following lemma says that this confusion in the levels is compatible with the type system.

Lemma 7 (Demotion). $\Sigma; \Delta^{+1}; \Gamma^{+1} \vdash v^{n+1} : t^{n+1}$ *implies* $\Sigma; \Delta; \Gamma \vdash v^{n+1} : t^n$.

Proof. By induction on the derivation of $\Sigma; \Delta^{+1}; \Gamma^{+1} \vdash v^{n+1} : t^{n+1}$.

The *reflective* nature of $\mathsf{MiniML}_{\mathsf{ref}}^{\mathsf{meta}}$ is fully captured by the Demotion Lemma and the following Promotion Lemma (which is not relevant to the proof of Type Safety).

Lemma 8. $\Sigma; \Delta; \Gamma \vdash e : t^n$ *implies* $e \in V^{n+1}$ *and* $\Sigma; \Delta^{+1}; \Gamma^{+1} \vdash e : t^{n+1}$.

Finally, we establish the key result relating the type system to the operational semantics. This result entails that evaluation of a well-typed program $\emptyset; \emptyset \vdash e : t^0$ cannot raise an error, i.e. $\emptyset, e \overset{0}{\hookrightarrow} \mathsf{err}$ is not derivable.

Theorem 2 (Safety). $\mu_0, e \overset{n}{\hookrightarrow} d$ *and* $\Sigma_0 \models \mu_0$ *and* $\Sigma_0; \Delta^{+1}; \Gamma^{+1} \vdash e : t^n$ *imply that there exist* μ_1 *and* v^n *and* Σ_1 *such that* $d \equiv (\mu_1, v^n)$ *and* $\Sigma_0, \Sigma_1 \models \mu_1$ *and* $\Sigma_0, \Sigma_1; \Delta^{+1}; \Gamma^{+1} \vdash v^n : t^n$.

Proof. By induction on the derivation of the evaluation judgement $\mu_0, e \overset{n}{\hookrightarrow} d$.

4   Conservative Extension Result

This section shows that $\mathsf{MiniML}_{\mathsf{ref}}^{\mathsf{meta}}$ is a *conservative extension* of $\mathsf{MiniML}_{\mathsf{ref}}$ w.r.t. typing and operational semantics. When we need to distinguish the syntactic categories of $\mathsf{MiniML}_{\mathsf{ref}}^{\mathsf{meta}}$ from those of $\mathsf{MiniML}_{\mathsf{ref}}$ we use a superscript $\_^{\mathsf{meta}}$ for the formers, e.g. $\mathsf{E}^{\mathsf{meta}}$ denotes the set of $\mathsf{MiniML}_{\mathsf{ref}}^{\mathsf{meta}}$ terms, while E denotes the set of $\mathsf{MiniML}_{\mathsf{ref}}$ terms. We have the following inclusions between the syntactic categories of the two languages:

Lemma 9. $\mathsf{T} \subseteq \mathsf{C}^{\mathsf{meta}}$ *and* $\mathsf{E} \subseteq \mathsf{E}^{\mathsf{meta}}$ *and* $\mathsf{V} \subseteq \mathsf{V}^{0\,\mathsf{meta}}$.

Proof. Easy induction on the structure of $t \in \mathsf{T}$, $e \in \mathsf{E}$ and $v \in \mathsf{V}$.

There are minor mismatches between the typing and evaluation judgements of the two languages, thus we introduce three derived predicates, which simplify the formulation of the conservative extension result:

- $e\colon t$, i.e. e is a program of type t;
- $e \Downarrow$, i.e. evaluation of e may lead to a value;
- $e \Downarrow \mathsf{err}$, i.e. evaluation of e may lead to a run-time error.

The following table defines the three predicates in $\mathsf{MiniML_{ref}}$ and $\mathsf{MiniML_{ref}^{meta}}$:

predicate	meaning in $\mathsf{MiniML_{ref}}$	meaning in $\mathsf{MiniML_{ref}^{meta}}$
$e\colon t$	$\emptyset; \emptyset \vdash e\colon t$	$\emptyset; \emptyset; \emptyset \vdash e\colon t^0$
$e \Downarrow$	$\exists \mu, v.\ \emptyset, e \hookrightarrow \mu, v$	$\exists \mu, v.\ \emptyset, e \overset{0}{\hookrightarrow} \mu, v$
$e \Downarrow \mathsf{err}$	$\emptyset, e \hookrightarrow \mathsf{err}$	$\emptyset, e \overset{0}{\hookrightarrow} \mathsf{err}$

The conservative extension result can be stated as follows (the rest of the section establishes several facts, which combined together imply the desired result)

Theorem 3 (Conservative Extension). $\mathsf{MiniML_{ref}}$ *and* $\mathsf{MiniML_{ref}^{meta}}$ *agree on the validity of the assertions* $e\colon t$, $e \Downarrow$ *and* $e \Downarrow \mathsf{err}$, *whenever* $e \in \mathsf{E}$ *and* $t \in \mathsf{T}$.

A typing judgement $\Sigma; \Gamma \vdash e\colon t$ for $\mathsf{MiniML_{ref}}$ it is not appropriate for $\mathsf{MiniML_{ref}^{meta}}$, because $\Gamma\colon \mathsf{X} \overset{fin}{\to} \mathsf{T}$ and e lack the level information. Therefore, we introduce the following operation to turn a type assignment into a type-and-level assignment

$$\{x_i\colon t_i | i \in m\}^n \overset{\Delta}{=} \{x_i\colon t_i^n | i \in m\}$$

i.e. Γ^n assigns level n to all variables declared in Γ.

Proposition 1. $\Sigma; \Gamma \vdash e\colon t$ *in* $\mathsf{MiniML_{ref}}$ *implies* $\Sigma; \emptyset; \Gamma^0 \vdash e\colon t^0$ *in* $\mathsf{MiniML_{ref}^{meta}}$.

Proof. Easy induction on the derivation of $\Sigma; \Gamma \vdash e\colon t$.

An immediate consequence of Proposition 1 is that $e\colon t$ in $\mathsf{MiniML_{ref}}$ implies $e\colon t$ in $\mathsf{MiniML_{ref}^{meta}}$. For the converse, we need to define a translation from $\mathsf{T^{meta}}$ to T.

Definition 2. *The function* $\|\_\|$ *from* $\mathsf{T^{meta}}$ *to* T *is defined as*

$$\|[o]\| \overset{\Delta}{=} \|o\|$$
$$\|\langle t \rangle\| \overset{\Delta}{=} \|t\|$$

and it commutes with all other type-constructs of $\mathsf{MiniML_{ref}^{meta}}$. *The extension to signatures* Σ *is point-wise;* $\|\Gamma\|(x) = \|t\|$ *when* $\Gamma(x) = t^n$ *and similarly for* Δ.

Proposition 2. $\Sigma; \Delta; \Gamma \vdash e\colon t^n$ *implies* $\|\Sigma\|; \|\Delta\|; \|\Gamma\| \vdash e\colon \|t\|$, *provided* $e \in \mathsf{E}$.

Proof. By induction on the derivation of $\Sigma; \Delta; \Gamma \vdash e\colon t^n$.

The operational semantics of $\mathsf{MiniML_{ref}^{meta}}$ may introduce Bullet (e.g. when manipulating the store), even when the evaluation starts in a configuration (μ, e) without occurrences of $\bullet$. Therefore, to relate the operational semantics of $\mathsf{MiniML_{ref}^{meta}}$ and $\mathsf{MiniML_{ref}}$, we introduce a partial function on $\mathsf{E^{meta}}$ which erases Bullet from $\bullet e$ when $\mathrm{FV}(e) = \emptyset$.

Definition 3 (Erasure). *The partial function $|\_|$ on $\mathsf{E}^{\mathsf{meta}}$ is defined as*

$$| \bullet e| \triangleq \begin{cases} |e| & \text{if } FV(e) = \emptyset \\ \text{undefined} & \text{otherwise} \end{cases}$$

and it commutes with all other term-constructs of $\mathsf{MiniML}^{\mathsf{meta}}_{\mathsf{ref}}$.

Lemma 10. *The erasure enjoys the following properties:*

- *If $\Sigma; \Delta; \Gamma \vdash e : t^n$ and $|e|$ is defined, then $\Sigma; \Delta; \Gamma \vdash |e| : t^n$;*
- *if $|e_2| \equiv e_2'$ and $|e_1| \equiv e_1'$ then $|e_2[x := e_1]| \equiv e_2'[x := e_1']$.*

Proof. The first part is by induction on the derivation of $\Sigma; \Delta; \Gamma \vdash e : t^n$; the second is by induction on the structure of e_2.

Definition 4 (Bisimulation). *The relation $\mathsf{R} \subseteq \mathsf{E}^{\mathsf{meta}} \times \mathsf{E}_0$ is given by*
$e \mathrel{\mathsf{R}} e' \overset{\triangle}{\iff} FV(e) = \emptyset$ *and $|e| \equiv e'$.*
    The relation is extended to stores μ and configurations d as follows:
$\mu \mathrel{\mathsf{R}} \mu' \overset{\triangle}{\iff} dom(\mu) = dom(\mu')$ *and $\mu(l) \mathrel{\mathsf{R}} \mu'(l)$ when $l \in dom(\mu)$;*
$d \mathrel{\mathsf{R}} d' \overset{\triangle}{\iff} d = \mathsf{err} = d'$ *or $(d = (\mu, e)$ and $d = (\mu', e')$ where $\mu \mathrel{\mathsf{R}} \mu'$ and $e \mathrel{\mathsf{R}} e')$.*

The following proposition says that R is a bisimulation between the operational semantics of $\mathsf{MiniML}^{\mathsf{meta}}_{\mathsf{ref}}$ and $\mathsf{MiniML}_{\mathsf{ref}}$.

Proposition 3. *If $\mu \mathrel{\mathsf{R}} \mu'$ and $e \mathrel{\mathsf{R}} e'$, then*

1. *$\mu, e \overset{0}{\hookrightarrow} d$ implies there exist (unique) d' such that $d \mathrel{\mathsf{R}} d'$ and $\mu', e' \hookrightarrow d'$;*
2. *$\mu', e' \hookrightarrow d'$ implies there exist d such that $d \mathrel{\mathsf{R}} d'$ and $\mu, e \overset{0}{\hookrightarrow} d$.*

Proof. The first part is by induction on the derivation of $\mu, e \overset{0}{\hookrightarrow} d$. The second part is by lexicographic induction on the derivation of $\mu', e' \hookrightarrow d'$ and the number of top-level Bullets in e (i.e. n such that $e \equiv \bullet^n w$).

This implies the conservative extension result for the predicates $e \Downarrow$ and $e \Downarrow \mathsf{err}$.

5   Conclusions and Further Research

In this section we discuss possible improvements to the type system and variations to the syntax and operational semantics of $\mathsf{MiniML}^{\mathsf{meta}}_{\mathsf{ref}}$.

Sub-typing. In $\text{MiniML}^{\text{meta}}_{\text{ref}}$ sub-typing arises naturally, e.g. one expects $[o] \leq o$ for any open type $o \in \mathsf{O}$.

Before adding a sub-sumption rule $\dfrac{\Sigma; \Delta; \Gamma \vdash e : t_1^n}{\Sigma; \Delta; \Gamma \vdash e : t_2^n}$ $t_1 \leq t_2$ to $\text{MiniML}^{\text{meta}}_{\text{ref}}$, it is better to adopt a more general syntax for types t and closed types c

$$t \in \mathsf{T} ::= \text{nat} \mid t_1 \to t_2 \mid \text{ref } c \mid \langle t \rangle \mid [t]$$
$$c \in \mathsf{C} ::= \text{nat} \mid t_1 \to c_2 \mid \text{ref } c \mid [t]$$

and let the sub-typing rule derive $[c] = c$. One expects the usual sub-typing rules for functional and references types, and it seems natural to require the Code and Closed type constructors to be covariant, i.e.

$$\frac{t_1' \leq t_1 \quad t_2 \leq t_2'}{t_1 \to t_2 \leq t_1' \to t_2'} \quad \frac{c' \leq c \quad c \leq c'}{\text{ref } c \leq \text{ref } c'} \quad \frac{t \leq t'}{\langle t \rangle \leq \langle t' \rangle} \quad \frac{t \leq t'}{[t] \leq [t']}$$

while sub-typing axioms, which generate non trivial relations, are

$$[t] \leq t \qquad c \leq [c] \qquad [t_1 \to t_2] \leq [t_1] \to [t_2] \qquad [\langle t \rangle] \leq \langle [t] \rangle$$

From the sub-typing axioms and rules above one can derive the following facts:

- $t \leq c$ implies $t \in \mathsf{C}$, by induction on the derivation of $t \leq c$;
- $[c] = c$ and $c \to [t] = [c \to t]$, while the following sub-typing are strict $[\langle t \rangle] < \langle t \rangle$ and $[\langle t_1 \rangle] \to [\langle t_2 \rangle] < [\langle t_1 \rangle \to \langle t_2 \rangle]$.

We plan to investigate the addition of sub-typing and its effects on type safety.

Useless-Variable Annotation. The binder $\bullet e$ of $\text{MiniML}^{\text{meta}}_{\text{ref}}$ takes an all or nothing approach. One could provide a more fine-grained annotation $(x)e$, which allows to name a useless variable. The typing rules for $(x)e$ are the obvious one:

$$\frac{\Sigma; \Delta; \Gamma, x : t^m \vdash e : c^n}{\Sigma; \Delta; \Gamma \vdash (x)e : c^n} \; m > n \qquad \frac{\Sigma; \Delta, x : t^m; \Gamma \vdash e : c^n}{\Sigma; \Delta; \Gamma \vdash (x)e : c^n} \; m > n$$

One can define the derived notation $(X)e$, where X is a finite set/sequence of variables, by induction on the cardinality of X: $(\emptyset)e \overset{\Delta}{\equiv} e$, $(x, X)e \overset{\Delta}{\equiv} (x)(X)e$. One might identify $\bullet e$ with $\tilde{e} \overset{\Delta}{\equiv} (X)e$, where $X = \text{FV}(e)$. However, at the operational level such identification is not right. In fact, the rule

$$\frac{\mu_0, e_1 \overset{0}{\hookrightarrow} \mu_1, \bullet \lambda x.e \quad \mu_1, e_2 \overset{0}{\hookrightarrow} \mu_2, v_2 \quad \mu_2, \bullet (e[x := v_2]) \overset{0}{\hookrightarrow} \mu_3, v}{\mu_0, e_1 \, e_2 \overset{0}{\hookrightarrow} \mu_3, v}$$

is not an instance of

$$\frac{\mu_0, e_1 \overset{0}{\hookrightarrow} \mu_1, (X)\lambda x.e \quad \mu_1, e_2 \overset{0}{\hookrightarrow} \mu_2, v_2 \quad \mu_2, ((X)e)[x := v_2] \overset{0}{\hookrightarrow} \mu_3, v}{\mu_0, e_1 \, e_2 \overset{0}{\hookrightarrow} \mu_3, v}$$

since the free variables in v_2 are bound by $\bullet_-$, but not by $(X)_-$. This seems to suggest that one might want to maintain $\bullet e$ even in the presence of $(x)e$. On the other hand, the conservative extension of MiniML$_{\mathsf{ref}}$ into MiniML$_{\mathsf{ref}}^{\mathsf{meta}}$ seems to become simpler if we use $(x)e$ (and a suitable adaptation of the operational semantics) instead of $\bullet e$.

Acknowledgements

We would like to thank the anonymous referees for their valuable comments (any failure to fully exploit them is our fault). This paper would not have been conceived without the previous work in collaboration with Zino Benaissa, Tim Sheard and Walid Taha, who have introduced us to the challenges of multi-stage programming. Finally, we would like to thank Tim Sheard for his stimulating criticisms on previous attempts, and Walid Taha for many discussions.

References

B97.   Zine El-Abidine Benaissa Explicit Substitution Calculi as a Foundation of Functional Programming Languages Implementations PhD thesis, INRIA, 1997.

BMTS99.   Zine El-Abidine Benaissa, Eugenio Moggi, Walid Taha, and Tim Sheard. Logical modalities and multi-stage programming. In *Federated Logic Conference (FLoC) Satellite Workshop on Intuitionistic Modal Logics and Applications (IMLA)*, July 1999.

CDDK86.   Dominique Clement, Joelle Despeyroux, Thierry Despeyroux, and Gilles Kahn. A simple applicative language: Mini-ML. In *Proceedings of the 1986 ACM Conference on Lisp and Functional Programming*, pages 13–27. ACM, ACM, August 1986.

CMT00.   Cristiano Calcagno, Eugenio Moggi, Walid Taha. Closed Types as a Simple Approach to Safe Imperative Multi-Stage Programming. In *Proceedings of ICALP 2000*, volume 1853 of LNCS, pages 25–36, Springer, 2000.

Dav96.   Rowan Davies. A temporal-logic approach to binding-time analysis. In *Proceedings, 11th Annual IEEE Symposium on Logic in Computer Science*, pages 184–195, New Brunswick, July 1996. IEEE Computer Society Press.

DP96.   Rowan Davies and Frank Pfenning. A modal analysis of staged computation. In *23rd Annual ACM Symposium on Principles of Programming Languages (POPL'96)*, pages 258–270, St. Petersburg Beach, January 1996.

LM99.   Jean-Jacques Levy and Luc Maranget. Explicit Substitutions and Programming Languages. In *19th Conference on Foundations of Software Technology and Theoretical Computer Science (FSTTCS)*, Chennai, India, December 1999.

Met00.   The MetaML Home Page, 2000. Provides source code and documentation online at
            http://www.cse.ogi.edu/PacSoft/projects/metaml/index.html.

MTBS99.   Eugenio Moggi, Walid Taha, Zine El-Abidine Benaissa, and Tim Sheard. An idealized MetaML: Simpler, and more expressive. In *European Symposium on Programming (ESOP)*, volume 1576 of *Lecture Notes in Computer Science*, pages 193–207. Springer-Verlag, 1999.

Tah99.   Walid Taha. *Multi-Stage Programming: Its Theory and Applications*. PhD thesis, Oregon Graduate Institute of Science and Technology, July 1999.

TBS98.   Walid Taha, Zine-El-Abidine Benaissa, and Tim Sheard. Multi-stage programming: Axiomatization and type-safety. In *25th International Colloquium on Automata, Languages, and Programming*, volume 1443 of *Lecture Notes in Computer Science*, pages 918–929, Aalborg, July 1998.

TS97.   Walid Taha and Tim Sheard. Multi-stage programming with explicit annotations. In *Proceedings of the ACM-SIGPLAN Symposium on Partial Evaluation and semantic based program manipulations PEPM'97, Amsterdam*, pages 203–217. ACM, 1997.

TS00.   Walid Taha and Tim Sheard. MetaML: Multi-stage programming with explicit annotations. *Theoretical Computer Science*, 248(1-2), 2000.

WS99.   Mitchell Wand, Igor Siveroni. Constraint Systems for Useless Variable Elimination. In *Proceedings of 26th ACM Symposium on Principles of Programming Languages (POPL)*, pages 291–302, 1999.

WF94.   Andrew K. Wright and Matthias Felleisen. A Syntactic Approach to Type Soundness. *Information and Computation*, 115(1):38–94, 1994.

A   MiniML$_{\text{ref}}^{\text{BN}}$

This section recalls the syntax and type system of MiniML$_{\text{ref}}^{\text{BN}}$, to help in a comparison with MiniML$_{\text{ref}}^{\text{meta}}$. The types t and closed types c of MiniML$_{\text{ref}}^{\text{BN}}$ are defined as

$$t \in \mathsf{T} ::= c \mid t_1 \to t_2 \mid \langle t \rangle \qquad c \in \mathsf{C} ::= \mathsf{nat} \mid [t] \mid \mathsf{ref}\, c$$

Remark 3. Function types are never closed, the types $[c]$ and c are not identified.

The set of MiniML$_{\text{ref}}^{\text{BN}}$ terms is defined as

$$
\begin{aligned}
e \in \mathsf{E} ::= &\; x \mid \lambda x.e \mid e_1\, e_2 \mid \mathsf{fix}\, x.e \mid \mathsf{z} \mid \mathsf{s}\, e \mid (\mathsf{case}\, e\, \mathsf{of}\, \mathsf{z} \to e_1 \mid \mathsf{s}\, x \to e_2) \mid \\
&\; \langle e \rangle \mid \tilde{\,}e \mid \mathsf{run}\, e \mid [e] \mid (\mathsf{let}\, [x] = e_1\, \mathsf{in}\, e_2) \mid \\
&\; \mathsf{ref}\, e \mid !\, e \mid e_1 := e_2 \mid l \mid \mathsf{fault}
\end{aligned}
$$

Remark 4. The constant fault leads to a run-time error when evaluated at level 0, and evaluates to itself at higher levels. Operationally, fault is equivalent to the MiniML$_{\text{ref}}^{\text{meta}}$ term $\bullet x$. There is an explicit closed construct $[e]$, and one let-binder $(\mathsf{let}\, [x] = e_1\, \mathsf{in}\, e_2)$.

Figure 5 summarizes the typing rules of MiniML$_{\text{ref}}^{\text{BN}}$ which differ from those of MiniML$_{\text{ref}}^{\text{meta}}$. The main differences are:

- (case*) corresponds to declare the bound variable in Δ, instead of Γ, and is only used to simplify the translation of MiniML$_{\text{ref}}$ in MiniML$_{\text{ref}}^{\text{BN}}$.
- (close*) is necessary because there is no identification of $[c]$ with c.

$$\text{(case*)} \quad \frac{\Sigma; \Delta; \Gamma \vdash e \colon \mathsf{nat}^n \quad \Sigma; \Delta; \Gamma \vdash e_1 \colon t^n \quad \Sigma; \Delta, x \colon \mathsf{nat}^n; \Gamma \vdash e_2 \colon t^n}{\Sigma; \Delta; \Gamma \vdash (\mathsf{case}\, e\, \mathsf{of}\, \mathsf{z} \to e_1 \mid \mathsf{s} x \to e_2) \colon t^n}$$

$$\frac{\Sigma; \Delta^{\leq n}; \emptyset \vdash e \colon t^n}{\Sigma; \Delta; \Gamma \vdash [e] \colon [t]^n} \qquad \frac{\Sigma; \Delta; \Gamma \vdash e_1 \colon [t_1]^n \quad \Sigma; \Delta, x \colon t_1^n; \Gamma \vdash e_2 \colon t_2^n}{\Sigma; \Delta; \Gamma \vdash (\mathsf{let}\, [x] = e_1 \,\mathsf{in}\, e_2) \colon t_2^n}$$

$$\text{(fix*)} \quad \frac{\Sigma; \Delta^{\leq n}, x \colon t^n; \emptyset \vdash e \colon t^n}{\Sigma; \Delta; \Gamma \vdash \blacksquare x x . e \colon t^n} \qquad \text{(close*)} \quad \frac{\Sigma; \Delta; \Gamma \vdash e \colon c^n}{\Sigma; \Delta; \Gamma \vdash [e] \colon [c]^n}$$

Fig. 5. Type System for $\mathsf{MiniML}_{\mathsf{ref}}^{\mathsf{BN}}$

– (fix*) can type recursive definitions (e.g. of closed functions) that are not typable with (fix). For instance, from $\emptyset; f' \colon [t_1 \to t_2]^n, x \colon t_1^n \vdash e \colon t_2^n$ one cannot derive $\mathsf{fix}\, f'.[\lambda x.e] \colon [t_1 \to t_2]^n$, while the following modified term $\mathsf{fix}\, f'.(\mathsf{let}\, [f] = f' \,\mathsf{in}\, [\lambda x.e[f' := [f]]])$ has the right type, but the wrong behavior (it diverges!). The rule (fix*) allows to type $[\mathsf{fix}\, f.\lambda x.e[f' := [f]]]$, which has the desired operational behavior.

In $\mathsf{MiniML}_{\mathsf{ref}}^{\mathsf{meta}}$ the (fix*) rule is not necessary: assuming a unit type (), one could write the term $\mathsf{fix}\, f'.(\mathsf{let}_c f = \lambda().f' \,\mathsf{in}\, \lambda x.e[f' := f()])$ which has the desired type and does not diverge; this term is not typable in $\mathsf{MiniML}_{\mathsf{ref}}^{\mathsf{BN}}$ because $f \colon () \to (t_1 \to t_2)$ would not have a closed type.

Specification and Correctness of Lambda Lifting[*]

Adam Fischbach and John Hannan

Department of Computer Science and Engineering
The Pennsylvania State University, University Park, PA 16802, USA
{fischbac,hannan}@cse.psu.edu

Abstract. We present a formal and general specification of lambda lifting and prove its correctness with respect to an operational semantics. Lambda lifting is a program transformation which eliminates free variables from functions by introducing additional formal parameters to function definition and additional actual parameters to function calls. This operation supports the transformation from a lexically-structured functional program into a set of recursive equations. Existing results provide specific algorithms with no flexibility, no general specification, and only limited correctness results. Our work provides a general specification of lambda lifting (and related operations) which supports flexible translation strategies which may result in new implementation techniques. Our work also supports a simple framework in which the interaction of lambda lifting and other optimizations can be studied and from which new algorithms might be obtained.

1 Introduction

Lambda lifting is a program transformation which eliminates free variables from functions by introducing additional formal parameters to function definitions and additional actual parameters to function calls. The operation finds application in the implementation of functional languages, where functions without free variables can be implemented more easily than those with free variables [10,1]. Another application for lambda lifting is partial evaluation, where recursive equations (the result of completely lambda lifting a program) provide a convenient representation [3].

In general, lambda lifting and its inverse, lambda dropping [3], are operations which modify the way in which the implementation of a function accesses the variables occurring in the body of the function and, consequently, the representation of data, including parameters and closures, used by the implementation. The particular choice of lexical structure of a program has no significant importance with respect to the meaning of a program, and we often assume that it has no consequence on the efficiency of the program. Lambda lifting and dropping, in part, provide the flexibility that allows an implementation to be indifferent to the choice of structure made by the programmer.

---

[*] This work is supported in part by NSF Award #CCR-9900918.

W. Taha (Ed.): SAIG 2000, LNCS 1924, pp. 108–128, 2000.

1.1   Motivation

The essential aspect of lambda lifting can be summarized by two statements:

1. Remove free variables from functions by inserting additional parameters to the definition of these functions;
2. Apply each occurrence of a function name to these additional parameters.

Descriptions of lambda lifting, as originally presented by Johnsson [10] and Hughes [9], and later by Peyton Jones [12,13], start with these simple concepts and then use algorithms, based on a kind of flow analysis, to fill in the details.

Because these are algorithms, they make specific decisions regarding which variables to lift from functions (just those necessary) and where to lift applications (only at the use of named lifted functions). These decisions reflect both the practical considerations of lambda lifting (in the context of compilation) and the limitations of a simple flow-based approach. These works do not provide general principles of lambda lifting from which specific algorithms can be derived and proved correct. They also do not accommodate different design choices (regarding what to lift and where to lift it) and their implications. They do not describe what kinds of operations are, in general, possible. In summary, they do not provide a foundation (i.e., specification) from which to base applications and implementations of lambda lifting.

The motivation for our work stems from these shortcomings of existing work.

1.2   Goals

Our goal is to provide a foundation, via a high-level, declarative specification, for lambda lifting and related operations. Such a presentation should be devoid of particular implementation or algorithmic decisions. Instead it should support the justification of any operation reasonably based on the informal description given by the two statements above. Proving this specification correct (with respect to a semantics for the language) justifies any operation or algorithm which conforms to this specification. I.e., for any given algorithm, we need only prove it correct with respect to the specification, rather than with respect to the semantics of the language.

We wish not only to explicate existing notions of lambda lifting, but also to explore alternatives which might provide better solutions in some applications. We intend to provide a specification which allows for experimenting with flexible strategies of lambda lifting. Also, we wish to provide a framework for exploring the interaction of lambda lifting and related operations including unCurrying [8], closure conversion [4], and arity raising [7].

1.3   Contributions

The specific contributions presented in this paper are:

1. A high-level, declarative specification of lambda lifting;
2. Proof of correctness of this specification;
3. An identification of a particular lambda lifting strategy which supports the unCurrying of the lifted parameters and does not introduce any new function-call sites;

   This work contributes towards a larger goal of studying the optimization of function-call protocols in higher-order languages. Our first steps in this effort have been providing formal descriptions of basic transformations (optimizations) which focus on the way in which a function is called (and hence defined). The current work falls into this category and our previous work on unCurrying [8] and arity raising [7] also contributed in this area. Subsequent steps include studying the interaction of these transformations and the practical impact of them in real implementations. This work addresses some fundamental and theoretical questions concerning minimizing certain aspects of function calls, measured either statically and/or dynamically, and it also provides additional tools to the arsenal of compiler writers for higher-order languages.

1.4   Outline

The remainder of the paper is organized as follows. In the next section we introduce basic concepts of lambda lifting. We introduce a simple language and an informal definition of lifting. In Section 3 we give a formal specification of lambda lifting as a deductive system. In Section 4 we give the correctness of our specification with respect to the type system and operational semantics of the language. In Section 5 we introduce dependent types for parameter lifting. In Section 6 we present a simple algorithm based on our approach and prove it correct. In Section 7 we discuss some applications for lambda lifting, and in Section 8 we conclude.

2   Overview of Lambda Lifting

Lambda lifting is a transformation on lexically scoped programs which provides a means for eliminating free variables from function definitions. The operation was developed independently by Hughes [9] and Johnsson [10], both in the context of compiling functional languages. Peyton Jones later provided a careful development of the operation [12,13] in the larger context of language implementation. Lambda dropping, the inverse of lambda lifting was more recently proposed by Danvy and Schultz [3] as an operation to restore the lexical block structure of programs following lambda lifting. In all cases the presentation of these operations is mostly algorithmic and restricted in their application to higher-order functions. With respect to correctness, only some preliminary results by Danvy [2] exist.

We present here an overview of the operations of lambda lifting and dropping described in these works, but we do not discuss the algorithms given there.

2.1   The Language

We present our specification of lambda lifting for a small higher-order functional language with let-polymorphism and traditional call-by-name semantics. The grammar for this language is

$$e ::= c \mid x \mid \lambda x.e \mid e_1 \mathbin{@} e_2 \mid \mathsf{let}\ x = e_1\ \mathsf{in}\ e_2$$

For simplicity of our presentation, we limit the form of let-expressions, disallowing simultaneous declarations.

The type system for this language is a traditional one and will be discussed in more detail in Section 4. We assume an operational semantics based on environments and function closures. It is the traditional one which axiomatizes the judgment $\rho \triangleright e \hookrightarrow v$, in which ρ is an environment mapping variables to values.

2.2   The Basics of Lambda Lifting

Lambda lifting has been described as a two step process, based on Johnsson's algorithm [3]:

1. *Parameter Lifting.* Free variables of a function are eliminated by introducing additional parameters to the function. Call sites of the function are correspondingly supplied with these variables as additional arguments.
2. *Block Floating.* Local function definitions with no free variables can be floated outwards through the block structure of the program until they become global definitions.

The block floating step is trivial once all free variables have been eliminated from functions. More generally, function definitions (possibly containing free variables) can be floated outwards (or inwards) as long as the function is not moved (outwards) outside the scope of the free variables or moved (inwards) inside the scope of a declaration of a variable with the same name as a free variable occurring in the function. The practical aspects of block floating have been studied by Peyton Jones et. al. [14]. The correctness of this operation is nearly trivial, and we do not address it here. Our results do not support any new notions of block floating and so we do not discuss it further.

The parameter lifting step is a more subtle operation and care must be taken to ensure correctness. When we insert a lifted (actual) parameter x, we must ensure that x is in the scope of its intended declaration (and not shadowed by another declaration of x).

Traditional lambda lifting strategies require the lifted parameters to be inserted at each occurrence of the lifted function. But another alternative is to delay the application of a lifted function to its lifted parameter until the function is applied to its original argument. For higher-order functions identifying all such applications and correctly performing the translation is difficult and not previously supported by any description of lambda lifting. Consider the term

```
let x = e1
in let f = λy.y(x)
   in let g = λh.λz.h(h(z))
      in g f e2 end
   end
end
```

We can apply h (which is bound to f) to the parameter x, and also lift x from g:

```
let x = e1
in let f = λx.λy.y(x)
   in let g = λx.λh.λz.(h x (h x z))
      in g x f e2 end
   end
end
```

This translation is, to our knowledge, not supported in general by any existing algorithms. Just as our previous work using type-based systems have extended results to support higher-order analyses and translations [7,8], our specification of parameter lifting also benefits from the nature of type systems.

2.3   Lambda Dropping

The inverse of lambda lifting has been called lambda dropping by Danvy and Schultz [3]. As the inverse of lifting, they describe it via two steps: block sinking and parameter dropping. They provide a definition of dropped programs and give an algorithm for lambda dropping. While the relation to lambda lifting is apparent, the authors only conjecture that lifting and dropping are inverses. Because previous works have presented lambda lifting and dropping algorithmically, this inverse correspondence has been obscured. If, instead, a specification of lambda lifting is given as a binary relation (between an input term and a lifted form of the term), then the specification also describes lambda dropping.

Rather than describing each of these operations as a distinct function, we represent them as a single relation defined by a set of inference rules. This approach has many advantages over previous descriptions of lifting and dropping:

1. it provides a natural correspondence between lifting and dropping;
2. it supports a general description, avoiding specific algorithmic decisions;
3. it supports reasonable proofs of correctness;

4. it supports the study of the lambda lifting translation with respect to other translations (e.g., unCurrying) given in a similar style.

3   Specification of Parameter Lifting

We give a formal specification of parameter lifting as a deductive system which axiomatizes a relation between two terms. The second term is a parameter-lifted form of the first. (Equivalently, the first term is a parameter-dropped form of the second). As our goal is to provide a general description of these operations we will not enforce any particular strategy of which parameters to lift or where to lift them. Our specification simply guarantees that the operation performed is correct. Hence, the system is non-deterministic in the sense that a given term can possibly be related to many lifted forms. We use type information to provide constraints between terms and to direct the definition of the relation between terms. Most of the inference rules follow the structure of a traditional type system for simple types, but the specification also contains additional rules unique to the problem of lambda lifting.

3.1   Annotated Types

Because every lifting of a parameter in a function declaration must be accompanied by the appropriate application of a term to that parameter, we need to generate constraints between terms. As already demonstrated, the names of variables have particular importance in these constraints and we must be careful with names. We extend the traditional definition of simple types to include annotations over function arrows which provide information regarding lifted parameters:

$$\tau ::= \iota \mid \alpha \mid \tau \rightarrow \tau \mid \tau \xrightarrow{x} \tau$$
$$\sigma ::= \tau \mid \forall \alpha.\sigma$$

We let ι and α range over base types and type variables, respectively. The type $\tau_1 \rightarrow \tau_2$ denotes the traditional function type, while the type $\tau_1 \xrightarrow{x} \tau_2$ denotes the type of a function obtained by lifting the free variable $x : \tau_1$ out of the body of a function of type τ_2. The schemas (σ) are defined as usual. We denote the free expression variables of τ by $FV(\tau)$.

3.2   Parameter Lifting

The specification in Figure 1 axiomatizes the relation for parameter lifting. The specification uses a judgment $\Gamma \rhd e : \tau \Rightarrow e'$ in which e and e' are terms, Γ is a context mapping variables to types and τ is a type. We read this judgment as stating that under the assumption of Γ, expression e has type τ and can be lifted to e'. We assume a signature Σ mapping constants to their types and these types do not contain any term variables over function arrows. The operator '$\succ$' creates an instance of a type scheme.

$$\frac{\Gamma(x) \succ \tau}{\Gamma \triangleright x : \tau \Rightarrow x} \text{ (var)} \qquad\qquad \frac{\Sigma(c) = \tau}{\Gamma \triangleright c : \tau \Rightarrow c} \text{ (const)}$$

$$\frac{\Gamma\{y{:}\tau\} \triangleright e : \tau_1 \Rightarrow e' \quad y \notin \mathrm{dom}\,(\Gamma) \quad FV(\tau \rightarrow \tau_1) \subseteq \mathrm{dom}\,(\Gamma)}{\Gamma \triangleright \lambda y.e : \tau \rightarrow \tau_1 \Rightarrow \lambda y.e'} \text{ (abs)}$$

$$\frac{\Gamma(x) \succ \tau_1 \quad \Gamma \triangleright \lambda y.e : \tau \Rightarrow \lambda z.e'}{\Gamma \triangleright \lambda y.e : \tau_1 \xrightarrow{x} \tau \Rightarrow \lambda x.\lambda z.e'} \text{ (lift-abs)}$$

$$\frac{\Gamma \triangleright e_1 : \tau_2 \rightarrow \tau \Rightarrow e_1' \quad \Gamma \triangleright e_2 : \tau_2 \Rightarrow e_2'}{\Gamma \triangleright e_1 \,@\, e_2 : \tau \Rightarrow e_1' \,@\, e_2'} \text{ (app)}$$

$$\frac{\Gamma \triangleright e : \tau_1 \xrightarrow{x} \tau \Rightarrow e' \quad \Gamma(x) \succ \tau_1}{\Gamma \triangleright e : \tau \Rightarrow e' \,@\, x} \text{ (lift-app)}$$

$$\frac{x \notin \mathrm{dom}\,(\Gamma) \quad FV(\tau) \subseteq \mathrm{dom}\,(\Gamma)}{\Gamma \triangleright e_1 : \tau_1 \Rightarrow e_1' \quad \sigma_1 = \mathrm{Gen}(\tau_1, \Gamma) \quad \Gamma\{x{:}\sigma_1\} \triangleright e_2 : \tau \Rightarrow e_2'}{\Gamma \triangleright \mathrm{let}\, x = e_1 \,\mathrm{in}\, e_2 : \tau \Rightarrow \mathrm{let}\, x = e_1' \,\mathrm{in}\, e_2'} \text{ (let)}$$

Fig. 1. Parameter Lifting

The rules (const), (var), (app), (abs), and (let) are simple extensions to the traditional typing rules for a language with let-polymorphism. The types in these rules do range over the annotated types defined above, but no use of those annotations is made. (The rules (app) and (abs), however, require that the top-most function arrow be unannotated.) The rules (abs) and (let) do include constraints to ensure that the introduction of a variable name does not shadow an existing declaration of the same name. (This ensures that we avoid one of the problems introduced in the previous section.) The rules (abs) and (let) include conditions to ensure that lifted parameters (occurring free in types) do not escape their scope. The Gen function used in the (let) rule is the traditional one in which $\mathrm{Gen}(\tau, \Gamma) = \forall \alpha_1 \cdots \forall \alpha_n.\tau$ for $\{\alpha_1 \cdots \alpha\}$ free in τ but not free in Γ. We comment on the interaction between such generalization and lambda lifting below.

Only the rules (lift-abs) and (lift-app) make use of annotated arrows, and these are the rules that introduce formal parameters and actual parameters, respectively. The rule (lift-abs) supports the parameter lifting of any variable x that is currently in scope ($x \in \mathrm{dom}(\Gamma)$). We annotate the type of the resulting expression by placing the name of this lifted parameter over the function arrow. In the conclusion of (lift-abs) the subject expression is a function, and this ensures that we only parameter lift at the point of function definitions. Observe that this same subject expression appears in the antecedent of the rule. This allows multiple parameters to be lifted from a function definition (which is the reason why we use z instead of y in the translated term). But this also complicates reasoning about correctness since a simple induction over terms will not work in this case.

The rule (lift-app) complements (lift-abs) by supporting the introduction of a new application to any term of the appropriate type. The rule ensures that $x \in \mathsf{dom}(\Gamma)$ to avoid one of the problems illustrated in the previous section. Observe that the rule (lift-app) allows any term of type $\tau_1 \xrightarrow{x} \tau$ (not just a variable) to be applied to lifted parameters.

This specification supports the example translation given in Section 2.2. In fact, the original term in that example can be related to several distinct terms (with varying amounts of lifted and varying placement of lifted parameters) by our specification.

4   Correctness

Having specified lambda lifting we now demonstrate its correctness by providing appropriate relationships between our specification and static and dynamic (operational) semantics for the language. (See the appendix for specification of the operational semantics.)

4.1   Type Correctness

We show that the system in Figure 1 derives judgments over exactly the typable terms (in a traditional type system). Additionally, we show that every typable source term can be related to some target term.

Let the judgment $\Gamma \rhd e : \tau$ denote the traditional typing system for the given fragment of a functional language.

Theorem 1 (Type Completeness). *If $\Gamma \rhd e : \tau$ then there exists a term e' such that $\Gamma \rhd e : \tau \Rightarrow e'$.*

The proof follows by constructing a deduction which performs no parameter lifting.

We additionally have that the specification relates only typable terms. To show this we first define two translations from annotated types to unannotated types:

Definition 1. *For any annotated type τ,*

1. *let $|\tau|$ be the type obtained by erasing all annotations occurring over function arrows in τ;*
2. *let $||\tau||$ be defined inductively as follows:*

$$||\iota|| = \iota$$
$$||\alpha|| = \alpha$$
$$||\tau_1 \to \tau_2|| = ||\tau_1|| \to ||\tau_2||$$
$$||\tau_1 \xrightarrow{x} \tau_2|| = ||\tau_2||$$

We extend these definitions to type schemas and type contexts in a natural way. The type $|\tau|$ is the erasure of τ and the type $||\tau||$ removes the lifting information from τ.

Theorem 2 (Type Correctness). *If* $\Gamma \rhd e : \tau \Rightarrow e'$ *then* $|\Gamma| \rhd e' : |\tau|$ *and* $||\Gamma|| \rhd e : ||\tau||$.

The proof of each part follows by induction over the deduction of $\Gamma \rhd e : \tau \Rightarrow e'$.

Type correctness tells us that we are, at least, constructing expressions which satisfy the constraints given by the type system. We still need to demonstrate that operationally, a parameter-lifted expression is equivalent to the original expression.

4.2   Operational Correctness

To understand the operational correctness is to understand one fundamental property which makes parameter-lifting work:

> Let e be an expression with free variable x (to be lifted). During the evaluation of e (starting with some environment ρ), the value of all occurrences of x (in the deduction) is $\rho(x)$, i.e. all environments constructed or introduced during the evaluation of e map x to $\rho(x)$.

In other words, it does not matter if we obtain the value of x from any environment naturally encountered during the evaluation of e (the unlifted situation) or if we initially get the value of x from the starting environment ρ (the lifted situation). This property does not, in fact, hold in general. We need to impose a constraint on ρ for it to hold. A parameter can only be lifted if this constraint is guaranteed to hold at run time.

To discuss operational correctness we need an operational semantics. We use a traditional operational semantics obtained by axiomatizing the judgment $\rho \rhd e \hookrightarrow v$, and this definition is given in the appendix. We assume a lazy (call-by-name) semantics, though the results that follow can be modified to support an eager (call-by-value) semantics.

We begin our discussion of correctness with some notation regarding the environments and values of the operational semantics. In our language an environment ρ is a mapping from variables to values, and a value is either a constant or a function closure $[\rho, \lambda x.e]$. We use '·' for the empty environment.

We need to refer to the restriction of the domain of an environment so we introduce the following.

Definition 2. *For any environment ρ and set S, let $\rho|_S$ be the restriction of ρ to domain S.*

Note that if S is empty then $\rho|_S$ is the empty environment.

We also need to extract the environment from a closure:

Definition 3. *Let* env *be a function on values which returns the environment of a function closure:*

$$env([\rho, \lambda x.e]) = \rho$$
$$env(c) = \cdot$$

Our specification of parameter lifting defines a relationship between an expression and a lifted form of the expression. To reason about correctness we need to define a relation between a value and a lifted form of the value, and also a relation between an environment and a lifted form of the environment. (The values in the environment have been lifted.)

Definition 4 (Value and Environment Relations). *Let* $v : \sigma \Rightarrow v'$ *and* $\rho : \Gamma \Rightarrow \rho'$ *be defined as the least relations satisfying the following:*

1. $v : \forall \overline{\alpha}.\tau \Rightarrow v'$ *if* $v : \tau \Rightarrow v'$;
2. $c : \tau \Rightarrow c$ *for all constants* $c{:}\tau \in \Sigma$;
3. $[\rho, \lambda x.e] : \tau \Rightarrow [\rho', \lambda y.e']$ *if there exists a* Γ *such that* $\rho : \Gamma \Rightarrow \rho'$ *and* $\Gamma \triangleright \lambda x.e : \tau \Rightarrow \lambda y.e'$.
4. $\rho : \Gamma \Rightarrow \rho'$ *if* $dom(\rho) = dom(\Gamma) = dom(\rho')$, *and for all* $y \in dom(\rho)$, $\rho(y) : \Gamma(y) \Rightarrow \rho'(y)$, $FV(\Gamma(y)) \subseteq dom(\Gamma)$, *and* $\rho'|_{FV(\Gamma(y))} = env(\rho'(y))|_{FV(\Gamma(y))}$.

The condition $\rho'|_{FV(\Gamma(y))} = env(v')|_{FV(\Gamma(y))}$ provides the essential constraint on environments and values to ensure the correctness of lifting parameters. Any lifted variables (which will occur free in $\Gamma(y)$) must have the same meaning in the initial environment ρ' and in the environment of the value v'.

To demonstrate operational correctness we must ensure that the translation of a term preserves the meaning (value) of a term. Since values can be function closures which, in the translated case, can contain parameter-lifted terms, we can only expect the values to be related via the translation. Preserving the meaning includes, in general, termination properties. So we must show that one term has a value iff its translation (in either direction) has a value.

Theorem 3. 1. *If* $\rho : \Gamma \Rightarrow \rho'$, $\rho \triangleright e \hookrightarrow v$, *and* $\Gamma \triangleright e : \tau \Rightarrow e'$ *then there exists a* v' *such that* $\rho' \triangleright e' \hookrightarrow v'$, $v : \tau \Rightarrow v'$, *and* $\rho'|_{FV(\tau)} = env(v')|_{FV(\tau)}$.
2. *If* $\rho : \Gamma \Rightarrow \rho'$, $\rho' \triangleright e' \hookrightarrow v'$, *and* $\Gamma \triangleright e : \tau \Rightarrow e'$ *then there exists a* v *such that* $\rho \triangleright e \hookrightarrow v$, $v : \tau \Rightarrow v'$, *and* $\rho'|_{FV(\tau)} = env(v')|_{FV(\tau)}$.

The proof of part (1) follows by well-founded induction on the lexicographical ordering of $(|\Pi|, |\Xi|)$, in which Π is the deduction of $\rho \triangleright e \hookrightarrow v$, Ξ is the deduction of $\Gamma \triangleright e : \tau \Rightarrow e'$, and $|\mathcal{D}|$ denote the height of deduction $\mathcal{D}$. The case in which the conclusion of Ξ is introduced by an instance of the (lift-app) rule is the one that makes essential use the requirement $\rho'|_{FV(\tau)} = env(v')|_{FV(\tau)}$.

The proof of part (2) proceeds similarly, only now by well-founded induction on $(|\Pi'|, |\Xi|)$. Again, only the case in which the conclusion of Ξ is introduced by an instance of the (lift-app) rule makes essential use of the condition $\rho'|_{FV(\tau)} = env(v')|_{FV(\tau)}$.

A simple corollary to the theorem gives us a desired result for closed programs of base type:

Corollary 1. *If $\cdot \rhd e : \iota \Rightarrow e'$ then*

$$\cdot \rhd e \hookrightarrow v \ \textit{iff} \ \cdot \rhd e' \hookrightarrow v.$$

The proof follows immediately from the theorem.

5   Dependent Types for Parameter Lifting

Consider the following program fragment which contains v and w free:

```
let f = λx.x+v
    g y = λy.y*w
    h k = λk.k 5
in (h f) + (h g)
```

This expression can be parameter lifted via Johnsson-style algorithms to

```
let f v x = λv.λx.x+v
    g w y = λw.λy.y*w
    h k = λk.k 5
in (h (f v)) + (h (g w))
```

in which f and g are partially applied to their arguments, and hence cannot be unCurried.

As already suggested, our specification supports a higher-order form of parameter lifting in which the names of parameter lifted functions can still be passed as arguments, allowing for unCurrying:

```
let f v w x = λv.λw.λx.x+v
    g v w y = λv.λw.λy.y*w
    h v w k = λv.λw.λk.k v w 5
in (h v w f) + (h v w g)
```

In this example we must lift parameters v and w from both f and g since both functions occur as the third argument to h. This is a kind of parameter lifting not supported by Johnsson-style algorithms. (Johnsson-style algorithms can lift out parameters not occurring free in a function but only when these parameters are needed by functions occurring in some call chain in which this function occurs.) Observe that the type of both f and g, as determined by our specification, is

$$\text{int} \xrightarrow{v} \text{int} \xrightarrow{w} \text{int} \to \text{int}.$$

Another possibility exists for parameter lifting which still supports the unCurrying of functions f and g:

```
let f v x = λv.λx.x+v
    g w y = λw.λy.y*w
    h a k = λa.λk.k a 5
in (h v f) + (h w g)
```

This version exploits the fact that f and g each have one, though not identical, lifted parameter. Our specification of parameter lifting does not support the translation of the original program to this one. This translation cannot be handled by simple types annotated with parameter-lifted variables. We cannot give the same type to f and g, which is required for them both to occur as the second argument to h.

To understand how to support this translation, consider the required types for the two occurrences of h. The first occurrence must have type

$$\mathsf{int} \to (\mathsf{int} \xrightarrow{v} \mathsf{int} \to \mathsf{int}) \to \mathsf{int}$$

while the second occurrence must have type

$$\mathsf{int} \to (\mathsf{int} \xrightarrow{w} \mathsf{int} \to \mathsf{int}) \to \mathsf{int}.$$

Observe that the type of the second argument to h *depends* on the first argument to h. This suggests *dependent types* which, in fact, provide a solution. We can enrich our type system with dependent types as follows

$$\tau ::= \cdots \mid \Pi x{:}\tau.\tau$$

(A dependent type $\Pi x{:}\tau_1.\tau_2$ denotes a function with formal parameter $x : \tau_1$ and whose result type depends of the actual parameter $v : \tau_1$ supplied at each function call. If f has type $\Pi x{:}\tau_1.\tau_2$ and v has type τ_1 then $(f\,v)$ has type $\tau_2[v/x]$.) Dependent types extend the notion of function types when expression variables can appear free in types. (If x does not occur free in τ_2 then $\Pi x{:}\tau_1.\tau_2$ is equivalent to $\tau_1 \to \tau_2$.) Since expression variables can appear free in our parameter lifting types, our use of dependent types is non-trivial.

We introduce the following rules which are adapted from the rules (lift-app) and (lift-abs) to use dependent types:

$$\frac{\Gamma \rhd e : \Pi x{:}\tau_1.\tau \Rightarrow e' \quad \Gamma(y) \succ \tau_1}{\Gamma \rhd e : \tau[y/x] \Rightarrow e' \,@\, y} \ (\Pi\text{-lift-app})$$

$$\frac{x \notin \mathsf{dom}(\Gamma) \quad \Gamma\{x{:}\tau_1\} \rhd \lambda y.e : \tau \Rightarrow \lambda z.e'}{\Gamma \rhd \lambda y.e : \Pi x{:}\tau_1.\tau \Rightarrow \lambda x.\lambda z.e'} \ (\Pi\text{-lift-abs})$$

Adding these rules to our system now allows us to translate the original program to the third translation above. The function h can be given type

$$\Pi a{:}\mathsf{int}.(\mathsf{int} \xrightarrow{a} \mathsf{int} \to \mathsf{int}) \to \mathsf{int}$$

and the expressions (h v f) and (h w g) can each be typed accordingly.

Both the second and third translations above support the unCurrying of lifted functions and do not increase the number of function applications at run time. Which of the two, then, should be preferred by an implementation? At first glance, the third requires one less parameter to the lifted form of function h, and so this case might be preferred. However, if we assume parameters are passed in registers if possible, then the second case actually might be preferable. If we assume that function h expects its three parameters in registers r_0, r_1, and r_2, then we need only copy v and w once into r_0 and r_1, respectively. Then each call to h need only copy the appropriate argument into r_3 (first f, then g). For this particular example, the difference between the two approaches is insignificant since both require exactly one copying of v and w. The practical importance of dependent types is a question for future study.

6   Simple Parameter Lifting Algorithm

Our specification provides a general, high-level description of parameter lifting that supports flexibility in the choice of which parameters to lift. Because of this property, many possible algorithms could be based on this specification. We present in this section one example of a simple parameter lifting algorithm for a restricted form of the language introduced in Section 2. We then demonstrate how the specification in Figure 1 can be used to prove that this algorithm is correct.

A parameter lifting algorithm must make specific choices as to which parameters to lift and where to insert applications. We choose the following: all free variables are lifted from the body of a named function, and each occurrence of a function name is applied directly to that function's lifted parameters.

For syntactic convenience, we add a letfun expression to the grammar in Section 2 (the operational semantics is the same as that for let):

$$e ::= \dots \mid \text{letfun } f = \lambda x.e_1 \text{ in } e_2$$

Since we wish to restrict parameter lifting to named functions, we require that functions only be defined by letfun expressions.

6.1   Two-Phase Specification

Following methods successfully employed in previous work (e.g. [8,7]), we first present a two-phase specification for parameter lifting from which a specific algorithm is more easily derivable than from the general specification in Figure 1.

The first phase of this specification deduces which variables are lifted and where new applications are inserted. The rules in Figure 2 define the judgment $\Gamma_1 \rhd e : (\tau, \theta) \Rightarrow m$ in which e is an input term, τ is a type, θ is an ordered set of variables, m is an annotated form of e, and Γ_1 maps variables to types and ordered sets. The annotated term m is the same as the input term e except that all variables and letfun expressions are annotated with sets of lifted parameters.

These annotations are then used in the second phase of the specification that does the actual lifting of parameters.

The set θ represents all free variables in m, including all annotations. In Γ_1, if a function name f maps to the pair $(\tau_1 \to \tau_2, \theta)$, then θ contains all the parameters lifted from the function f. Note that if f is not a function name then θ is empty. Since θ is an *ordered* set, all set operations must be order-preserving.

$$\frac{\Gamma_1(x) \succ (\tau,\theta)}{\Gamma_1 \triangleright x : (\tau, \{x\} \cup \theta) \Rightarrow x^\theta} \qquad\qquad \frac{\Sigma(c) = \tau}{\Gamma_1 \triangleright c : (\tau, \emptyset) \Rightarrow c}$$

$$\frac{\Gamma_1\{y{:}(\tau,\emptyset)\} \triangleright e : (\tau_1, \theta) \Rightarrow m \quad y \notin \mathrm{dom}\,(\Gamma_1)}{\Gamma_1 \triangleright \lambda y.e : (\tau \to \tau_1, \theta - \{y\}) \Rightarrow \lambda y.m}$$

$$\frac{\Gamma_1 \triangleright e_1 : (\tau_2 \to \tau, \theta_1) \Rightarrow m_1 \quad \Gamma_1 \triangleright e_2 : (\tau_2, \theta_2) \Rightarrow m_2}{\Gamma_1 \triangleright e_1 \,@\, e_2 : (\tau, \theta_1 \cup \theta_2) \Rightarrow m_1 \,@\, m_2}$$

$$\frac{\sigma = \mathrm{Gen}(\tau_1 \to \tau_2, \Gamma_1) \quad f \notin \mathrm{dom}\,(\Gamma_1)}{\Gamma_1 \triangleright \lambda y.e_1 : (\tau_1 \to \tau_2, \theta_1) \Rightarrow \lambda y.m_1 \quad \Gamma_1\{f{:}(\sigma, \theta_1)\} \triangleright e_2 : (\tau, \theta_2) \Rightarrow m_2}{\Gamma_1 \triangleright \mathrm{letfun}\ f = \lambda y.e_1\ \mathrm{in}\ e_2 : (\tau, \theta_1 \cup (\theta_2 - \{f\})) \Rightarrow \mathrm{letfun}\ ^{\theta_1} f = \lambda y.m_1\ \mathrm{in}\ m_2}$$

$$\frac{\sigma = \mathrm{Gen}(\tau_1, \Gamma_1) \quad x \notin \mathrm{dom}\,(\Gamma_1)}{\Gamma_1 \triangleright e_1 : (\tau_1, \theta_1) \Rightarrow m_1 \quad \Gamma_1\{x{:}(\sigma, \emptyset)\} \triangleright e_2 : (\tau, \theta_2) \Rightarrow m_2}{\Gamma_1 \triangleright \mathrm{let}\, x = e_1\ \mathrm{in}\ e_2 : (\tau, \theta_1 \cup (\theta_2 - \{x\})) \Rightarrow \mathrm{let}\, x = m_1\ \mathrm{in}\ m_2}$$

Fig. 2. Parameter Lifting Annotation Phase

The rules for variables and letfun in Figure 2 are the only rules that actually annotate terms. In the letfun rule, θ_1 contains all the free variables occurring in $\lambda y.m_1$. These are all the parameters that will be lifted from the function. The function name f must then map to, and the letfun term must be annotated with, the set θ_1.

The variable rule forces each occurrence of a variable to be annotated with its corresponding list of lifted parameters.

The translation phase defines the judgment $m \Rightarrow_t e$ in which m is an annotated term and e is the translated (parameter lifted) form of m. The rules for translation are straightforward and can be found in the appendix.

Again, the only interesting cases are those for variables and letfun. Each variable must be applied to all of the lifted parameters occurring in its annotation. Similarly, all functions (which are defined by letfun) must include bindings for all lifted parameters.

We can prove that this two-phase specification is sound with respect to the more general specification in Figure 1. In order to do this, we need to add a rule for letfun to the original specification. This rule is identical to the (let) rule in Figure 1, except it requires a function declaration. We also must define a correspondence between the contexts used in the specification of Figure 2 and the contexts used in the specification of Figure 1, which includes a correspondence between the ranges of these contexts.

First we provide a translation from type schemas and sets to annotated types.

Definition 5. *Let* $\mathcal{L}(\sigma, \theta, \Gamma)$ *be defined inductively as*

$$\mathcal{L}(\forall \overline{\alpha}.\tau, y::\theta, \Gamma) = \mathcal{L}(\forall \overline{\beta} \forall \overline{\alpha}.\tau_y \xrightarrow{y} \tau, \theta, \Gamma)$$
$$\text{where } \Gamma(y) = \forall \overline{\beta}.\tau_y \text{ and } \{\overline{\alpha}\} \cap \{\overline{\beta}\} = \emptyset$$
$$\mathcal{L}(\sigma, \emptyset, \Gamma) = \sigma$$

Next we define a translation on contexts.

Definition 6. *For any context* Γ_1 *mapping variables to pairs* (σ, θ)*, let* $\mathcal{T}(\Gamma_1)$ *be the context such that for all* $x \in dom(\Gamma_1)$*, if* $\Gamma_1(x) = (\sigma_x, \theta_x)$ *then*

$$\mathcal{T}(\Gamma_1)(x) = \mathcal{L}(\sigma_x, \theta_x, \Gamma_1)$$

Finally, we introduce a notion of *closed* contexts that provides a reasonable (and required) constraint on the sets occurring in contexts.

Definition 7 (Closed Contexts). *A context* Γ_1 *is* closed, *written* Closed(Γ_1)*, iff for all* $x \in dom(\Gamma_1)$*, if* $\Gamma_1(x) = (\sigma, \theta)$ *then* $\theta \subseteq dom(\Gamma_1)$*.*

We need only deal with closed contexts because the free variables in a type (of a function) refer to lifted variables, and these variables must be declared in an enclosing scope, and hence in the context.

We can then state the soundness property of the two-phase system.

Lemma 1. *If* Closed(Γ_1)*,* $\Gamma_1 \triangleright e : (\tau, \theta) \Rightarrow m$ *and* $m \Rightarrow_t e'$ *then* $\mathcal{T}(\Gamma_1) \triangleright e : \tau \Rightarrow e'$*.*

The proof proceeds by induction on the structure of the typing deduction.

6.2   Example Algorithm

We can now define a recursive algorithm based on this two-phase specification and prove its correctness. The algorithm is also partitioned into two phases (see Figure 3): $\mathcal{PL}$, which annotates the input term, and *translate*, which introduces variable bindings and applies function names to the function's lifted parameters.

$\mathcal{PL}$ takes a context Γ_2, which maps variables to ordered sets of variables, and an input term e, and returns an ordered set θ and an annotated form of e. $\mathcal{PL}$ corresponds to the rules in Figure 2. Notice that types in Figure 2 do not play a role in computing annotations. So, if we assume the input term is well-typed, the algorithm can safely ignore types altogether. We also assume that all variables in the input term are distinct.

$\mathcal{PL}(\Gamma_2, c) = (\emptyset, c)$

$\mathcal{PL}(\Gamma_2, x) = \text{if } x \notin \text{dom}(\Gamma_2) \text{ then fail}$
$\quad\quad\text{else let } \theta = \Gamma_2(x)$
$\text{in } (\{x\} \cup \theta, x^\theta)$

$\mathcal{PL}(\Gamma_2, \lambda y.e) = \text{let}$
$\quad\quad (\theta, m) = \mathcal{PL}(\Gamma_2\{y : \emptyset\}, e)$
$\text{in } (\theta - \{y\}, \lambda y.m)$

$\mathcal{PL}(\Gamma_2, e_1 @ e_2) = \text{let}$
$\quad\quad (\theta_1, m_1) = \mathcal{PL}(\Gamma_2, e_1)$
$\quad\quad (\theta_2, m_2) = \mathcal{PL}(\Gamma_2, e_2)$
$\text{in } (\theta_1 \cup \theta_2, m_1 @ m_2)$

$\mathcal{PL}(\Gamma_2, \text{letfun } f = \lambda y.e_1 \text{ in } e_2) = \text{let}$
$\quad\quad (\theta_1, m_1) = \mathcal{PL}(\Gamma_2, \lambda y.e_1)$
$\quad\quad (\theta_2, m_2) = \mathcal{PL}(\Gamma_2\{f : \theta_1\}, e_2)$
$\text{in } (\theta_1 \cup (\theta_2 - \{f\}), \text{letfun}^{\theta_1} f = m_1 \text{ in } m_2)$

$\mathcal{PL}(\Gamma_2, \text{let } x = e_1 \text{ in } e_2) = \text{let}$
$\quad\quad (\theta_1, m_1) = \mathcal{PL}(\Gamma_2, e_1)$
$\quad\quad (\theta_2, m_2) = \mathcal{PL}(\Gamma_2\{x : \emptyset\}, e_2)$
$\text{in } (\theta_1 \cup (\theta_2 - \{x\}), \text{let } x = m_1 \text{ in } m_2)$

$translate(y^{x::s}) = translate(y^s) @ x$
$translate(y^\emptyset) = y$

$translate(\text{letfun}^{x::s} f = m_1 \text{ in } m_2) =$
$\quad\quad translate(\text{letfun}^s f = \lambda x.m_1 \text{ in } m_2)$
$translate(\text{letfun}^\emptyset f = m_1 \text{ in } m_2) =$
$\quad\quad \text{letfun } f = translate(m_1) \text{ in } translate(m_2)$

$translate(\lambda y.m) = \lambda y.translate(m)$
$translate(m_1 @ m_2) = translate(m_1) @ translate(m_2)$
$translate(\text{let } x = m_1 \text{ in } m_2) = \text{let } x = translate(m_1) \text{ in } translate(m_2)$
$translate(c) = c$

Fig. 3. Simple Algorithm

The function *translate* is straightforward. The syntax $y :: s$ represents an ordered set where y is the first element in the set and s is the remainder of the set.

In order to prove this algorithm correct, we first need to prove that it is sound with respect to the two-phase specification of the previous subsection. Again, we need to define a correspondence between different types of contexts:

Definition 8. *Let Γ be a context mapping variables to types and Γ_2 be a context mapping variables to sets, such that $dom(\Gamma) = dom(\Gamma_2)$. Then $\Gamma \star \Gamma_2$ is the context such that, for all $x \in dom(\Gamma)$:*

$$(\Gamma \star \Gamma_2)(x) = (\Gamma(x), \Gamma_2(x))$$

Lemma 2.   *1. If $\mathcal{PL}(\Gamma_2, e) = (\theta, m)$, and $\Gamma \triangleright e : \tau$ then $(\Gamma \star \Gamma_2) \triangleright e : (\tau, \theta) \Rightarrow m$.
2. If $translate(m) = e$ then $m \Rightarrow_t e$.*

The proof of part (1) follows by induction on the definition of $\mathcal{PL}$ and the structure of the typing deduction. The proof of part (2) follows by induction on the definition of *translate*.

Theorem 4 (Algorithm Correctness). *If for some well-typed, closed term e, $\mathcal{PL}(\cdot, e) = (\emptyset, m)$ and $translate(m) = e'$ then $\cdot \triangleright e \hookrightarrow v$ iff $\cdot \triangleright e' \hookrightarrow v$.*

The proof follows immediately from Lemma 2, Lemma 1, and Corollary 1.

The algorithm presented in this section is a very limited one, but serves to demonstrate how the parameter lifting specification in Section 3 can be used to facilitate proofs of correctness.

This algorithm is particularly limited in the fact that function names are applied directly to lifted variables. Because of this limitation and the simplicity of the source language, types are essentially ignored. As noted in previous sections, our specification supports other possible placements of these applications. In these cases, simply mapping the function name to θ in the context is insufficient. Instead, the set of lifted variables must be included in the function's type. In previous work we studied type systems for specifying closure conversion [4], an escape analysis [5], and a live-variable analysis [6]. In each of these, we use types annotated with sets of variables corresponding to the variables needed by a function. We can adapt these specifications to capture the set of variables we need to lift from function definitions. Instead of placing a single variable over a function arrow (as done in Figure 1), we can place a set of variables over a single function arrow.

In the case of higher-order functions, judicious placement of applications can avoid the introduction of new function calls. To ensure that lifting inserts no new function-call sites requires, at least, that parameter lifting be intertwined with block floating to avoid lifting parameters outside of their scope. Defining a reasonable algorithm which places the lifted parameters only at existing function-call sites is non-trivial and is the subject of future work.

7   Future Work

The language considered in this work is particularly simple, consisting of only the core fragment of a lazy functional programming language. Future work will address scaling up this work to larger languages and utilizing it in practical applications.

7.1   Extensions to Real Languages

Including additional language features, such as recursive function declarations and references, complicates the specification and implementation of lambda lifting. We plan to consider extending our results to deal with a rich set of language features so that our work can be applied to real languages. Recursion does not significantly complicate the high-level specification of lambda lifting, but it does introduce new issues into the algorithm. References and imperative features introduce a new issue. Lifting is safe, in part, because of referential transparency: we are free to replace a variable with a new variable whose value is the same as the original value. But languages with imperative features do not enjoy this property. Lifting out a parameter which has a reference to it may not be safe because the reference still refers to the original variable not the new lifted parameter. Updates to the reference will not be reflected in the lifted parameter. So lifting must be done carefully to ensure proper behaviour of references and imperative operations.

7.2   Applications

Partial Evaluation. In addition to constant folding and propagation, partial evaluators may unfold procedure calls and specialize functions (generating perhaps many different versions of the same function) to take advantage of static data. In order to perform such optimizations efficiently, many partial evaluators require that a program consist of a list of recursive equations. Lambda lifting is used to transform a block-structured program into one suitable for partial evaluation. The specialized program (in the form of recursive equations) can then be trasformed back into a block structured program via lambda dropping [3]. We hope that our work will find some application in the development of lambda lifting and dropping for partial evaluators.

UnCurrying. Traditional approaches to lambda lifting use a simple strategy for lifting applications: all occurrences of a function name are applied to its lifted parameters. In the case of a function name which is an argument to another function, this necessarily means that lambda lifting introduces a new function call point and the need to handle the partial application of the function. UnCurrying (the lifted parameters with the original parameters) is not possible. Our specification supports more general placement of the application to lifted parameters and can often avoid these problems. The cost is an increase in the number of function parameters.

We wish to further study the interaction of lambda lifting and unCurrying, along with other transformations. In particular, we would like to investigate whether there is some reasonable notion or measurement of a minimal number of function calls of a lambda lifted program. Similarly, we would like to understand if there is a notion of minimal number of function parameters under these conditions. Perhaps most importantly, we want to investigate a compilation technique in which aggressive application of λ-lifting and unCurrying produces a program in which all functions are completely λ-lifted and unCurryed.

Flexible Closure Representation. Functional programs are often implemented using closures which allow functions to be treated as first-class values. Closures provide the mechanism by which functions can access their free variables upon evaluation. However, closures can be computationally expensive to create and maintain. As a result, there has been a significant amount of work devoted to finding more efficient ways of representing and implementing closures (for example, [15] and [17]).

We are currently investigating ways in which lambda lifting, in conjunction with other optimizations (including unCurrying [8] and arity raising [7]), can be used to improve upon current techniques for closure representation. For instance, completely lambda lifting a program (parameterizing all free variables in each function) and postponing function application until all actual parameters are available can eliminate the need for some closures. Every time a function is called, all nonlocal variables needed in the body of that function are passed as parameters. This approach can significantly increase the number of variables passed as parameters, but eliminates much of the overhead of creating and accessing closures. While eliminating *all* closures in this manner may not be practically useful, this approach does allow us to provide a more flexible representation which eliminates some closures and allows more variables to be accessed locally.

8   Conclusion

We have presented a declarative specification for lambda lifting and proven it correct with respect to an operational semantics. The specification provides a general relation between a term and a lifted form of the term, without enforcing a single lifting strategy. The symmetry between lifting and dropping is evident from the relational nature of the specification. Thus, this specification provides a foundation from which existing algorithms may be proved correct, and also a starting point for the development of new, type-inference-based, algorithms.

Acknowledgements. We thank Olivier Danvy and the referees for their comments and suggestions.

References

1. CLINGER, W., AND HANSEN, L. T. Lambda, the ultimate label, or a simple optimizing compiler for scheme. In *1994 Conference on Lisp and Functional Programming* (1994), C. Talcott, Ed., ACM Press, pp. 128–139.
2. DANVY, O. An extensional characterization of lambda lifting. Tech. Rep. RS-98-2, BRICS, January 1998.
3. DANVY, O., AND SCHULTZ, U. P. Lambda dropping: Transforming recursive equations into programs with block structure. Tech. Rep. RS-99-27, BRICS, September 1999. To appear in the November 2000 issue of Theoretical Computer Science.
4. HANNAN, J. Type systems for closure conversions. In *Participants' Proceedings of the Workshop on Types for Program Analysis* (May 1995), H. R. Nielson and K. L. Solberg, Eds., Aarhus University, DAIMI PB-493, pp. 48–62.
5. HANNAN, J. A type-based escape analysis for functional languages. *Journal of Functional Programming 8*, 3 (May 1998).
6. HANNAN, J., AND HICKS, P. Live variable analysis using types. In *Workshop on Types in Compilation* (1997), Computer Science Department, Boston College. Available as a technical report.
7. HANNAN, J., AND HICKS, P. Higher-order arity raising. In *Proceedings of the Third International Conference on Functional Programming* (September 1998), P. Hudak and C. Queinnec, Eds., ACM SIGPLAN, pp. 27–38.
8. HANNAN, J., AND HICKS, P. Higher-order unCurrying. In *Proceedings of the 25th Annual ACM SIGPLAN-SIGACT Symposium on Principles of Programming Languages* (January 1998), pp. 1–11.
9. HUGHES, J. Super combinators: A new implementation method for applicative languages. In *Conference Record of the 1982 ACM Symposium on Lisp and Functional Programming* (August 1982), D. S. Wise, Ed., pp. 1–10.
10. JOHNSSON, T. Lambda lifting: Transforming programs to recursive equations. In *Functional Programming Languages and Computer Architecture* (1985), J.-P. Jouannaud, Ed., vol. 201 of *Lecture Notes in Computer Science*, Springer Verlag, pp. 190–203.
11. MILNER, R., AND TOFTE, M. Co-induction in relational semantics. *Theoretical Computer Science 87*, 1 (1991), 209–220.
12. PEYTON JONES, S. L. *The Implementation of Functional Programming Languages.* Prentice Hall International Series in Computer Science. Prentice Hall International, 1987.
13. PEYTON JONES, S. L., AND LESTER, D. R. *Implementing Functional Languages.* Prentice Hall International Series in Computer Science. Prentice Hall International, 1992.
14. PEYTON JONES, S. L., PARTAIN, W., AND SANTOS, A. Let-floating: Moving bindings to give faster programs. In *Proceedings of the ACM SIGPLAN International Conference on Functional Languages* (1996), R. Harper, Ed., pp. 1–12.
15. SHAO, Z., AND APPEL, A. Space-efficient closure representations. In *Proceedings of the 1994 ACM Conference on Lisp and Functional Programming* (June 1994), pp. 150–161.
16. SHIVERS, O. *Control-Flow Analysis of Higher-Order Languages.* PhD thesis, Carnegie-Mellon University, May 1991.
17. WAND, M., AND STECKLER, P. Lightweight Closure Conversion. In *ACM Transactions on Programming Languages and Systems* (January 1997), pp. 48–86.

A   Operational Semantics

$$\overline{\rho \triangleright c \hookrightarrow c}$$

$$\frac{\rho(x) = [\rho_1, e_1] \quad \rho_1 \triangleright e_1 \hookrightarrow v}{\rho \triangleright x \hookrightarrow v}$$

$$\overline{\rho \triangleright \lambda x.e \hookrightarrow [\rho, \lambda x.e]}$$

$$\frac{\rho \triangleright e_1 \hookrightarrow [\rho_1, \lambda x.e] \quad \rho_1\{x \mapsto [\rho, e_2]\} \triangleright e \hookrightarrow v}{\rho \triangleright e_1 @ e_2 \hookrightarrow v}$$

$$\frac{\rho\{x \mapsto [\rho, e_1]\} \triangleright e_2 \hookrightarrow v}{\rho \triangleright \text{let } x = e_1 \text{ in } e_2 \hookrightarrow v}$$

B   Parameter Lifting Translation Phase

$$\overline{c \Rightarrow_t c} \qquad \overline{y^\emptyset \Rightarrow_t y} \qquad \frac{y^s \Rightarrow_t e}{y^{x::s} \Rightarrow_t e @ x}$$

$$\frac{m \Rightarrow_t e}{\lambda y.m \Rightarrow_t \lambda y.e} \qquad \frac{m_1 \Rightarrow_t e_2 \quad m_2 \Rightarrow_t e_2}{m_1 @ m_2 \Rightarrow_t e_1 @ e_2}$$

$$\frac{\text{letfun}^s \ f = \lambda x.m_1 \text{ in } m_2 \Rightarrow_t e}{\text{letfun}^{x::s} \ f = m_1 \text{ in } m_2 \Rightarrow_t e}$$

$$\frac{m_1 \Rightarrow_t e_1 \quad m_2 \Rightarrow_t e_2}{\text{letfun}^\emptyset \ f = m_1 \text{ in } m_2 \Rightarrow_t \text{letfun } f = e_1 \text{ in } e_2}$$

$$\frac{m_1 \Rightarrow_t e_1 \quad m_2 \Rightarrow e_2}{\text{let } x = m_1 \text{ in } m_2 \Rightarrow_t \text{let } x = e_1 \text{ in } e_2}$$

On Jones-Optimal Specialization
for Strongly Typed Languages

Henning Makholm⋆

DIKU, University of Copenhagen
Universitetsparken 1, DK-2100 København Ø, Denmark
henning@makholm.net

Abstract. The phrase "optimal program specialization" was defined by Jones et al. in 1993 to capture the idea of a specializer being strong enough to remove entire layers of interpretation. As it has become clear that it does not imply "optimality" in the everyday meaning of the word, we propose to rename the concept "Jones-optimality".

We argue that the 1993 definition of Jones-optimality is in principle impossible to fulfil for strongly typed languages due to necessary encodings on the inputs and outputs of a well-typed self-interpreter. We propose a technical correction of the definition which allows Jones-optimality to remain a meaningful concept for typed languages.

We extend recent work by Hughes and by Taha and Makholm on the long-unsolved problem of Jones-optimal specialization for strongly typed languages. The methods of Taha and Makholm are enhanced to allow "almost optimal" results when a self-interpreter is specialized to a type-incorrect program; how to do this has been an open problem since 1987. Neither Hughes' nor Taha–Makholm's methods are by themselves sufficient for Jones-optimal specialization when the language contains primitive operations that produce or consume complex data types. A simple postprocess is proposed to solve the problem.

An implementation of the proposed techniques has been produced and used for the first successful practical experiments with truly Jones-optimal specialization for strongly typed languages.

1 Introduction

1.1 Program Specialization

A **program specializer** is a software system that given a program and some of its input produces a new program whose behaviour on the remaining input is identical to that of the original program.

We can express this in algebraic guise:

$$\forall p, d_1, d_2 : \quad [\![p]\!](d_1, d_2) = [\![\,[\![spec]\!](p, d_1)\,]\!](d_2) \tag{1}$$

⋆ Supported in part by the Danish National Science Research Council via project PLT (Programming Language Technology)

W. Taha (Ed.): SAIG 2000, LNCS 1924, pp. 129–148, 2000.

Here $[\![\cdot]\!]$ is the mapping that takes a program text to its meaning as a function from input to output. That is, $[\![p]\!](d)$ denotes the output produced by the program p when it is run with input d. We call p is the **subject program** and $[\![spec]\!](p, d_1)$ the **specialized program**.

Programs may diverge, so $[\![p]\!](d)$ is not always defined. This means that (1) must be accompanied with a specification of how it is to be interpreted in the presence of non-termination. We think an ideal program specializer ought to have the the following properties:

i) **Totality.** $[\![spec]\!](p, d_1)$ should be defined for any correctly formed program p and any d_1 that can meaningfully be input to p.

ii) **Correctness.** $[\![\,[\![spec]\!](p, d_1)\,]\!](d_2)$ must be defined exactly when $[\![p]\!](d_1, d_2)$ is (in which case (1) says their values must be equal).

There is a general consensus that what we have called correctness is a good requirement. Though sometimes one sees a specializer which allows the specialized program to terminate more often than the subject program, that property is always the subject of a couple of apologising and/or defensive sentences in the accompanying paper.

The agreement about totality is much less universal. Indeed, most actual program specializers are not total; the last decade of research in automatic program specialization has shown that totality is not easily achieved together with efficiency of the specialized program and the specialization process itself. Opinions even differ about whether it is a desirable property in its own right.

Apart from the two "hard" conditions of totality and correctness there are some less formal requirements that can reasonably be applied to a program specializer:

iii) **Strength.** The specialized program should be as least as efficient as the subject program. There should be a nontrivial class of interesting subject programs for which the specialized programs are substantially more efficient as the subject program.

iv) **Fairness.** The behaviour of the specializer should be free of gratuitous discontinuities: Similar subject programs ought to be specialized similarly, unless there is a rational excuse for doing things differently. If the specializer can't handle some part of the subject program by its preferred technique, it should be able to fall back to a cruder method without affecting the specialization of unrelated parts of the subject program

There are many different measures of strength; in this article we focus on *Jones' optimality criterion*, as described in the next subsection.

Fairness is the most vaguely defined of the criteria we have presented. Still we maintain that it is a real and very desirable property, though we do not currently know how to characterise it completely formally.

We consider as the eventual goal of our research area to produce automatic program transformers that non-expert software developers can use with the same ease as they use other development tools such as compilers or parser generators. Thus we seek to construct specializers that are strong enough to solve real problems while still being total, correct, and fair. This does not mean that every novel solution to a subproblem *must* have all of these ideal properties initially – but we consider it a problem worth solving if a proposed technique is apparently incompatible with one of these goals.

1.2   Jones' Optimality Criterion

Above we have assumed that all the occurring programs were written in the same fixed but arbitrary language $\mathcal{L}_1$. Now let another language $\mathcal{L}_2$ enter the discussion and imagine that we have an $\mathcal{L}_2$-interpreter int written in $\mathcal{L}_1$. That, is, int should satisfy

$$\forall p \in \mathcal{L}_2\text{-programs}, \forall d : \quad [\![int]\!](p, d) = [\![p]\!]_2(d) \ , \tag{2}$$

where $[\![\cdot]\!]_2$ is the meaning function for $\mathcal{L}_2$, and each side of the equation should be defined for the same p and d.

Note in passing that (2) does not specify how int should behave when p is not an $\mathcal{L}_2$-program. Some people maintain that a correct $\mathcal{L}_2$-interpreter ought to check its input and report an error if it is not a correct program. We think this view is too restrictive; it is commonly accepted that at least the toy interpreters one usually encounters in research papers simply start interpreting their input program right away and only report errors if the program tries to actually execute a problematic statement – even if the interpreted language is supposed to be typed. We do not argue against static checking of programs, but we claim that it should be thought of as a separate activity rather than an inherent part of any interpreter.

Futamura [5] observed that one can combine an interpreter int with the specializer $spec$ to achieve automatic translation of arbitrary programs from $\mathcal{L}_2$ to $\mathcal{L}_1$: Combining (1) and (2) we find

$$\forall p \in \mathcal{L}_2\text{-programs}, \forall d : \quad [\![\, [\![spec]\!](int, p)]\!](d) = [\![int]\!](p, d) = [\![p]\!]_2(d) \ , \tag{3}$$

that is, $[\![spec]\!](int, p)$ is an $\mathcal{L}_1$-program that behaves identically to the $\mathcal{L}_2$-program p. As before we call $[\![spec]\!](int, p)$ the **specialized program**, and we call the p in (3) the **source program** (cf. the "subject program" which is int here).

When is $spec$ strong enough to make this trick interesting? A logical goal is that $[\![spec]\!](int, p)$ should be as efficient as if it had been manually translated from p by a human programmer who knows how the language $\mathcal{L}_2$ works (notice that $spec$ does not know that – that knowledge is only implicit in int which is data for $spec$). This has been expressed by the catch phrase that the specializer "removes an entire layer of interpretation".

Jones' optimality criterion is a popular formalisation of the kind of strength that makes a specializer able to remove entire layers of interpretation.

The intuitive idea is that it is impossible to check that *spec* can remove *any* layer of interpretation, but we can get a good estimate of how good *spec* is at specializing away interpretation layers in general by looking at how it treats one particular interpreter, namely a self-interpreter for $\mathcal{L}_1$.

A self-interpreter is an interpreter that is written in the language it interprets. Thus the effect of considering a self-interpreter is to make $\mathcal{L}_2$ equal $\mathcal{L}_1$. Choose a self-interpreter *sint* for $\mathcal{L}_1$; Equation (3) then becomes

$$\forall p \in \mathcal{L}_1\text{-programs}, \forall d : \quad [\![\,[\![spec]\!](sint, p)\,]\!](d) = [\![p]\!](d) \ . \tag{4}$$

The equivalent programs p and $[\![spec]\!](sint, p)$ are both $\mathcal{L}_1$-programs, so we can meaningfully compare their efficiency and thus measure how much of *sint*'s interpretative overhead has been removed by the specialization.

The original version of the optimality criterion appeared in [14, Problem 3.8] which called a specializer "strong enough" if p and $[\![spec]\!](sint, p)$ were "essentially the same program", where "essentially" was intended to cover such minor differences as variable names and the order of function definitions, etc.

Later, Jones et al. [15, Section 6.4] refined the criterion by calling a specializer **optimal** if $[\![spec]\!](sint, p)$ is *at least as* efficient on all inputs as p. This new definition allowed the specializer to be "more than strong enough" – and indeed some of the specializers of the time were that, mostly because they sometimes continued to apply small local optimizations after having reached a specialized program that was essentially p.

This notion of "optimality" has proved to be a very productive engineering standard, but the subsequent history has also shown that it is by no means the ultimate measure of specializer strength. In particular, it has been found that even rather weak specializers can be "optimal" – for example, the Lambdamix system [9] is optimal though it does not even do value-polyvariant program-point specialization. This has caused much confusion because people (quite reasonably) think that the word "optimal" ought to imply that nothing can conceivably be better. It is too late to completely change the word, but we propose at least to warn that something uncommon is going on by saying **Jones-optimal** instead of just "optimal".

Jones et al. [15] remark that the definition of optimality is not perfect: It can be "cheated" by a specializer which simply returns the static input if the subject program compares equal to the text of a fixed self-interpreter and otherwise specializes the subject program by a bad technique. Our reaction to this scenario is that Jones-optimality is a measure of strength alone, and it must be combined with a requirement of fairness before it really has practical value. Clearly a specializer that cheats is fundamentally unfair.

1.3   Binding-Time Analyses and Off-Line Specialization

The specializers we consider in this paper are all **off-line**, meaning that the subject program presented to *spec* must be augmented with **annotations** that guide *spec* by telling it which of several methods should be employed when specializing each of the subject program's operations.

Real specializers include a **binding-time analysis** which automatically constructs suitable annotations for the subject program, so that the entire system implements a source-to-source transformation of unannotated programs.

This paper does not detail how binding-time analyses work; there is a large and still growing literature on the subject, and one of the virtues of the design we propose here is that existing binding-time analysis techniques can be reused unmodified.

1.4 Jones-Optimal Specialization for Typed Languages

This paper concerns Jones-optimal specialization for (strongly) *typed* languages. Whereas Jones-optimality was achieved quickly for untyped languages ([15] describes several examples), it was found to be a much harder problem for typed languages.

The reason for that is that a self-interpreter for a typed language is a more complex piece of software than for an untyped language. Some expressions in the interpreter must be able to represent any value the source program manipulates. These expressions must have a type; and in a strong type system there is no single type that encompasses every value a program can construct. Therefore the self-interpreter needs to represent the interpreted program's values in an encoded form, such that the entire set of values any program can produce is injected into the set of values admitted by a single **universal type**.

Partial evaluation [15], which is the most popular technique for program specialization,[1] cannot remove the injections into (and case analyses on) the universal type from the specialized program, because partial evaluation does not in general change the type of expressions. If one expression has, for example, type integer and another has the universal type, there has to be an injection operation to connect them when the two types cannot be changed.

This problem is related, but not identical, to problems that arise when one tries to construct an (efficient) program stager – also known as a generating-extension generator, or "cogen" – for a typed language by self-applying a partial evaluator [5,15]. In fact, Jones et al. [15] present optimality chiefly as a milestone on the way to a self-applicable partial evaluator, which may have led some people to think that the *only* value of Jones-optimality was to help with self-application.

Research about program stagers for typed languages [16, 1, 2] eventually reached the conclusion that a better strategy would be to bypass self-application

---

[1] This terminology follows Hughes [13] but is not standard. Traditionally, there has been no need to distinguish strictly between the extensional specification of a specializer, which is (1), and its internal workings – because there has only been one basic technique: the one described by [15]. However, given that Hughes [11] as well as Danvy [4] have proposed specialization techniques that are very different from traditional ones, we think it is important to keep the "what"s separate from the "how"s. Thus we use "specialization" about anything that realizes (1) and "partial evaluation" with the implied restriction that this is done by traditional methods.

completely and write cogen by hand. We wish to point out that though this approach makes self-application unnecessary, Jones-optimality is still a desirable property in its own right, because it abstracts the ability of the specializer to produce efficient target code when one translates programs by specializing an interpreter. That is a question of strength, which is independent of whether or not the specializer uses a hand-written cogen.

1.5   Previous Solutions

In 1996 Hughes [11, 12] managed to get rid of the residual tagging and untagging operations by leaving the partial-evaluation paradigm. His **type specializer** works by constructing a type derivation for the subject program in a non-standard type system which includes information about statically known data. A specialized program is then extracted from the type derivation such that the type of each specialized expression is derived from, but not identical to, the type of an expression in the subject program.

Hughes conjectured his type specializer to be Jones-optimal after an experiment with an interpreter for a subset of the subject language showed that the interpretative overhead was removed completely. The experiment was not repeated with a complete self-interpreter, so while we find the conjecture plausible, the question has not yet been settled conclusively. In particular the termination properties of the type specializer itself are not fully understood, so it is possible that it does not always terminate when applied to a complete self-interpreter.

There is a more serious problem with the type specializer: It obtains its strength by sacrificing totality. The type specializer uses annotations on the subject program to decide precisely which tags are to be removed. If, during the specialization process, the type specializer discovers that removing these tags will harm the correctness of the specialized program, it simply gives up, outputting an error message instead of a specialized program. Hughes argues that this happens only when the source program is ill-typed (which is true) and that the lack of totality is not a problem when the goal is Jones-optimality. We think, conversely, that Jones-optimality is a measure of strength, and that strength and totality are orthogonal goals which ought to be achievable simultaneously. (Additionally, the user of the type specializer must select a trade-off between totality and strength by his selection of annotations on the subject programs; this makes it unlikely that a satisfactory, fully automatic binding-time analysis for the type specializer can be constructed).

Inspired by Hughes' work, the author and Walid Taha independently discovered that the complexity of Hughes' solution can be greatly reduced by removing the type tags as a post-process rather than during the specialization phase. That led to a joint paper [19] which proposed essentially the following specializer structure:

$$spec(p, d) = \textbf{let } p' = PE(p, d) \textbf{ in if } SafeToErase(p')$$
$$\textbf{then } TagErasure(p')$$
$$\textbf{else } p'$$

where PE is a traditional partial evaluator (which may include binding-time improvers, a hand-written cogen, or other existing or future refinements) that is Jones-optimal except for leaving tagging and untagging operations in the residual program p'. As with Hughes' system, the subject program p is annotated with information about which tags ought to be removed in the specialized program, but in addition the annotations try to predict which particular instance of each tag are met in each of the case analyses that are used for untagging operations. PE passes these extra annotations unchanged through to p', after which the post-transformation *TagErasure* simply removes the indicated tagging and untagging operations (replacing untagging case analyses with the indicated branches). This tag erasure takes place only if a special type-based analysis *SafeToErase* can prove that erasing the tags will not change the behaviour of p'. If it is found that erasing tags is unsafe, p' is simply used as it is.[2]

The Taha–Makholm proposal sacrificed some of the strength of Hughes' system by separating the tag elimination from the specialization process, but managed to improve the totality of the specializer by using the fall-back option of not removing tags in situations where Hughes' specializer would simply reject its input. On the other hand the fact that the fall-back decision is made globally means that the design is not fair: if the tags do not match up in even a tiny bit of a big specialized program, *all* tags in the entire program will be left in.

The design does not in itself guarantee totality, because the partial evaluator PE might itself diverge – but it is *no less total* than PE. Thus unlike for Hughes' system, there is hope that a clever binding-time analysis (see, e.g., [8, 7]) might guarantee termination of PE without hurting the Jones-optimality of the entire system.

1.6   Organization of this Paper: Summary of Contributions

Section 2. We point out that necessary encodings of input and output in a typed self-interpreter prevents (4) from being true in a strict sense. We analyse this phenomenon and propose how the definition should be repaired to make Jones-optimality a meaningful property for typed languages.

Section 3. We briefly present the small PEL language, the subject language of our prototype specializer MiXIMUM which we are using for experiments in Jones-optimal specialization for typed languages.

PEL is a first-order language. The previous work [11, 12, 19] has all been formulated for higher-order languages, but we think that the restriction to a first-order language makes the essential properties of our techniques clearer. We conjecture that our techniques will be relatively easy to extend to higher-order languages.

---

[2] This description of the Taha–Makholm design is somewhat simplified. What really happens in that paper is that the tag erasure is allowed to change the behaviour of the program in a controlled way, and in the **else** branch extra "wrapper" code is added to p' to change its behaviour similarly.

Section 4. We show how the Taha–Makholm proposal can be extended to *improve the fairness* of the system while preserving Jones-optimality. The practical relevance of this is that MiXIMUM can specialize an interpreter for an untyped version of PEL with respect to a not-well-typed source program, and the specialized program will contain type tags only where absolutely necessary. MiXIMUM introduces no extraneous tags in the parts of the source program that happen to be well-typed. To the best of our knowledge this is the first serious answer to Problem 11.2 of [14][3].

Section 5. We point out a problem that has not been addressed in the previous work cited in Sect. 1.5: The previous methods work only for the cases where the embedding into the universal type can be constructed in parallel with the computation of the value that gets embedded. When the language contains primitive operations that work on compound values, the self-interpreter must contain "deep" tagging and untagging operations which cannot be eliminated totally by prior methods. We propose an "identity elimination" that can take care of this.

Section 6. MiXIMUM has been used to specialize a self-interpreter in practise, yielding Jones-optimal results for all of the source programs we tried (including the self-interpreter itself). To our knowledge, this is the first successful experiment with Jones-optimality for a typed language; the previous work has used source languages that were proper subsets of the language the interpreter was written in.

Finally, Sect. 7 concludes.

2   Jones-Optimality with a Typed Self-Interpreter

In typed languages, input and output are typed just as well as the variables inside the program. A program that expects an integer as input cannot be applied at all to a list of integers.

This has consequences for Jones-optimality experiments. Namely, it means that the self-interpreter must accept and produce the interpreted program's input and output wrapped in the "universal type" encoding. That again means that the self-interpreter will use the same wrapping on input and output when it has been specialized – so the specialized program is not directly comparable to the source program; they do not even work on the same data!

This argument is subtle enough to deserve being recast in formulas. We use a informal notion of types to clarify what is going on. First we write down the type of a program specializer:

$$[\![spec]\!] : Pgm \times Data \to Pgm \ , \tag{5}$$

---

[3] The problem, reading "Achieve type security and yet do as few run time type tests as possible", does not not explicitly mention that this is to be achieved in the context of compiling by specializing an interpreter, but we consider that to be implicit in its context. Without that qualification the problem has of course long since been solved by "soft typing" systems such as [10].

where *Pgm* is the type of all program texts and *Data* is whatever type *spec* uses for encoding the static input to a program (assume that *spec* itself is written in a typed language and so need an encoding here).

Equation (5) is correct but does not tell the whole story. In particular, the second argument to *spec* must encode a value of the type the program given as the first argument to *spec* expects as its first argument. And there is a certain relation between the types of the subject program and the specialized program.

To express this, we introduce a notion of subtyping – reminiscent of the "underbar types" used by [15, Section 16.2] – into our informal type language: $\frac{\alpha \rightarrow \beta}{Pgm}$ is the type of the *text* of a program which it itself has type $\alpha \rightarrow \beta$. That is, $\frac{\alpha \rightarrow \beta}{Pgm}$ is a subtype of *Pgm*. Similarly, let $\frac{\alpha}{Data}$ be the subtype of *Data* consisting of the encodings of all values of type α.

With this notation we can refine (5) to

$$\forall \alpha, \beta, \gamma : \quad [\![spec]\!] : \frac{\alpha \times \beta \rightarrow \gamma}{Pgm} \times \frac{\alpha}{Data} \rightarrow \frac{\beta \rightarrow \gamma}{Pgm} \ . \tag{6}$$

Notice that if we remove everything above the bars we arrive back at (5).

Similarly to (6) we can give the type of the self-interpreter:

$$\forall \alpha, \beta : \quad [\![sint]\!] : \frac{\alpha \rightarrow \beta}{Pgm} \times \frac{\alpha}{Univ} \rightarrow \frac{\beta}{Univ} \tag{7}$$

This is the type of the *meaning* of the self-interpreter. The type of the *text* of the self-interpreter (which we give as input to the specializer) has a third layer:

$$\forall \alpha, \beta : \quad sint : \frac{\frac{\alpha \rightarrow \beta}{Pgm} \times \frac{\alpha}{Univ} \rightarrow \frac{\beta}{Univ}}{Pgm} \tag{8}$$

Now say that we want to compute $[\![spec]\!](sint, d)$ for some d. Equations (6) and (8) imply that d must have type $\frac{\frac{\alpha \rightarrow \beta}{Pgm}}{Data}$; that is, d must be the *Data* encoding of a program p. However $[\![p]\!]$ has type $\alpha \rightarrow \beta$ whereas

$$[\![\,[\![spec]\!](sint, d)\,]\!] : \frac{\alpha}{Univ} \rightarrow \frac{\beta}{Univ} \ , \tag{9}$$

so the comparison between p and $[\![spec]\!](sint, d)$ that is the core of Jones' optimality criterion is inherently unfair. For some programs p, for example one that efficiently constructs a list of the first n natural numbers, $[\![spec]\!](sint, d)$ is *necessarily* slower than p, simply because it has to construct a bigger output value. Thus Jones-optimal specialization of an encoding interpreter is impossible!

Earlier work does not, as far as we are aware, address this problem directly. Nevertheless, it has been dealt with in different ways.

Hughes allows his type specializer to replace the types of the specialized program's input and output with *specialized* versions of the subject program's types. This means that the extensional specification of the specializer (1) is not quite true; $[\![\,[\![spec]\!](p, d_1)]\!](d_2)$ must be replaced by $W([\![\,[\![spec]\!](p, d_1)]\!](U(d_2)))$, where U and W are coercions that can be derived from a "residual type" that is a by-product of the type specialization. It may be argued that when we translate programs by specializing interpreters we *want* the type to change to reflect the type of the source program. However from our perspective the eventual goal is a generally usable specializer which simply happens to be strong enough to specialize interpreters well. Allowing a general specializer to make its own guess at which type we want for the specialized program would make it difficult to automate the use of the specialized program.

The earlier Taha–Makholm design [19] modified this solution by suggesting that the specification of the U and W coercions should be an *input* to the specialization process rather than something the specializer decides for itself. That is better, because it gives control back to the user. But we still consider it clumsy to expect the user of a generally usable specializer to learn a separate notation for specifying how the type of the specialized program should relate to the subject program's type.

So instead of changing the behaviour of the specializer, we propose to solve the problem by using a different interpreter in the optimality test. Instead of a self-interpreter with type (7) we use a variant $sint_{\alpha \to \beta}$ with type

$$[\![sint_{\alpha \to \beta}]\!] : \frac{\alpha \to \beta}{Pgm} \times \alpha \to \beta \ . \tag{10}$$

The interpreter text $sint_{\alpha \to \beta}$ must depend on α and β, but once we know these it is easy to construct $sint_{\alpha \to \beta}$ mechanically:

$$sint_{\alpha \to \beta} = decode_\beta \circ sint \circ \langle Id, encode_\alpha \rangle \ , \tag{11}$$

where $encode_\alpha : \alpha \to Univ$ and $decode_\beta : Univ \to \beta$ are the natural injection and extraction functions, and "$\circ$" is symbolic function composition – implemented naïvely by simply generating a program whose main function applies the two composants to the input sequentially.

We propose that this construction be used to adjust Jones' optimality criterion when used in a typed context: a specializer for a typed language should be called **Jones-optimal** if for any types α, β and any program $p : \dfrac{\alpha \to \beta}{Pgm}$, the program $[\![spec]\!](sint_{\alpha \to \beta}, p)$ is at least as efficient as p on any input.

This solution is more general than the one proposed by [19], because it can be seen as simply programming the U and W coercions into the subject program before the specialization. Our solution means that the user of the specializer does not have to learn an independent notation for specifying the coercions. It is also more flexible because the subject language is generally more expressive than a special-purpose notation for coercions. On the other hand it requires more from the specializer to obtain Jones-optimality with this strategy – but in Sect. 5 we show that the required strength is in general necessary for other reasons anyway.

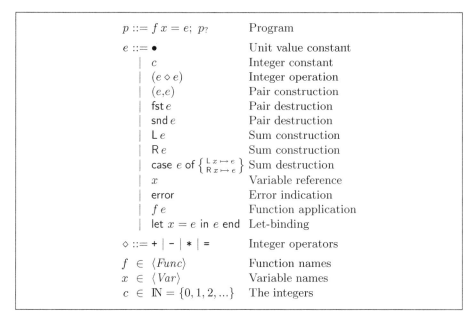

Fig. 1. Abstract Syntax of PEL

3   Language

We use the PEL language defined by Welinder [20], extended for technical reasons with an explicit unit type. It is a minimal, call-by-value functional language which manipulates first-order values built from this grammar:

$$\langle \mathit{Val} \rangle \ni v ::= \bullet \mid 0 \mid 1 \mid 2 \mid \dots \mid (v,v) \mid \mathsf{L}\, v \mid \mathsf{R}\, v$$

The language is attractive for our purposes because of its simplicity and because we can use Welinder's PEL self-interpreter, which has been formally proven correct, in optimality experiments. Using an existing self-interpreter[4] should vindicates us of the possible critique of having programmed the self-interpreter in unnatural ways to compensate for idiosyncrasies in the specializer.

The syntax of PEL expressions is given in Fig. 1, and the dynamic semantics in Fig. 2. A program is a set of mutually recursive functions, the first of which defines the meaning of the program – the only nontrivial feature of the semantics is that the equality test operator "=" delivers its result encoded using the sum type; L• represents false and R• represents true. Thus the case expression can be used as an if-then-else construct. For full details see [20, Section 3.3].

---

[4]   The self-interpreter in [20] does not use or support the "•" value; Welinder kindly added support for • to his interpreter and adjusted his mechanical proof of its correctness to work with the new interpreter.

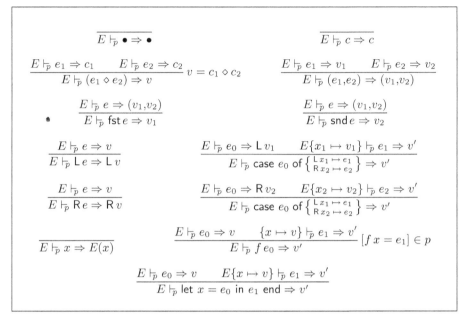

Fig. 2. Dynamic Semantics for PEL. There is intentionally no rule for error

3.1 Type System

Because we are concerned with specialization of typed languages, we add a (monomorphic) type system to PEL. A **type** in our system is a finite or (regularly) infinite tree built from this grammar:

$$\langle Typ \rangle \ni \tau \quad ::= \quad \text{unit} \mid \text{int} \mid \langle L\,\tau + R\,\tau \rangle \mid (\tau, \tau)$$

Our implementation represents infinite types as graphs; this representation is isomorphic to Welinder's construction (which uses explicit syntax for recursion and a co-inductively defined equivalence relation) but more convenient in implementations.

The typing rules for PEL expressions are given in Fig. 3. They define a judgement "$\Gamma \vdash_T e : \tau$" where $\Gamma : \langle Var \rangle \rightarrow \langle Typ \rangle$ and $T : \langle Func \rangle \rightarrow \langle Typ \rangle \times \langle Typ \rangle$ are type environments that give types to the program's variables and functions, respectively.

4   An Erasure Analysis for Improving Fairness

Recall the specializer structure proposed by [19]:

$$spec(p, d) = \textbf{let } p' = PE(p, d) \textbf{ in if } SafeToErase(p')$$
$$\textbf{then } TagErasure(p')$$
$$\textbf{else } p'$$

$$\frac{}{\Gamma \vdash_T \bullet : \mathsf{unit}} \qquad\qquad \frac{}{\Gamma \vdash_T c : \mathsf{int}}$$

$$\frac{\Gamma \vdash_T e_1 : \mathsf{int} \qquad \Gamma \vdash_T e_2 : \mathsf{int}}{\Gamma \vdash_T (e_1 \diamond e_2) : \mathsf{int}}\, \diamond \neq\, = \qquad \frac{\Gamma \vdash_T e_1 : \mathsf{int} \qquad \Gamma \vdash_T e_2 : \mathsf{int}}{\Gamma \vdash_T (e_1 = e_2) : \langle \mathsf{L\,unit} + \mathsf{R\,unit}\rangle}$$

$$\frac{\Gamma \vdash_T e_1 : \tau_1 \qquad \Gamma \vdash_T e_2 : \tau_2}{\Gamma \vdash_T (e_1, e_2) : (\tau_1, \tau_2)} \qquad \frac{\Gamma \vdash_T e : (\tau_1, \tau_2)}{\Gamma \vdash_T \mathsf{fst}\, e : \tau_1} \qquad \frac{\Gamma \vdash_T e : (\tau_1, \tau_2)}{\Gamma \vdash_T \mathsf{snd}\, e : \tau_2}$$

$$\frac{\Gamma \vdash_T e : \tau_1}{\Gamma \vdash_T \mathsf{L}\, e : \langle \mathsf{L}\,\tau_1 + \mathsf{R}\,\tau_2\rangle} \qquad\qquad \frac{\Gamma \vdash_T e : \tau_2}{\Gamma \vdash_T \mathsf{R}\, e : \langle \mathsf{L}\,\tau_1 + \mathsf{R}\,\tau_2\rangle}$$

$$\frac{\Gamma \vdash_T e_0 : \langle \mathsf{L}\,\tau_1 + \mathsf{R}\,\tau_2\rangle \qquad \Gamma\{x_1 \mapsto \tau_1\} \vdash_T e_1 : \tau \qquad \Gamma\{x_2 \mapsto \tau_2\} \vdash_T e_2 : \tau}{\Gamma \vdash_T \mathsf{case}\, e_0\, \mathsf{of}\, \left\{ \begin{smallmatrix} \mathsf{L}\,x_1 \mapsto e_1 \\ \mathsf{R}\,x_2 \mapsto e_2 \end{smallmatrix} \right\} : \tau}$$

$$\frac{}{\Gamma \vdash_T x : \Gamma(x)} \qquad\qquad \frac{}{\Gamma \vdash_T \mathsf{error} : \tau}$$

$$\frac{\Gamma \vdash_T e_0 : \tau_0}{\Gamma \vdash_T f\, e_0 : \tau_1}\, T(f) = \tau_0 \to \tau_1 \qquad \frac{\Gamma \vdash_T e_0 : \tau_0 \qquad \Gamma\{x \mapsto \tau_0\} \vdash_T e_1 : \tau_1}{\Gamma \vdash_T \mathsf{let}\, x = e_0\, \mathsf{in}\, e_1\, \mathsf{end} : \tau_1}$$

Fig. 3. Typing Rules for PEL

The global test on $SafeToErase(p')$ hurts the fairness of the system, so in MiX-IMUM we use a different structure

$$spec(p, d) = \mathbf{let}\ p' = PE(p, d)$$
$$p'' = ErasureAnalysis(p')$$
$$\mathbf{in}\ TagErasure(p'')$$

The annotations on p are now only used to guide the partial evaluator, and p' is an unannotated program. The analysis $ErasureAnalysis$ then analyses p' to find out which injections and case analyses can safely be erased without changing the meaning of p'. The output of $ErasureAnalysis$ is an annotated program p'' which except for the annotations that guide $TagErasure$ is the same program as p'.

The advantage of this design is that it allows the erasure annotations to be more fine-grained than in the Taha–Makholm proposal. There the erasure annotations on p' came from the annotated subject program p, so two tagging operations in p' which originated in the same tagging operation in p had to have the same annotation. MiXIMUM can give them different erasure annotations because the erasure annotations are created only after the partial evaluation.

The erasure analysis works by doing a non-standard type inference using the non-standard type system defined in Fig. 4. Here types (finite or infinite) are built from the grammar

$$\langle STyp\rangle \ni \check\tau ::= \mathsf{unit} \mid \mathsf{int} \mid \langle \mathsf{L}_\sigma\, \check\tau + \mathsf{R}_\sigma\, \check\tau\rangle \mid (\check\tau, \check\tau)$$
$$\langle Sign\rangle \ni \sigma ::= \oplus \mid \ominus$$

$$\overline{\check\Gamma \vdash_{\check T} \bullet : \mathsf{unit}} \qquad\qquad \overline{\check\Gamma \vdash_{\check T} c : \mathsf{int}}$$

$$\frac{\check\Gamma \vdash_{\check T} e_1 : \mathsf{int} \qquad \check\Gamma \vdash_{\check T} e_2 : \mathsf{int}}{\check\Gamma \vdash_{\check T} (e_1 \diamond e_2) : \mathsf{int}} \diamond \neq\; = \qquad \frac{\check\Gamma \vdash_{\check T} e_1 : \mathsf{int} \qquad \check\Gamma \vdash_{\check T} e_2 : \mathsf{int}}{\check\Gamma \vdash_{\check T} (e_1 = e_2) : \langle \mathsf{L}_\oplus \mathsf{unit} + \mathsf{R}_\oplus \mathsf{unit}\rangle}$$

$$\frac{\check\Gamma \vdash_{\check T} e_1 : \check\tau_1 \qquad \check\Gamma \vdash_{\check T} e_2 : \check\tau_2}{\check\Gamma \vdash_{\check T} (e_1,e_2) : (\check\tau_1,\check\tau_2)} \qquad \frac{\check\Gamma \vdash_{\check T} e : (\check\tau_1,\check\tau_2)}{\check\Gamma \vdash_{\check T} \mathsf{fst}\, e : \check\tau_1} \qquad \frac{\check\Gamma \vdash_{\check T} e : (\check\tau_1,\check\tau_2)}{\check\Gamma \vdash_{\check T} \mathsf{snd}\, e : \check\tau_2}$$

$$\frac{\check\Gamma \vdash_{\check T} e : \check\tau_1}{\check\Gamma \vdash_{\check T} \mathsf{L}\, e : \langle \mathsf{L}_\oplus \check\tau_1 + \mathsf{R}_\sigma \check\tau_2 \rangle} \qquad\qquad \frac{\check\Gamma \vdash_{\check T} e : \check\tau_2}{\check\Gamma \vdash_{\check T} \mathsf{R}\, e : \langle \mathsf{L}_\sigma \check\tau_1 + \mathsf{R}_\oplus \check\tau_2 \rangle}$$

$$\frac{\check\Gamma \vdash_{\check T} e_0 : \langle \mathsf{L}_{\sigma_1} \check\tau_1 + \mathsf{R}_{\sigma_2} \check\tau_2 \rangle \qquad \check\Gamma\{x_1 \mapsto \check\tau_1\} \vdash_{\check T} e_1 : \check\tau \qquad \check\Gamma\{x_2 \mapsto \check\tau_2\} \vdash_{\check T} e_2 : \check\tau}{\check\Gamma \vdash_{\check T} \mathsf{case}\, e_0 \,\mathsf{of}\, \left\{ {\mathsf{L}\, x_1\, \mapsto\, e_1 \atop \mathsf{R}\, x_2\, \mapsto\, e_2} \right\} : \check\tau}$$

$$\overline{\check\Gamma \vdash_{\check T} x : \check\Gamma(x)} \qquad\qquad \overline{\check\Gamma \vdash_{\check T} \mathsf{error} : \check\tau}$$

$$\frac{\check\Gamma \vdash_{\check T} e_0 : \check\tau_0}{\check\Gamma \vdash_{\check T} f\, e_0 : \check\tau_1} \check T(f) = \check\tau_0 \to \check\tau_1 \qquad \frac{\check\Gamma \vdash_{\check T} e_0 : \check\tau_0 \qquad \check\Gamma\{x \mapsto \check\tau_0\} \vdash_{\check T} e_1 : \check\tau_1}{\check\Gamma \vdash_{\check T} \mathsf{let}\, x = e_0 \,\mathsf{in}\, e_1 \,\mathsf{end} : \check\tau_1}$$

Fig. 4. Non-standard type system for the erasure analysis. Apart from the signs in the sum types these rules are identical to the ones in Fig. 3

The intuitive meaning of the σs in the sum types is that, for example, the type $\langle \mathsf{L}_\oplus \check\tau_1 + \mathsf{R}_\ominus \check\tau_2 \rangle$ is a sum type where only the $\mathsf{L}\,\check\tau_1$ component is ever constructed. Such a type can safely be replaced with $\check\tau_1$ and the injections and case analyses for that sum type can be removed.

A non-standard type derivation for the program can be constructed by a straightforward unification-based type inference (which uses a graph unification algorithm to construct recursive types where necessary). The unifications never fail: We assume the program to be conventionally well-typed before the analysis, so there is at least one valid derivation by the rules in Fig. 4, given by attaching $\oplus$s to each sum type in the conventional derivation (note that none of the typing rules require any σ to be $\ominus$).

In general, however, some σ variables have not yet been unified with $\oplus$ after the non-standard type inference. These are then artificially set to $\ominus$ (except that all σs that appear in the type of the main function must be $\oplus$, which means that no tags that can be seen from outside the program will be erased). The result is a "maximally $\oplus$-free" typing for the program.

The actual tag erasure now consists of applying the $\|\cdot\|$ mapping defined in Fig. 5 to each function body in the program. This mapping is guided by the type annotations from the non-standard type analysis.

We remark that the work necessary to do the erasure analysis we have presented does not significantly exceed the work needed to compute the *SafeToErase*

$$\lfloor \bullet \rfloor = \bullet$$

$$\lfloor c \rfloor = c$$

$$\lfloor (e_1 \diamond e_2) \rfloor = (\lfloor e_1 \rfloor \diamond \lfloor e_2 \rfloor)$$

$$\lfloor (e_1, e_2) \rfloor = (\lfloor e_1 \rfloor, \lfloor e_2 \rfloor)$$

$$\lfloor \mathsf{fst}\, e \rfloor = \mathsf{fst}\, \lfloor e \rfloor$$

$$\lfloor \mathsf{snd}\, e \rfloor = \mathsf{snd}\, \lfloor e \rfloor$$

$$\lfloor (\mathsf{L}\, e)^{\oplus\oplus} \rfloor = \mathsf{L}\, \lfloor e \rfloor$$

$$\lfloor (\mathsf{L}\, e)^{\oplus\ominus} \rfloor = \lfloor e \rfloor$$

$$\lfloor (\mathsf{R}\, e)^{\oplus\oplus} \rfloor = \mathsf{R}\, \lfloor e \rfloor$$

$$\lfloor (\mathsf{R}\, e)^{\ominus\oplus} \rfloor = \lfloor e \rfloor$$

$$\left\lfloor \mathsf{case}\, e_0{}^{\oplus\oplus}\, \mathsf{of}\, \left\{ \begin{smallmatrix} \mathsf{L}\, x_1 \mapsto e_1 \\ \mathsf{R}\, x_2 \mapsto e_2 \end{smallmatrix} \right\} \right\rfloor = \mathsf{case}\, \lfloor e_0 \rfloor\, \mathsf{of}\, \left\{ \begin{smallmatrix} \mathsf{L}\, x_1 \mapsto \lfloor e_1 \rfloor \\ \mathsf{R}\, x_2 \mapsto \lfloor e_2 \rfloor \end{smallmatrix} \right\}$$

$$\left\lfloor \mathsf{case}\, e_0{}^{\oplus\ominus}\, \mathsf{of}\, \left\{ \begin{smallmatrix} \mathsf{L}\, x_1 \mapsto e_1 \\ \mathsf{R}\, x_2 \mapsto e_2 \end{smallmatrix} \right\} \right\rfloor = \mathsf{let}\, x_1 = \lfloor e_0 \rfloor\, \mathsf{in}\, \lfloor e_1 \rfloor\, \mathsf{end}$$

$$\left\lfloor \mathsf{case}\, e_0{}^{\ominus\oplus}\, \mathsf{of}\, \left\{ \begin{smallmatrix} \mathsf{L}\, x_1 \mapsto e_1 \\ \mathsf{R}\, x_2 \mapsto e_2 \end{smallmatrix} \right\} \right\rfloor = \mathsf{let}\, x_2 = \lfloor e_0 \rfloor\, \mathsf{in}\, \lfloor e_2 \rfloor\, \mathsf{end}$$

$$\left\lfloor \mathsf{case}\, e_0{}^{\ominus\ominus}\, \mathsf{of}\, \left\{ \begin{smallmatrix} \mathsf{L}\, x_1 \mapsto e_1 \\ \mathsf{R}\, x_2 \mapsto e_2 \end{smallmatrix} \right\} \right\rfloor = \mathsf{let}\, x = \lfloor e_0 \rfloor\, \mathsf{in}\, \mathsf{error}\, \mathsf{end}$$

$$\lfloor x \rfloor = x$$

$$\lfloor \mathsf{error} \rfloor = \mathsf{error}$$

$$\lfloor f\, e \rfloor = f\, \lfloor e \rfloor$$

$$\lfloor \mathsf{let}\, x = e_0\, \mathsf{in}\, e_1\, \mathsf{end} \rfloor = \mathsf{let}\, x = \lfloor e_0 \rfloor\, \mathsf{in}\, \lfloor e_1 \rfloor\, \mathsf{end}$$

Fig. 5. Specification of the tag erasure. The expressions inside the $\lfloor \rfloor$s are supposed to be annotated with sum-reduction types; the pattern "$e^{\sigma_1 \sigma_2}$" matches an e that annotated with type $\langle \mathsf{L}_{\sigma_1}\, \breve{\tau}_1 + \mathsf{R}_{\sigma_2}\, \breve{\tau}_2 \rangle$ for some $\breve{\tau}_{1,2}$

function in the Taha–Makholm proposal; essentially our new design improves fairness for free!

5   Identity Elimination

The design presented in the previous section is not actually strong enough to specialize PEL Jones-optimally. The problem is PEL's "=" operator which takes two int operands and produces an $\langle \mathsf{L}\, \mathsf{unit} + \mathsf{R}\, \mathsf{unit} \rangle$ result. The self-interpreter must inject this compound result into the universal type, which means that the source expression $(e_1 = e_2)$ after the initial partial evaluation becomes

$$\mathsf{case}\, (e_1 = e_2)\, \mathsf{of}\, \left\{ \begin{matrix} \mathsf{L}\, x \mapsto \mathsf{R}\mathsf{R}\mathsf{R}\mathsf{L}\mathsf{L}\bullet \\ \mathsf{R}\, x \mapsto \mathsf{R}\mathsf{R}\mathsf{R}\mathsf{R}\mathsf{L}\bullet \end{matrix} \right\} \tag{12}$$

which can be broken down as

$$\mathsf{case}\, (e_1 = e_2)\, \mathsf{of}\, \left\{ \begin{matrix} \mathsf{L}\, x \mapsto TagAsSum(\mathsf{L}\, TagAsUnit(\bullet)) \\ \mathsf{R}\, x \mapsto TagAsSum(\mathsf{R}\, TagAsUnit(\bullet)) \end{matrix} \right\} \tag{13}$$

or just

$$encode_{\langle \mathsf{L}\,\mathrm{unit}+\mathsf{R}\,\mathrm{unit}\rangle}(e_1 = e_2) \ . \tag{14}$$

After tag elimination that becomes

$$\mathsf{case}\ (e_1 = e_2)\ \mathsf{of} \left\{ \begin{array}{l} \mathsf{L}\,x \ \mapsto\ \mathsf{L}\,\bullet \\ \mathsf{R}\,x \ \mapsto\ \mathsf{R}\,\bullet \end{array} \right\} \ , \tag{15}$$

where the (by now superfluous) case analysis makes the expression less efficient than the source expression $(e_1 = e_2)$. Therefore the result is not Jones-optimal.

Note that the resulting expression (15) is independent of the particular value encoding used by the self-interpreter. It may look like the "encoding of booleans as tagged units" comes from the self-interpreter, but the fact is that this "encoding" is part of the language specification – and the value encoding that the self-interpreter puts *atop* that one disappeared in the tag elimination phase that took (12) to (15).

The moral of this example is that though tag elimination in itself can remove tagging and untagging operations, it cannot completely remove entire $encode_\tau$ or $decode_\tau$ computations. They get reduced to code that meticulously breaks a value apart to is primitive components, only to build an identical value from scratch!

It is seen that a situation similar to (15) will arise in natural self-interpreters for *any* primitive operation that delivers or expects a value of a complex type. In PEL the only occurrence of the problem is with the equality test, but other languages might have primitive operations for arbitrary complex types; each must be accompanied by an $encode_\tau$ or $decode_\tau$ in a self-interpreter. In general these conversions may even be recursive: Consider for example a primitive operation that finds the least element of a list of integers. Then the self-interpreter's case for that function must use a recursive function $decode_{[\mathrm{int}]}$ which after tag erasure becomes a recursive identity mapping which might look like

$$f_{\mathrm{d}}\,x = \mathsf{case}\ x\ \mathsf{of} \left\{ \begin{array}{l} \mathsf{L}\,y \ \mapsto\ \mathsf{L}\,\bullet \\ \mathsf{R}\,z \ \mapsto\ \mathsf{R}\,(\mathsf{fst}\,z, f_{\mathrm{d}}\,\mathsf{snd}\,z) \end{array} \right\} \ . \tag{16}$$

Our solution is yet another postprocess which we call **identity elimination**. This phase solves not only the problem outlined above, but also takes care of the $encode_\alpha$ and $decode_\beta$ components of (11), which the tag elimination also reduce to identity mappings akin to (16).

The identity elimination proceeds in several phases. In the first phase, every $\bullet$ in the program is replaced with the innermost enclosing variable whose type is unit, if such one exists. This transforms (16) to

$$f_{\mathrm{d}}\,x = \mathsf{case}\ x\ \mathsf{of} \left\{ \begin{array}{l} \mathsf{L}\,y \ \mapsto\ \mathsf{L}\,y \\ \mathsf{R}\,z \ \mapsto\ \mathsf{R}\,(\mathsf{fst}\,z, f_{\mathrm{d}}\,\mathsf{snd}\,z) \end{array} \right\} \tag{17}$$

which makes it more explicit that f_{d} is really a identity function. The f_{d} defined by (16) is not an identity function when applied to, say, $\mathsf{R}\,(4, \mathsf{L}\,2)$ – but replacing the $\bullet$ by y localizes the global knowledge that f_{d} will not be applied to such a

$$(\mathsf{fst}\ \pi_1...\pi_n x, \mathsf{snd}\ \pi_1...\pi_n x) \rightarrow \pi_1...\pi_n x \quad \text{where each } \pi_i \in \{\mathsf{fst}, \mathsf{snd}\}$$

$$\mathsf{case}\ e\ \mathsf{of} \left\{ \begin{array}{l} \mathsf{L}\,x_1 \mapsto \mathsf{L}\,x_1 \\ \mathsf{R}\,x_2 \mapsto \mathsf{R}\,x_2 \end{array} \right\} \rightarrow e$$

$$\mathsf{case}\ e\ \mathsf{of} \left\{ \begin{array}{l} \mathsf{L}\,x_1 \mapsto \mathsf{L}\,e_1 \\ \mathsf{R}\,x_2 \mapsto \mathsf{L}\,e_2 \end{array} \right\} \rightarrow \mathsf{L}\ \mathsf{case}\ e\ \mathsf{of} \left\{ \begin{array}{l} \mathsf{L}\,x_1 \mapsto e_1 \\ \mathsf{R}\,x_2 \mapsto e_2 \end{array} \right\}$$

$$\mathsf{case}\ e\ \mathsf{of} \left\{ \begin{array}{l} \mathsf{L}\,x_1 \mapsto \mathsf{R}\,e_1 \\ \mathsf{R}\,x_2 \mapsto \mathsf{R}\,e_2 \end{array} \right\} \rightarrow \mathsf{R}\ \mathsf{case}\ e\ \mathsf{of} \left\{ \begin{array}{l} \mathsf{L}\,x_1 \mapsto e_1 \\ \mathsf{R}\,x_2 \mapsto e_2 \end{array} \right\}$$

$$f\,e \rightarrow e \quad \text{if } f \in \mathcal{F}$$

Fig. 6. Reduction rules for the identity elimination. The two first rules might be construed a form of η-reduction for product and sum types. In the last rule $\mathcal{F}$ is a set of names of functions which are supposed to be identity functions

value. This phase could be avoided by consistently writing all *encode* and *decode* operations to reuse unit values, but that would hardly be a natural programming style.

The main part of the identity elimination consists of repeatedly applying the reductions in Fig. 6 to the program. The last of these reductions refers to a set $\mathcal{F}$ of names of functions that are supposed to be identity functions. Intuitively, the functions meant to be in $\mathcal{F}$ are the ones like f_{d} that are used for the necessary recursion in $encode_\tau$ or $decode_\tau$ when τ is recursive.

Formally we want $\mathcal{F}$ to be a safe approximation to the set of functions f such that $f\,e$ and e are always equivalent (assuming that $f\,e$ is well-typed). How can we compute such an $\mathcal{F}$? A first attempt would be to use the largest $\mathcal{F}$ such that $\mathcal{F}$ allows the definitions for all $f \in \mathcal{F}$ to be reduced to "$f\,x = x$" – but that alone would not be sound, because it would allow the function

$$f_0\,x = f_0\,x \tag{18}$$

to be classified as an identity function, despite being non-terminating for all inputs.

We do not have an *elegant* way to compute $\mathcal{F}$, but we do have a safe one that seems to work in practise: $\mathcal{F}$ must allow the definitions for all $f \in \mathcal{F}$ to be reduced to "$f\,x = x$" under the constraint that the reduction $f\,e \rightarrow e$ may be used only if $f \in \mathcal{F}$ *and* simple syntactic conditions can ensure that the value of e is always smaller than the argument to the function where the reduction is applied. For example, in (17) that is true of the call to f_{d} because the argument is $\mathsf{fst}\,z$, which is smaller than z, which by the case expression is smaller than x.

With this condition a largest possible $\mathcal{F}$ can be found by fixed-point iteration. In the final reduction after a safe $\mathcal{F}$ has been computed, we allow $f\,e \rightarrow e$ to be applied whenever $f \in \mathcal{F}$.

Finally, any remaining references to variables of type unit are replaced with $\bullet$ expressions. Aside from making the program more readable, this means that the entire identity elimination never makes a program *less* efficient under the not unreasonable assumption that constructing a constant • might be faster than retrieving it from a variable.

6   Experiments with MiXIMUM

MiXIMUM is a prototype implementation of the design presented above. The system is implemented in Moscow ML [18] and is available electronically as `http://www.diku.dk/~makholm/miximum.tar.gz`[5].

We have used MiXIMUM to perform the Jones-optimality experiment described in Sect. 2 with Welinder's self-interpreter [20] and a number of source programs p, the biggest of which was the self-interpreter itself. In each case the result of specializing the self-interpreter to p was alpha-equivalent to the result of running p itself through MiXIMUM's post-processes, none of which can degrade the performance of the program. In other words, MiXIMUM meets the definition of Jones-optimality – at least in the examples we have tried.

MiXIMUM takes care to preserve the subject program's termination properties, that is, to be "correct" in the sense of Sect. 1.1. The partial evaluator never discards code or reduces let bindings, so a subject expression such as

$$\text{let } x = 17 \text{ in } (x + 42) \text{ end}$$

will, as a first approximation, be specialized to

$$\text{let } x = 17 \text{ in let } x' = x \text{ in let } x'' = 42 \text{ in } 59 \text{ end end end}$$

and after the main specialization an eventual reduction pass reduces all let bindings where it can be proved (by simple syntactic conditions) that reduction can neither change the termination properties of the program nor degrade its efficiency. That reduces the example expression above to the constant expression 59.

It is hardly surprising that such simple techniques preserve the subject program's termination properties, but we can offer the less trivial observation that they apparently do not interfere with Jones-optimality. In particular, the let bindings that result from erasing an untagging operation (Fig. 5) appear always to be eligible for reduction.

---

[5] Readers who download MiXIMUM will discover that the system is not quite faithful to the design in Sect. 4. The partial evaluator in the prototype has been split into two phases, the second of which occurs after the tag erasure. This has historical reasons, and we're presently working on bringing the structure of MiXIMUM closer to the ideal structure we have presented here. There is also another postprocess which unfolds spurious let bindings and functions as a local arity raiser. This was found to be necessary for achieving Jones-optimality but does not in itself contain novel ideas.

7 Conclusion

We have shown how to extend the design of Taha and Makholm [19] to be more fair without sacrificing Jones-optimality. We have implemented our proposed design and conducted experiments which strongly suggest that it is Jones-optimal.

Two directions of further work immediately suggest themselves here: to extend the MiXIMUM implementation to work with a higher-order language, and to produce actual proofs of its correctness and Jones-optimality. Both of these lines of work are being investigated presently.

A third direction would be to investigate how our methods could be extended to deal with languages with user-defined n-ary sum types. The simplicity of the methods presented here are to some extent due to the fact that PEL has only binary sums. Achieving Jones-optimality with a self-interpreter that handles arbitrary sum types would probably require adding a variant of constructor specialization [17] and integrate it with the methods presented here. (We note that Hughes' type specializer [11] does include constructor specialization).

Acknowledgements

I thank Arne Glenstrup, John Hughes, Neil D. Jones, Walid Taha, Peter Thiemann, and Morten Welinder for constructive discussions and helpful advice on presenting and improving the results reported here. Thanks also to the anonymous referees who pointed out numerous points in the draft version that needed better explanation.

References

1. Andersen, L. O.: Program Analysis and Specialization for the C Programming Language. PhD thesis, Department of Computer Science, University of Copenhagen (1994). DIKU-TR-94/19
2. Birkedal, L. and Welinder, M.: Hand-writing program generator generators. In: Hermenegildo, M. and Penjam, J. (eds.): Programming Language Implementation and Logic Programming: 6th International Symposium, PLILP '94. Lecture Notes in Computer Science, Vol. 844. Springer-Verlag, Berlin Heidelberg New York, 198–214. ftp://ftp.diku.dk/diku/semantics/papers/D-199.dvi.Z
3. Bjørner, D., Ershov, A. P., and Jones, N. D. (eds.): Partial Evaluation and Mixed Computation: selected papers from the IFIP TC2 Workshop, October 1987. Special issue of New Generation Computing **6:2–3**
4. Danvy, O.: Type-directed partial evaluation. In: Principles of Programming Languages: 23rd ACM SIGPLAN-SIGACT Symposium, POPL '96. ACM Press, New York, NY, USA, 242–257.
ftp://ftp.daimi.au.dk/pub/empl/danvy/Papers/danvy-popl96.ps.gz
5. Futamura, Y.: Partial evaluation of computation process – an approach to a compiler-compiler. Systems, Computers, Controls **2** (1971) 45–50. Reprinted as [6]
6. Futamura, Y.: Partial evaluation of computation process—an approach to a compiler-compiler. Higher-Order and Symbolic Computation **14** (1999) 381–391. Reprint of [5]

7. Glenstrup, A. J.: Terminator II: Stopping Partial Evaluation of Fully Recursive Programs. Master's thesis, Department of Computer Science, University of Copenhagen (1999). DIKU-TR-99/8. http://www.diku.dk/~panic/TerminatorII/

8. Glenstrup, A. J. and Jones, N. D.: BTA algorithms to ensure termination of off-line partial evaluation. In: Bjørner, D., Broy, M., and Pottosin, I. V. (eds.): Perspectives of System Informatics: 2nd International Andrei Ershov Memorial Conference, PSI '96. Lecture Notes in Computer Science, Vol. 1181. Springer-Verlag, Berlin Heidelberg New York, 273–284. ftp://ftp.diku.dk/diku/semantics/papers/D-274.ps.gz

9. Gomard, C. K. and Jones, N. D.: A partial evaluator for the untyped lambda-calculus. Journal of Functional Programming **1** (1991) 21–69

10. Henglein, F.: Global tagging optimization by type inference. In: Lisp and Functional Programming: 1992 ACM Conference, LFP '92. Special issue of ACM LISP Pointers **5:1**. ACM Press, New York, NY, USA, 205–215

11. Hughes, J.: Type specialization for the λ-calculus; or, A new paradigm for partial evaluation based on type inference. In: Danvy, O., Glück, R., and Thiemann, P. (eds.): Partial Evaluation: International Seminar. Lecture Notes in Computer Science, Vol. 1110. Springer-Verlag, Berlin Heidelberg New York (1996) 183–251. http://www.cs.chalmers.se/~rjmh/Papers/typed-pe.ps

12. Hughes, J.: An introduction to program specialization by type inference. In: Glasgow Workshop on Functional Programming. Glasgow University (1996). http://www.cs.chalmers.se/~rjmh/Papers/glasgow-96.dvi

13. Hughes, J.: The correctness of type specialization. In: Smolka, G. (ed.): 9th European Symposium on Programming: ESOP '00. Lecture Notes in Computer Science, Vol. 1782. Springer-Verlag, Berlin Heidelberg New York, 215–229

14. Jones, N. D. et al.: Challenging problems in partial evaluation and mixed computation. In: Bjørner, D., Ershov, A. P., and Jones, N. D. (eds.): Partial Evaluation and Mixed Computation: IFIP TC2 Workshop. North-Holland, Amsterdam, The Netherlands (1987) 1–14. Also pages 291–303 of [3]

15. Jones, N. D., Gomard, C. K., and Sestoft, P.: Partial Evaluation and Automatic Program Generation. Prentice Hall, Englewood Cliff, NJ, USA (1993). http://www.dina.kvl.dk/~sestoft/pebook/pebook.html

16. Launchbury, J.: A strongly-typed self-applicable partial evaluator. In: Hughes, J. (ed.): Functional Programming Languages and Computer Architecture: 5th ACM Conference, FPCA '91. Lecture Notes in Computer Science, Vol. 523. Springer-Verlag, Berlin Heidelberg New York, 145–164

17. Mogensen, T. Æ.: Constructor specialization. In: Schmidt, D. (ed.): Partial Evaluation and Semantics-Based Program Manipulation: ACM SIGPLAN Symposium, PEPM '93. 22–32

18. Romanenko, S. and Sestoft, P.: Moscow ML version 1.44. A light-weight implementation of Standard ML (1999). http://www.dina.kvl.dk/~sestoft/mosml.html

19. Taha, W. and Makholm, H.: Tag elimination; or, Type specialisation is a type-indexed effect. In: Subtyping & Dependent Types in Programming: APPSEM Workshop, DTP '00. INRIA technical report. http://www-sop.inria.fr/oasis/DTP00/Proceedings/taha.ps

20. Welinder, M.: Partial Evalutation and Correctness. PhD thesis, Department of Computer Science, University of Copenhagen (1998). DIKU-TR-98/13

Pragmatic Aspects
of Reusable Program Generators
Position Paper

Norman Ramsey

Division of Engineering and Applied Sciences
Harvard University
nr@eecs.harvard.edu

Abstract. When writing a program generator requires considerable in-
tellectual effort, it is pleasant to amortize that effort by using the generator to build more than one application. When a program generator
serves multiple clients, however, the implementor must address pragmatic questions that implementors of single-use program generators can
ignore. In how many languages should generated code be written? How
should code be packaged? What should the interfaces to the client code
look like? How should a user control variations? This paper uses examples from SLED, λ-RTL, and ASDL to elaborate on these questions. It
is hoped that the paper will stimulate discussion and the development of
better techniques. Most urgently needed is a simple, clear way to control
interfaces to generated code.

1   Introduction

There are many ways to deploy program generators; not all are alike. For example, some may be used only once, while others are used over and over. This paper
examines program generators that are intended to be reused—what properties
they should have and how they might be structured.

1.1   Why Reuse?

Not all program generators need to be reusable. Many are simple tools that are
unknown to all but their authors; writing programs that generate programs
is a technique every experienced programmer should use from time to time
(Hunt and Thomas 1999, Section 20). Even program generators that become
known to many programmers are not necessarily reusable. The `lburg` tool used
to generate `lcc`'s code generators (Fraser and Hanson 1995), the *spawn* tool used
to generate executable editors (Larus and Schnarr 1995), and the tool that `gcc`
uses to compile its machine descriptions (Stallman 1992) are all examples. Some-

W. Taha (Ed.): SAIG 2000, LNCS 1924, pp. 149–171, 2000.

one building a new code generator, a new executable editor, or a new peephole optimizer[1] would have to create a new program generator.

A few program generators are intended for reuse. Examples include the lexer generator Lex (Lesk and Schmidt 1975), the parser generator Yacc (Johnson 1975), and the code-generator generator BURG (Fraser, Henry, and Proebsting 1992). The effort required to create a reusable program generator is much greater than that required to create a single-use program generator, so it is worth examining what might justify such an effort.

- Generating a lexical analyzer requires algorithms that manipulate finite automata, e.g., they translate regular expressions to NFAs, convert NFAs to DFAs, and minimize states of DFAs. These algorithms are worth reusing. Perhaps more importantly, the lexical analyzer is a significant performance bottleneck in many compilers (Waite 1986), and it is worth trying to automate the expertise needed to make this component efficient. Newer lexer generators attempt to provide not only good automata, but also efficient code (Gray 1988Bumbulis and Cowan 1993).
- Generating a parser requires analysis of the grammar and construction of the lookahead sets. Writing an LR parser and building SLR(1) parsing tables is fairly straightforward (Aho and Johnson 1974), but building the more useful LALR(1) tables is harder, especially if one wishes to do so efficiently (DeRemer and Pennello 1982).
- Some code generators select instructions by finding minimum-cost covers of intermediate-code trees. A typical code generator might use dynamic programming to find a minimum-cost cover, and it is fairly easy to write a program to generate such a code generator. But to squeeze the last ounce of performance out of the code generator, getting the fastest possible compiler, it is desirable to do the dynamic programming at program-generation time. Doing so efficiently is not so easy (Proebsting 1992).

These examples show that if a nontrivial algorithm or technique is required to create efficient code, that algorithm or technique may be worth embodying in a program generator. *How* to do so is the central question of any particular program-generation problem. This paper discusses a different, pragmatic question: how can we arrange for generated code to work well with the client code? A reusable program generator should generate code that can fit into a variety of applications, written in a variety of implementation languages.

This paper presents problems, not solutions. It reports on experience with the program generators behind the New Jersey Machine-Code Toolkit (Ramsey and Fernández 1995) and the λ-RTL translator (Ramsey and Davidson 1999), as well as the ASDL program generator (Wang et al. 1997). This experience shows the significance of the problems, even if the solutions used in the tools are often unsatisfying.

---

[1] Gcc's machine descriptions contain all manner of information used to generate the compiler, but the core of the system is based on instruction selection by peephole optimization (Davidson and Fraser 1984).

1.2   Requirements for Reuse

What properties should a program generator have if it is to be used?

- The generated code should be *written in the programming language of the client's choice*. Foreign-function calls may suffice in some cases, but for most purposes, the generated code needs to work in the client's native language. This requirement explains the repeated pleas for "Yacc-alikes" on the Usenet newsgroup `comp.compilers`.
- The generated code should be *idiomatic and readable*. Wise programmers distrust generated code that they don't understand (Hunt and Thomas 1999, Section 35). Readable code is doubly important when an author is debugging a program generator that is new or that involves experimental algorithms. Prettyprinting code nicely is not enough; the code must use programming conventions that are native to the target language. Such conventions encompass decisions ranging from the spelling of identifiers (use of capital letters and underscores) to the representations of common data structures (lists, tables) to input/output conventions.
- The user should *control the interfaces* between generated code and client code. In many modern programming languages, even simple procedural interfaces offer considerable scope for variation. Should a C procedure be called directly or through a pointer? Should a Modula-3 procedure be called through a procedure appearing in an interface or through a method appearing in an object type? Should C++ procedures be generated at top level, in their own class, or in their own namespace?
  These choices are not always matters of personal preference. For example, if the client program will contain multiple instances of an abstraction (some of which may be generated automatically), the indirect call, the object type, or the class are the better alternatives. But if there is to be only one instance of the abstraction, and if performance is critical, the cost of indirection may be too high. These tradeoffs are illustrated below with examples from the New Jersey Machine-Code Toolkit (Ramsey and Fernández 1995).
- A user may wish to *control internals* of the generated code, for example, to adjust space/time tradeoffs or other properties that affect performance.

In a single-use program generator written by its user, these properties should emerge naturally. They are much harder to achieve in a program generator intended for reuse; after all, these properties appear peripheral to a program generator's main job, which is to embody some useful algorithm or technique. The primary claim of this paper is that these pragmatic aspects of program generation are every bit as important as the central, algorithmic aspects. The primary source of evidence supporting this claim is experience with the New Jersey Machine-Code Toolkit.

2   Case Study: The New Jersey Machine-Code Toolkit

The New Jersey Machine-Code Toolkit is a program generator that helps programmers create applications that process machine code—assemblers, disassemblers, code generators, tracers, profilers, debuggers, and executable editors, for example. Writing low-level bit-fiddling code by hand is tedious and error-prone; generating this code automatically reduces retargeting effort and eliminates a significant source of errors.

Applications use the Toolkit for encoding, decoding, or both. For example, assemblers encode, disassemblers decode, and executable editors do both. The Toolkit has been used to build a retargetable debugger
(Ramsey and Hanson 1992), a retargetable, optimizing linker (Fernández 1995), a run-time code generator, a decompiler, an execution-time analyzer (Braun 1996), an optimizing compiler for object-oriented languages (Dean et al. 1996), a binary translator
(Cifuentes, van Emmerik, and Ramsey 1999), and other applications. All applications work with *streams* of instructions. Streams can take many forms; for example, a debugger can treat the text segment of a target process as an instruction stream.

2.1   Coupling Generated Code to Applications

Decoding applications use *matching statements* to read instructions from a stream and identify them. A matching statement is like a case statement, except its alternatives are labelled with patterns that match instructions or sequences of instructions. Client programmers insert matching statements directly into hand-written source code. The Toolkit transforms matching statements into efficient decoders.

Encoding applications call C procedures generated by the toolkit. These procedures encode instructions and emit them into a stream; e.g., the SPARC call `fnegs(r2, r7)` emits the word `0x8fa000a2`. The Toolkit can also create encoding procedures that emit assembly language.

The Toolkit includes two program generators, which share infrastructure. The *translator* translates matching statements in a C or Modula-3 program into ordinary code. The *generator* generates encoding and relocation procedures in C.

Generated code couples to applications' code at both higher and lower levels of abstraction. Application code at high levels of abstraction calls generated code to encode or decode instructions. Generated code calls application code at lower levels of abstraction to manage the details of reading and writing the bytes in the *instruction stream*, which is the Toolkit's model of binary representation.

Low-Level Coupling: Generated Code to Instruction Streams. The Toolkit dictates the semantics, but not the representation, of instruction streams. An instruction stream is like a byte stream, except that the units may be "tokens" of any size, not just 8-bit bytes. Because machine instructions don't always fit in a machine word, an instruction is a sequence of one or more tokens; for example, a SPARC instruction is always one 32-bit token, but a Pentium instruction might include several 8-bit prefixes, an 8-bit opcode, 8-bit format bytes, and a 32-bit immediate operand.

Decoders generated by the Toolkit examine tokens in instruction streams. Each decoder treats an *address* within a stream as an abstract type; application code supplies a representation, as well as code to perform three operations: add an integer to an address, fetch a token from an address, and convert an address to an integer (e.g., so a decoder can extract bits from the program counter). The Toolkit's decoders do not use linguistic abstraction mechanisms (e.g., C procedures or C preprocessor macros) to manipulate an application's instruction stream; instead, the Toolkit uses its own form of macros. Users provide "code templates" that perform the basic operations above, and the Toolkit instantiates these templates as needed.

The templates define the interface between the generated code and the lower-level application code. For example, these templates are used in a debugger, which is written in Modula-3 (Ramsey and Hanson 1992):

```
address type        is    "Word.T"
address add         using "Word.Plus(%a, %o)"
address to integer  using "%a"
fetch any using "FetchAbs(m, %a, Type.I%w).n"
```

The instruction stream, m, is built directly into the fetch template.

As another example, these templates are used in a binary translator, written in C (Cifuentes, van Emmerik, and Ramsey 1999); the instruction stream is implicit in the getDword operation.

```
address type        is "unsigned"
address to integer  using "%a"
address add         using "%a+%o"
fetch 32            using "getDword(%a)"
```

Encoding procedures generated by the Toolkit have a different low-level interface, which is a single C procedure or macro. Each encoding procedure calls that procedure to emit a token into the instruction stream; the Toolkit's user can choose the name of that procedure at program-generation time. The Toolkit includes a 600-line library that implements an instruction-stream abstraction and several emission procedures and macros, but application programmers can replace that library with their own code.

High-Level Coupling: Application to Generated Code. At the high level, there is no formal interface between an application and a generated decoder. Matching statements act just like statements in the source language (C or Modula-3), and each action within a matching statement may be any statement in the source language. In effect, the Toolkit extends the source language with a new construct.

The Toolkit generates a procedural interface for access to encoders. Applications call through this interface to emit binary representations into an instruction stream. The Toolkit supports not only direct calls, but also indirect calls, which go through function pointers stored in a structure. The indirect method is the standard encoding of object-orientation in C.

The alternatives that we have implemented are not the only alternatives; Section 3.1 discusses high-level interfaces further.

2.2   History and Requirements

The Toolkit evolved from single-use program generators used to help retarget Standard ML of New Jersey (Appel and MacQueen 1991) and the debugger `ldb` (Ramsey and Hanson 1992). Standard ML of New Jersey uses run-time code generation, and `ldb` uses control-flow analysis of machine instructions to implement breakpoints (Ramsey 1994). Fernández's (1995) work on link-time optimization needed a fast, link-time assembler for performance, and this need provided the motivation to merge and adapt the original generators to create the Toolkit. Because the original applications were written in Standard ML, Modula-3, and C, support for multiple languages was a goal from the beginning.

Because the work was experimental, we placed a high premium on the readability of the generated code. Readable code not only helped us debug the program generator; it also helped us understand the performance and behavior of the generated code. Reading the generated decoders was especially important, because it helped us compare them with hand-written decoders, which made it easier to develop the decoding heuristics that make generated decoders perform as well as hand-written decoders.

We were also aware early that generated code should be idiomatic, i.e., where possible it should resemble code that a fluent programmer would write by hand. For example, the Toolkit should not require its own printing abstraction in order to emit assembly language; in C, it should use `printf`, and in Modula-3, it should use writers.

The need for users to control the interfaces to the generated code and some internals of the generated code was not obvious early. It become clear only as the Toolkit acquired other clients.

3   Needs of Clients

Of the requirements in Section 1.2, the most problematic have been the need to support multiple languages and the need to adjust generated code to interoperate cleanly with client code. This section illustrates some of these needs, using examples drawn from the Toolkit and from other program generators. The section then moves to more general issues of concrete types, interfaces, and languages.

3.1   Examples from the Toolkit

Needs of Decoding Applications. The design of the Toolkit's matching statements simplifies not only the program generator, but also the coupling to client code. Because the application programmer drops matching statements inline wherever decoders are needed, there is no need to wrap a generated decoder in a procedural abstraction, and therefore there is no need to provide different interfaces to different clients. The code templates make it unnecessary to decide how to package the instruction-stream abstraction, and they support multiple languages effortlessly.

These properties provide enormous flexibility while keeping the program generator simple. For example, clients can easily arrange for decoders to manipulate instruction streams without the overhead of procedure calls. No special command-line options or configuration parameters are needed, and the client need not rely on a compiler to inline procedure calls or method calls.

One penalty of the approach is that errors in matching statements or in templates can be detected only *after* the program generator runs, and some error messages may be mystifying. The Toolkit mitigates the problem by careful use of line-numbering pragmas (e.g., `#line` in C), which make it possible for some error messages to refer to source-code locations in the original matching statements.

Needs of Encoding Applications. Despite the advantages we realized by making the decoder generator a preprocessor, it never occurred to us to design the encoder generator that way. In both cases we were thinking not about the problem of coupling generated code to client code (the "pragmatic aspects" that are the subject of this paper) but about the best model for the program generator itself. For decoding, we wanted "ML-like pattern matching over binary representations of machine instructions." For encoding, we wanted "something just like assembly language, but more flexible than a traditional assembler." In particular, we wanted to emit instructions by name, and to have the assembler make sure the types and values of the operands were sensible. This thinking led us to associate an encoding procedure with each machine instruction.

This model serves the task of encoding instructions: check that the operands are sensible, and produce the bits. But we failed to consider that different applications may take different views of the *interface* to encoding.

- In the *applicative view*, instructions are abstractions, which are built up by applying constructors. To get binary code, the client program applies a function to an instruction, or to a sequence of instructions. This view is congenial to clients written in applicative style, like the Standard ML of New Jersey compiler.
- In the *imperative view*, there is no abstraction representing instructions, and instructions are not constructed; instead, to each instruction there corresponds a procedure, which is executed for its side effect, i.e., emission of the binary representation of the instruction. This view is congenial to traditional assemblers.
- Our original view is a hybrid view. The "effective address[2]" is treated as an abstraction, and each addressing mode corresponds to an applicative

---

[2] For those unfamiliar with CISC assembly languages, an effective address is a fragment of a machine instruction that identifies the location of an operand or result. In typical instruction sets, this location may refer either to a machine register or to a location in memory.

Where	*Who decides*	*What is decided*	*Possible language constructs*
Above	application	what to encode when	procedures, objects, (macros)
Gen. code	generator	encoding logic	
Below	application	how to emit bits	procedures, macros

Table 1. Interface Layers for Encoding Applications

constructor for effective addresses. Each instruction, however, corresponds to an imperative procedure, which is executed to cause binary emission.
– There are other ways to mix alternatives. For example, one might construct abstract instructions, but emit their binary representations as side effects. Or one might construct binary representations (sequences of tokens) directly, allowing the application to concatenate them explicitly.

The semantics of the interfaces is not all that can vary; the language constructs used to express the interfaces can also vary, as Table 1 illustrates. For the interface from above, the Toolkit enables the user to control the names of the generated procedures, and whether the procedures are called at the top level or indirectly through function pointers. The interface from below is simpler; the generated code needs to call only one emission procedure or macro.

Do these interfaces matter? Unfortunately, yes. Applications that generate code dynamically, such as DyC (Auslander et al. 1996), Fabius (Lee and Leone 1996), and VCODE (Engler 1996), all want the absolute best in performance. Overhead for indirect calls would be unacceptable. In the case of VCODE, even procedure-call overhead is unacceptable; VCODE cannot be implemented using the Toolkit because it requires macros.[3] More traditional applications, like static compilers, may prefer to call encoding procedures indirectly, so they can easily get both binary code (for speed) and assembly language (for debugging) from the same compiler.

We and our users paid for our oversight. When the Toolkit was first distributed, each new user asked for a new variation. We implemented several, but each addition increased the complexity not only of the Toolkit's implementation, but also the complexity of the interface used to control the program generator. The Toolkit uses command-line options to control variations (applicative or imperative, direct or indirect) and naming (of procedures, of types, and of structures). To achieve even the incomplete control provided by the Toolkit, there are 9 options that affect the interfaces to encoding procedures. Another 3 affect internals (e.g., logging), and perhaps a half dozen affect the closely related relocation procedures.

This situation is intolerable. The plethora of possibilities baffles even the Toolkit's authors; never mind what it does to novices. Clearly, some alternative is needed. I have considered a configuration language, but have not been enthusiastic; why should a big set of configuration variables be significantly better

---

[3] Private communication from Dawson Engler, 1995.

than a big set of command-line options? What is surprising is that the decoder generator avoids these problems completely, by requiring the client to provide source code both above (surrounding) matching statements and below matching statements (the code templates). What I really desire for the encoder generator is some sort of "program generation by example" that would banish command-line options and configuration variables, enabling users to say "generate code that looks like *this*." I wish I knew what such a facility might look like.

3.2   Examples from ASDL

The Abstract Syntax Description Language (ASDL) describes recursive, tree-like data structures, such as are used in compilers to represent abstract syntax, intermediate code, etc. (Wang et al. 1997). The corresponding program generator, asdlGen, emits code to create trees, pickle them (write them to files), and unpickle them (read them from files). Because the pickle format is independent of the programming language in which the trees are created, written, and read, components implemented in a variety of programming languages can exchange trees. AsdlGen 2.0 supports C, C++, Haskell, Icon, Java, Objective Caml, and Standard ML.

ASDL describes trees using a restricted form of algebraic datatypes, derived from types found in ML and Haskell. The value of the program generator is twofold:

– It generates an applicative interface for the creation of trees. While tree creation is trivial in languages like ML and Haskell, languages like C require explicit, separate allocation and initialization. The program generator supplies code that would be tedious to write by hand.
– It generates picklers and unpicklers for serialization, which would be very tedious to write by hand. Even better, the serialization code guarantees interoperability.

AsdlGen does these jobs well, but like the Toolkit, it does not work so well when it comes to the interfaces between generated code and client code.

Basic Structure of Interfaces. The original version of asdlGen interleaved type definitions, constructors, and serialization code in a single interface. This choice violated the requirement that generated code be idiomatic and easy to understand. While any module using the generated code will need access to the type definition, most will use either constructors, picklers, or unpicklers, not all three. Some clients may use *only* the type definition and no generated operations. Merging all into one interface makes it harder to understand and use the generated code. Worse, it creates a configuration problem: code generated with asdlGen can't be compiled without an installation of asdlGen that provides serialization libraries.

A later version of asdlGen split the output into two interfaces: one for definition and construction, one for serialization. This split simplified the migration of existing projects to ASDL, since it become possible for an ASDL expert to generate definitions of types and constructors, then ship the generated code to another site to be used.

Interfaces and Modularity. One of the most significant defects in ASDL is that it is difficult to define trees that contain subtrees of types defined in different modules. For example, if a programmer is designing a compiler, he might want to define statements and expressions in different modules. Because statements may contain expressions, this structure is difficult to achieve using ASDL, even if both expressions and statements are defined in ASDL. The situation worsens if a programmer wants to define some types using hand-written code, e.g., to exploit features that are available in the target implementation language but not in ASDL. Code generated by `asdlGen` cannot easily refer to such types, even when there is hand-written serialization code available to support them.

ASDL's "view" mechanism partly addresses both problems. In the main part of the ASDL description, the programmer must pretend that an abstract type is some concrete type, e.g., a string. The "view" mechanism, which works by adding fragments of hand-written code to the ASDL description, makes it possible to override the pretend type with the actual type, and to provide conversion routines between the pretend type and the actual type. It is not possible to provide picklers and unpicklers directly, nor is it possible to assert that values of the pretend type will never be serialized. The program generator would benefit from a cleaner way to interface to types for which the definitions, constructors, picklers, and unpicklers were defined by the programmer in ordinary source files.

Abstract Types and Existing Trees: Unforeseen Applications and Effects. One way to view an ASDL pickle is that it says which constructors should be called, in what order, to reproduce a tree. In this view, it should not matter whether the constructors build `asdlGen`'s concrete representation of trees, or whether they build a value of some abstract type. According to the algebraic approach to data abstraction, the concrete representation should be irrelevant; there is an obvious one-to-one mapping between trees of some concrete algebraic data type and a corresponding abstraction (Liskov and Guttag 1986). Unfortunately, the designers of `asdlGen` overlooked this possibility; generated picklers and unpicklers cannot couple to abstractions, but only to `asdlGen`'s concrete representation. The only way to pickle and unpickle a value of an abstract type is to write "transducers" by hand. For example, a generated unpickler produces ASDL's concrete representation; an unpickling transducer walks that representation and produces a value of an abstract type.

Unhappily, transducers are needed not only for abstraction, but also to interface to existing compilers. Hanson (1999) reports on experience with ASDL and `lcc`.

> This duplication of effort [the transducer] is an onerous side effect of retrofitting an existing compiler with ASDL... Most of the code in the

ASDL back end is devoted to building copies of [the compiler's] data structures—that is, building a different, but logically equivalent representation for nearly everything.

Simon Peyton Jones and I have found that transducers are necessary even when designing a new compiler from scratch. Because we want to couple a back end to front ends written in different languages, we attempted to use ASDL to describe an intermediate form. We do not, however, want the representation defined by ASDL—only the abstract interface. Our internal representation includes private annotations: sets of registers read and written, sets of source-language variables live at a control point, lists of registers whose last use is at a given assignment ("dead lists"), etc. Such annotations, which are likely to change as the compiler evolves, should not be visible from the external interface, which should not change as the compiler evolves. Because we cannot couple asdlGen's generated code to an abstraction, we must write transducers.

These needs for transducers arise not from fundamental limitations of program generation, but from an accident of asdlGen's design: generated serialization code can be coupled only to ASDL's concrete representation, not to an abstraction. AsdlGen could easily be modified to emit a type-definition interface giving only an abstraction, not a representation. It could also emit picklers and unpicklers parameterized by the abstraction. Although it is not immediately obvious how to encode such parameterization in C, many object-oriented and functional languages provide natural, idiomatic parameterization mechanisms (e.g., classes, functors, generics, and templates). The flaw in the program generator lies not in the fundamental model or the underlying algorithms, but in the limitations on the possible interfaces to the generated code.

3.3   Concrete Types, Polymorphic, and Otherwise

Both the Toolkit and asdlgen share with parser generators and with other program generators the need to create sequences of things. In some target languages, like ML and Haskell, polymorphic list types provide natural representations. In other languages, there is no obvious natural representation. In C, for example, there are at least three alternatives: linked list, null-terminated array of pointers, or dynamic-array abstraction. Different applications have different needs; for example, the lcc back end needs an implementation in which appending to a list takes constant time (Hanson 1999).

Sequences offer choices not only of representation, but also of type. *Heterogenous* generation creates a specialized sequence type for each different kind of sequence. This choice preserves type safety at the cost of code bloat. *Homogeneous* generation uses a generic sequence type that contains something like C's void * or Java's Object. This choice abandons type safety, but does not duplicate code. Again, no single choice is always suitable; for example, when translating polymorphic types into Java, the Pizza translator uses both alternatives (Odersky and Wadler 1997).

Even simple, monomorphic types can provide pitfalls for the unwary author of a program generator. Should integers have arbitrary precision (bignums), some fixed precision (e.g., 32 bits), or the native precision of integers in the target language (not specified in C, and perhaps 31 or 63 bits in a functional or object-oriented language that uses tags for garbage collection)? Should C strings be null-terminated, or should they carry an explicit length? What codes should be used to represent the enumerations that asdlGen uses to distinguish different constructors? How can one match codes used in an existing application? How can one make codes distinct across *all* types, so each code identifies not only a constructor but also a type?

In sum, different clients need different representations, and there are surprisingly many choices. Finding a simple, clear way even to *specify* the clients' needs, let alone satisfy them, appears to be an unsolved problem.

3.4   Interfacing to Abstractions

Once the author of a program generator recognizes the need to couple generated code to hand-written abstractions, the next question is what language constructs should be used at the interface. In object-oriented languages, objects with methods are natural. In functional languages, functions and closures may be more natural. Some traditional imperative languages, as well as many functional and object-oriented languages, provide modules, which may be more better representations of complex abstractions. In C, an abstraction can be represented by a group of functions, plus a pointer of unknown type (void *). The pointer, which corresponds to the environment pointer used to form closures in functional languages, is passed as an additional argument to each function. Using void * to turn a function pointer into a closure is a bit of a trick, but it is one that is often used to help make C code reusable (Hanson 1996).

The proper representation of an abstraction is influenced not only by the features available in the target language, but also by the idioms commonly used in that language. As an example, consider the problem of generating encoding procedures that print assembly language.

- In C, the use of void * can be made to fit the interfaces defined by fprintf and sprintf.

  ```
  void (*asmprintf)(void *cl, const char *fmt, ...);
  void *asmprintfd;  /* first arg to asmprintf */
  ```

  The variable asmprintf can point to fprintf or to sprintf, as well as to other functions. To avoid passing extra arguments to encoding procedures, asmprintf and asmprintfd are global variables. This choice is not just convenient; it enables the encoding procedures for binary and assembly language to have identical interfaces.
- In ML, one might expect to use a closure to print assembly language, but in practice, this is not idiomatic—most ML programmers would find it more natural to return a string, or perhaps a list or tree of strings.

– In Modula-3, one might expect to use an object with a print method, but in practice, Modula-3 programmers use a "writer" abstraction, making calls through the Wr interface.

The point of these examples is that language paradigm alone is not enough to determine the most idiomatic representation of abstractions. Two semantically similar abstractions might have different idiomatic representations, even in the same target language. Producing idiomatic code is difficult for the program generator. In asdlGen, for example, one of the hardest problems has been to hide differences between target-language idioms, even for a problem as seemingly straightfoward as printing.[4]

These details are language-dependent, and they may seem obscure or picky, but they matter because they are exposed at the interfaces between generated code and client code. For example, a Modula-3 programmer who is forced to use a "printing object" instead of a writer is also forced to write glue code by hand in order to exploit the rich support for writers found in the Modula-3 library. These kinds of requirements seem to call for very fine control over program generation.

4   Implementations

No program generator I have written or used does a great job providing multiple interfaces to generated code, in multiple languages. Still, my attempts have identified some questions for implementors to consider. Many of these questions revolve around intermediate representations that might be used inside a program generator.

– How many layers of intermediate representation should be inserted between the program-generation algorithm and the eventual emission of code?
– What should the intermediate representations look like? Should they represent the intersection of the target languages and interfaces, the union of the target languages and interfaces, or some abstraction of the target languages and interfaces? Or perhaps a combination?
– What intermediate representations can usefully be shared to generate code in different implementation languages?
– What intermediate representations can usefully be shared among program generators?

The Toolkit's implementation may suggest some answers, as discussed below.

The other important questions involve controlling interfaces to generated code. What in the program generator needs to be parameterized by the client's needs? How should these parameters be expressed? How can we control the complexity of a program generator that serves diverse clients?

---

[4] Private communication from Dan Wang, 21 May 2000.

4.1   Implementation of the Toolkit

The Toolkit has two implementations. The original, official implementation was written in Icon (Griswold and Griswold 1996). We chose Icon because it was an excellent match for the central problems of our original decoder generator; Icon's evaluation model made it easy to write backtracking, heuristic searches for good decoders, and Icon's string facilities made it easy to write preprocessors. As we added support for multiple languages and for alternative interfaces, and as the program generators grew more complex, Icon's lack of static typing and lack of modules made the implementation more and more unwieldy, and finally intractable. Icon was a poor match for handling the pragmatic aspects of program generation, the importance of which we had underestimated.

I undertook a new implementation of the Toolkit in Standard ML, where I could exploit static typing, polymorphism, and parameterized modules. I had two goals: write new, clean implementations of the algorithms, so we could add improvements, and build a serious infrastructure to support the pragmatic aspects of program generation. I have used the infrastructure not only for the Toolkit, but also for the λ-RTL project (Ramsey and Davidson 1998). I have been disappointed in the results, and I would not recommend that anyone use either my Icon code or my ML code. The rest of this section explains why.

4.2   The Icon Toolkit: Trees and Templates

Because Icon is a dynamically typed language, boundaries between intermediate representations are not precise or formal, but they can still be identified.

The program generator reads a machine description and produces equations relating abstract machine instructions and binary representations. The encoder generator uses an equation solver (Ramsey 1996) to compute the binary representation as a function of an abstraction. The decoder generator uses the same equation solver to compute the values of pattern variables (e.g., arguments to abstract constructors) in terms of the binary. Both the inputs to and outputs from the solver are expressed in a simple expression language. Most expressions are represented as trees, but to simplify the solver, linear combinations are represented as tables in which the keys are expressions and the values are coefficients. The equation solver is critical to the program generator's job, but it was a mistake to let the needs of the solver warp the representation of expressions used throughout the entire generator.

The program generators use the solver's expressions to create statements. The encoder generator uses relatively few statements: sequences, conditionals (for conditional assembly), case statements (for analyzing abstract effective addresses), and token emission. There are also statements that announce errors and emit relocation information. The decoder generator uses a greater variety of expressions, statements, and miscellaneous constructs. Additions include range tests, blocks with local variables, assignments, declarations of initialized data (arrays of names of instructions matched), comments, and line-number directives (`#line`). Many of these statements would be useful in a general-purpose

```
procedure emit_create_instance_body(pp, cons)
  a := []
  every i := inputs_of(cons).name do
    put(a, template_to_list("instance-assignment.t", "l", i, "r", i,
                            "name", Cnoreserve(cons.name)))
  emit_template(pp, "create-instance-body.t",
                    "safename", Cnoreserve(cons.name),
                    "name", cons.name, "type", cons.type.name,
                    "args", arg_decls(cons), "assignments", a,
                    "class", if \indirectname then "static " else "",
                    "input-tests", input_width_tests(cons))
  return
end
```

Fig. 1. Code that Instantiates an Encoding-Procedure Template

infrastructure for program generation; some would not. Identifying a good set of statements for general-purpose use is a significant unsolved problem, as is how best to extend such a set for use in any particular program generator.

The next layer of program generator, like the solver, is shared by the encoder generator and decoder generator. It converts expressions, statements, and directives into a "prettyprinting stream," which is represented as a string containing target-language code and embedded escape sequences. The escape sequences direct the insertion of indentation and line breaks; the interface is based on Pugh and Sinofsky (1987). The conversion happens in two stages. First, trees (and tables) are converted to prettyprinting streams. Second, prettyprinting streams are inserted into code templates, which can be thought of as prettyprinting streams with "holes." Both the encoder generator and the decoder generator convert trees, but only the encoder generator uses templates. The module that converts trees to C is 330 lines of Icon; the converter to Modula-3 is 243 lines. The encoder generator uses about 20 templates, which are 1–5 lines of code each.

Here, for example, is the template for an applicative encoding procedure, which returns a value of an abstract type representing an "instance" of an instruction.

```
%{class}%{type}_Instance %safename(%args) {$t
%{type}_Instance _i = { %{name}_TAG };
%{input-tests}%{assignments}return _i;$b
}
```

The % signs mark holes that are to be instantiated. The marks $t (tab) and $b (backtab) are escape sequences that control prettyprinting. Figure 1 shows the code that uses the template to emit an encoding procedure. The parameter cons contains information about the constructor being emitted. Each assignment to an instance variable is created by instantiating the instance-assignment.t template, which contains the string "_i.u.%name.%l = %r;." The functions `template_to_list` and `emit_template` instantiate templates; they are generated automatically by a single-use program generator. The function `Cnoreserve` mangles the name of the instruction to insure that it that doesn't collide with any of C's reserved words. The flag `indirectname` controls the visibility of the generated procedure. If the encoding procedure is intended to be called indirectly, through a function pointer, it is made `static`, so it won't be visible outside the generated compilation unit. Otherwise, it is exported.

The final step in program generation is to run the prettyprinter.

4.3   The ML Toolkit: A More Abstract Infrastructure

Rewriting the Toolkit in ML made it possible to separate intermediate forms explicitly, and to enforce that separation using ML's type and modules systems. Out of desire to enforce the separation, I abandoned templates, since all templates would have the same type.[5]

The ML implementation introduced an explicit representation of types in generated code. The representation includes all the types I could think of using in any target language: integers (signed and unsigned, and of arbitrary widths), Booleans, strings, characters, records, arrays, both safe and unsafe unions, functions, pointers, named abstract types, instances of machine instructions or effective addresses, a unit type (equivalent to C's `void`), and objects with inheritance. Integer types can be made "relocatable;" values of relocatable types have later binding times than values of ordinary integer types. By including both general-purpose types and Toolkit-specific types, I prevented intermediate forms from proliferating, but I also made the infrastructure harder to reuse. Were I to repeat the experiment, I might try to separate these two layers, but avoid duplication, by using some form of polymorphic extension, analogous to the "tower" of term representations used in Steele (1994).

As does the Icon implementation, the ML implementation uses a unique constructor for each operator in the term language. For example, left shift is represented not by a general "apply" node, but by a special `SHIFT` node. This representation made it easier to write the equation solver and algebraic simplifier, but it makes tree walking tedious. Accordingly, tree-walking functions are generated automatically by another single-use program generator. This generator also creates the type definitions for expressions, and functions that type-check expressions, rewrite trees, substitute for identifiers, and convert trees to LISP-like symbolic expressions. Unlike the Icon representation, the ML representation is not warped by the equation solver; although the equation solver requires ordered linear combinations (Derman and Van Wyk 1984), they are used only within the solver, which requires about 30 lines of code to convert back and forth.

Expressions are embedded in statements, which also represent a union of target-language facilities. For example, they are translatable into C statements or ML expressions. They include general-purpose assignments, conditionals, case

---

[5] In the ML implementation, the type of a prettyprinting stream is `PP.pretty`, and the type of a template would be `(string * PP.pretty) list -> PP.pretty`.

statements, block comments and commented statements, nested blocks with local variables, return statements, and an empty statement. They also include many special-purpose statements that are useful only in the context of the Toolkit, include statements that emit a token, discriminate on an abstract instruction, branch to an arm of a matching statement, etc.

Statements are included in procedure definitions. The program-generation abstraction can declare and define not only procedures, but also types, variables, constants, and exceptions. Declarations are collected into *interfaces*; definitions are collected into *implementations*, which import and export interfaces. Both interfaces and implementations can be parameterized. The interface abstraction has special-purpose values that represent hand-written code, including an encoding library, standard I/O, support for emitting assembly language, a sign-extension routine, and other miscellany.

The emitters for C and for ML are about 600 and 800 lines, respectively, or about double the size of the emitters in the Icon implementation. These numbers are probably affected most by the change of implementation language, by the larger domain of the new emitters (not just expressions and statements but also types, interfaces, and implementations), and by the elimination of templates, which can emit prettyprinted code very concisely.

5   Conclusions and Lessons Learned

Authors of program generators should explore not only the design space of possible generated code, but the design space of possible interfaces to that code. It is too easy to make mistakes if one does not know what interfaces clients will need. Were I to attempt another reusable program generator, I would undertake discount usability tests (Nielsen 1993) with potential users. ("Please write on the board the code you would like to use to exploit my new frobozz generator.") Until then, it is possible to draw a few conclusions about implementations.

5.1   Prettyprinting

Prettyprinting engines are well studied; optimal methods that use dynamic programming have long been known (Oppen 1980), and the problem is a favorite of functional programmers (Hughes 1995Wadler 1999). The maturity of this technology might lure an implementor into thinking it is easy to apply, but in practice there does not appear to be a well-established body of knowledge on how to exploit prettyprinting engines to produce readable, idiomatic results. I have found little discussion of techniques or alternatives, but Baecker and Marcus (1990) does survey previous work and present suggestions for C, and Blaschek and Sametinger (1989) presents a prettyprinter designed to be adapted to different conventions.

The difficulty of producing readable output can be exacerbated by idiosyncratic characteristics of automatically generated code. For example, the λ-RTL translator uses the Toolkit's infrastructure to generate RTL-creation procedures.

These procedures are like encoding procedures, but they emit the register-transfer lists (RTLs) that are used as intermediate code in the optimizer vpo (Benitez and Davidson 1988). Creating these RTLs requires function calls that are nested more deeply than calls C programmers typically write by hand, and the prettyprinted code is very difficult to read.

In the interests of parsimony, the original Toolkit translates directly from its intermediate form to target-language prettyprinting streams. This design has made it surprisingly difficult to get code that is well prettyprinted; for example, the output from the Toolkit still contains occasional unwanted newlines. A better design would separate the problem of translating into the target language from the problem of prettyprinting the target language. For example, one might introduce yet another intermediate form, to represent code in the target programming language. Dan Wang, implementor of `asdlGen`, reports satisfactory experience with this sort of design.[6] The ML implementation of the Toolkit takes a few steps in this direction; it has special intermediate forms to represent C types and ML pattern matches, for example.

Although adding an intermediate form for each target language might seem superficially unattractive, it does offer advantages. For example, type checking in the program generator might prevent one from generating syntatically incorrect code, as Thiemann (2000) demonstrates for HTML. Another advantage is the possibility of reusing the intermediate form and its prettyprinter in multiple program generators.

Some existing prettyprinting engines are limited, so program generators may not be able to use them without modification. For example, the original Toolkit's prettyprinter required a special hack to enable it to insert `#line` in column 1. One reason the original Toolkit does not emit macros for encoding is that its prettyprinter cannot easily escape internal newlines with backslashes.

5.2   Intermediate Representations

The original Toolkit tried to minimize the number of different intermediate representations used in the program generators. A single representation of expressions is used to solve equations, to simplify expressions, and to emit code. That representation is mapped directly to strings with prettyprinting escapes, with no abstract representation of the target programming language. These choices made it difficult to adjust the output of the program generator, and they make it unlikely that any of the code can be used in another program generator. Most of the choices have been repeated in the second implementation, with similar results.

The Toolkit's intermediate representations are "union languages," containing all the features that might be used from each target language. This design simplifies high levels of the program generator, but it can make the emitters larger and more complex. For example, the intermediate representation includes record-valued expressions and safe unions. Because these constructs cannot be

---

[6] Private communication, 1998.

expressed in C, they must be rewritten in terms of record variables and unsafe unions; the rewriter is another 300 lines of ML.

Intersection languages have the advantage of simplicity. Because the intersection language is a subset of every target language (for generated code), it is easy to write emitters. If the source language is an intersection language, as is ASDL, it is easy for users to predict the results of program generation. But intersection languages may make it harder to generate idiomatic, readable code; natural idioms in the target language may not be expressible directly in the intersection language. Also, users may chafe at restrictions imposed by the use of intersection languages; after all, while the author of a program generator may want to support multiple languages, any single user may be interested in just one language. For example, one of my biggest frustrations in using ASDL to create ML code was not having Booleans or characters built in. All I wanted was to save and restore my compiler's intermediate codes, and I was furious to have to write crippled ML code just because (in my perception) C doesn't have Booleans. Other users report similar frustrations.[7]

In the ML implementation of the Toolkit, I tried to build a reusable infrastructure for program generation. Although I successfully used the infrastructure a second time, I consider it a failed experiment. It is always difficult to learn from negative results, but here are the most pressing concerns I would try to address in another attempt.

- The intermediate form tries to generalize over many target languages. This choice makes the code-generation interfaces large and complex, without clear benefit.
- The intermediate form intermixes general-purpose and special-purpose constructs promiscuously. There should be a single, extensible representation for general-purpose constructs, which would then be extended with special-purpose constructs. Therefore not only should the intermediate-tree datatype be extensible; all the language-dependent emitters should also be extensible.
- A program generator needs to walk intermediate trees both in ways that are unaware of the semantics of particular operators (e.g., to find free variables) and in ways that are aware of the semantics of particular operators (e.g., to perform algebraic simplification). In today's programming languages, it is difficult to choose a representation that makes both kinds of tree walks simple. I tried to address this problem by using program generation for one set of tree walks (the set that is unaware of operators' semantics), but the results are baroque. This problem warrants further investigation.
- I would use an explicit, abstract representation of each target language, and I would create prettyprinters to work with those representations, not with my general-purpose intermediate form. At least the prettyprinters would almost certainly be reused.
- Both the ML and C emitters contain special-purpose transducers. Since these appear to be needed even when using a big union language, I would be tempted to try a small intersection language.

---

[7] Private communication from Dan Wang, May 2000.

– I abandoned code templates because I thought a fully abstract tree representation would be more principled and easier to port. But in the implementation of a program generator, templates are *much* easier to read, understand, and change than is code that emits code. And it is hard to design an abstraction that really works for multiple target languages. So I would try to find a solution that offered more of the clarity and simplicity of templates, even if the porting cost were greater.

5.3   Controlling Interfaces

Instantiating code templates by textual substitution has no semantic basis, making it almost impossible to detect and report errors in terms of the original sources. But templates not only simplify life for the implementor; they can also make things easier for the clients. Because it uses code templates, the interface to the Toolkit's decoder generator is very simple. In combination with the matching statements, the templates make the decoder generator easy and pleasant to use.

The contrast with the Toolkit's encoder generator is shocking. The problem is how to control all the potential variations: applicative vs. imperative, direct vs. indirect, objects vs. closures, etc. Command-line options, and probably also configuration variables, are too complex. The complexity makes a mess of documentation and intimidates users. A fixed interface is no better; for example, the fixed interfaces of code generated by Yacc and Lex make it hard to have multiple lexers or parsers in one application. The need for simple, clear ways of controlling interfaces to generated code may be the most pressing problem identified in this paper.

Acknowledgments

In this paper, the first-person plural describes joint work with Mary Fernández, co-creator of the New Jersey Machine-Code Toolkit. Thanks to Dan Wang for comments on the paper and for many vigorous discussions about ASDL. Thanks to Dave Hanson for his analysis of ASDL, and for suggesting using distinct codes for all enumerations. I borrowed the terms *heterogeneous* and *homogeneous* from Odersky and Wadler (1997). Comments from the program committee, and especially the many questions asked by reviewer 3, have helped me improve the paper. My work on the Toolkit and on other program generators has been supported by a Fannie and John Hertz Fellowship, an AT&T PhD Fellowship, Bellcore, Bell Labs, DARPA Contract MDA904-97-C-0247, and NSF Grants ASC-9612756 and CCR-9733974.

References

Aho, Alfred V. and Steve C. Johnson. 1974 (June). LR parsing. *Computing Surveys*, 6(2):99–124.

Appel, Andrew W. and David B. MacQueen. 1991 (August). Standard ML of New Jersey. In Wirsing, Martin, editor, *Third Int'l Symp. on Prog. Lang. Implementation and Logic Programming*, pages 1–13, New York.

Auslander, Joel, Matthai Philipose, Craig Chambers, Susan Eggers, and Brian Bershad. 1996 (May). Fast, effective dynamic compilation. *Proceedings of the ACM SIGPLAN '96 Conference on Programming Language Design and Implementation, in SIGPLAN Notices*, 31(5):149–159.

Baecker, Ronald M. and Aaron Marcus. 1990. *Human Factors and Typography for More Readable Programs*. Reading, MA: Addison-Wesley.

Benitez, Manuel E. and Jack W. Davidson. 1988 (July). A portable global optimizer and linker. *Proceedings of the ACM SIGPLAN '88 Conference on Programming Language Design and Implementation, in SIGPLAN Notices*, 23(7):329–338.

Blaschek, Günther and Johannes Sametinger. 1989 (July). User-adaptable prettyprinting. *Software—Practice & Experience*, 19(7):687–702.

Braun, Owen C. 1996 (May). Retargetability issues in worst-case timing analysis of embedded systems. Bachelor's thesis, Dept of Computer Science, Princeton University.

Bumbulis, Peter and Donald D. Cowan. 1993 (March). RE2C: A more versatile scanner generator. *ACM Letters on Programming Languages and Systems*, 2(4):70–84.

Cifuentes, Cristina, Mike van Emmerik, and Norman Ramsey. 1999 (October). The design of a resourceable and retargetable binary translator. In *Proceedings of the Working Conference on Reverse Engineering (WCRE'99)*, pages 280–291. IEEE CS Press.

Davidson, J. W. and C. W. Fraser. 1984 (October). Code selection through object code optimization. *ACM Transactions on Programming Languages and Systems*, 6(4):505–526.

Dean, Jeffrey, Greg DeFouw, David Grove, Vassily Litvinov, and Craig Chambers. 1996 (October). Vortex: An optimizing compiler for object-oriented languages. *OOPSLA '96 Conference Proceedings, in SIGPLAN Notices*, 31(10):83–100.

DeRemer, Frank and Thomas Pennello. 1982 (October). Efficient computation of LALR(1) look-ahead sets. *ACM Transactions on Programming Languages and Systems*, 4(4):615–649.

Derman, Emanuel and Christopher Van Wyk. 1984 (December). A simple equation solver and its application to financial modelling. *Software—Practice & Experience*, 14(12):1169–1181.

Engler, Dawson R. 1996 (May). VCODE: a retargetable, extensible, very fast dynamic code generation system. *Proceedings of the ACM SIGPLAN '96 Conference on Programming Language Design and Implementation, in SIGPLAN Notices*, 31(5):160–170.

Fernández, Mary F. 1995 (June). Simple and effective link-time optimization of Modula-3 programs. *Proceedings of the ACM SIGPLAN '95 Conference on Programming Language Design and Implementation,* in *SIGPLAN Notices,* 30(6):103–115.

Fraser, Christopher W. and David R. Hanson. 1995. *A Retargetable C Compiler: Design and Implementation.* Redwood City, CA: Benjamin/Cummings.

Fraser, Christopher W., Robert R. Henry, and Todd A. Proebsting. 1992 (April). BURG—fast optimal instruction selection and tree parsing. *SIGPLAN Notices,* 27(4):68–76.

Gray, Robert W. 1988 (June). γ-GLA: A generator for lexical analyzers that programmers can use. In *Proceedings of the Summer USENIX Conference,* pages 147–160, Berkeley, CA, USA.

Griswold, Ralph E. and Madge T. Griswold. 1996. *The Icon Programming Language.* Third edition. San Jose, CA: Peer-to-Peer Communications.

Hanson, David R. 1996. *C Interfaces and Implementations.* Benjamin/Cummings.

————. 1999 (April). Early experience with ASDL in lcc. *Software—Practice & Experience,* 29(5):417–435. See also Technical Report MSR-TR-98-50, Microsoft Research.

Hughes, John. 1995. The design of a pretty-printing library. In Jeuring, J. and E. Meijer, editors, *Advanced Functional Programming,* Vol. 925 of *LNCS.* Springer Verlag.

Hunt, Andrew and David Thomas. 1999. *The Pragmatic Programmer: From Journeyman to Master.* Reading, MA: Addison-Wesley.

Johnson, Steve C. 1975. Yacc—yet another compiler compiler. Technical Report 32, Computer Science, AT&T Bell Laboratories, Murray Hill, New Jersey.

Larus, James R. and Eric Schnarr. 1995 (June). EEL: machine-independent executable editing. *Proceedings of the ACM SIGPLAN '95 Conference on Programming Language Design and Implementation,* in *SIGPLAN Notices,* 30(6):291–300.

Lee, Peter and Mark Leone. 1996 (May). Optimizing ML with run-time code generation. *Proceedings of the ACM SIGPLAN '96 Conference on Programming Language Design and Implementation,* in *SIGPLAN Notices,* 31(5):137–148.

Lesk, M. E. and E. Schmidt. 1975. Lex — A lexical analyzer generator. Computer Science Technical Report 39, Bell Laboratories, Murray Hill, NJ.

Liskov, Barbara and John Guttag. 1986. *Abstraction and Specification in Program Development.* MIT Press / McGraw-Hill.

Nielsen, Jakob. 1993. *Usability Engineering.* Boston, MA: Academic Press.

Odersky, Martin and Philip Wadler. 1997. Pizza into Java: Translating theory into practice. In *Conference Record of the 24th Annual ACM Symposium on Principles of Programming Languages,* pages 146–159. ACM SIGACT and SIGPLAN, ACM Press.

Oppen, Derek C. 1980 (October). Prettyprinting. *ACM Transactions on Programming Languages and Systems,* 2(4):465–483.

Proebsting, Todd A. 1992 (June). Simple and efficient BURS table generation. *Proceedings of the ACM SIGPLAN '92 Conference on Programming Language Design and Implementation,* in *SIGPLAN Notices,* 27(6):331–340.

Pugh, William W. and Steven J. Sinofsky. 1987 (January). A new language-independent prettyprinting algorithm. Technical Report TR 87-808, Cornell University.

Ramsey, Norman. 1994 (January). Correctness of trap-based breakpoint implementations. In *Proceedings of the 21st ACM Symposium on the Principles of Programming Languages*, pages 15–24, Portland, OR.

———. 1996 (April). A simple solver for linear equations containing nonlinear operators. *Software—Practice & Experience*, 26(4):467–487.

Ramsey, Norman and Jack W. Davidson. 1998 (June). Machine descriptions to build tools for embedded systems. In *ACM SIGPLAN Workshop on Languages, Compilers, and Tools for Embedded Systems (LCTES'98)*, Vol. 1474 of *LNCS*, pages 172–188. Springer Verlag.

———. 1999 (December). Specifying instructions' semantics using λ-RTL (interim report). See http://www.cs.virginia.edu/zephyr/csdl/lrtlindex.html.

Ramsey, Norman and Mary F. Fernández. 1995 (January). The New Jersey Machine-Code Toolkit. In *Proceedings of the 1995 USENIX Technical Conference*, pages 289–302, New Orleans, LA.

Ramsey, Norman and David R. Hanson. 1992 (July). A retargetable debugger. *ACM SIGPLAN '92 Conference on Programming Language Design and Implementation*, in *SIGPLAN Notices*, 27(7):22–31.

Stallman, Richard M. 1992 (February). *Using and Porting GNU CC (Version 2.0)*. Free Software Foundation.

Steele, Jr., Guy L. 1994. Building interpreters by composing monads. In ACM, editor, *Conference Record of the 21st Annual ACM Symposium on Principles of Programming Languages*, pages 472–492, New York, NY, USA.

Thiemann, Peter. 2000 (January). Modeling HTML in Haskell. In Pontelli, Enrico and Vítor Santos Costa, editors, *Practical Aspects of Declarative Languages (PADL 2000)*, Vol. 1753 of *LNCS*, pages 263–277. Berlin: Springer.

Wadler, Philip. 1999. A prettier printer. Unpublished note available from the author's Web site.

Waite, William M. 1986 (May). The cost of lexical analysis. *Software—Practice & Experience*, 16(5):473–488.

Wang, Daniel C., Andrew W. Appel, Jeff L. Korn, and Christopher S. Serra. 1997 (October). The Zephyr Abstract Syntax Description Language. In *Proceedings of the 2nd USENIX Conference on Domain-Specific Languages*, pages 213–227, Santa Barbara, CA.

Type-Based Useless-Code Elimination
for Functional Programs
Position Paper

Stefano Berardi[1], Mario Coppo[1], Ferruccio Damiani[1], and Paola Giannini[2]

[1] Dipartimento di Informatica, Università di Torino
Corso Svizzera 185, 10149 Torino, Italy
[2] DISTA, Università del Piemonte Orientale
Corso Borsalino 54, 15100 Alessandria, Italy
{stefano,coppo,damiani,giannini}@di.unito.it
http://www.di.unito.it/~lambda

Abstract. In this paper we present a survey of the work on type-based useless-code elimination for higher-order functional programs. After some historical remarks on the motivations and early approaches we give an informal but complete account of the techniques and results developed at the Computer Science Department of the University of Torino. In particular, we focus on the fact that, for each of the type-based techniques developed, there is an optimal program simplification.

1 Useless-Code Elimination for Higher-Order Programs: Motivations, First Attempts

By static *useless-code elimination (UCE)* (which we improperly called *dead-code elimination* in some earlier papers) we mean detecting and removing, at compile time, those parts of a program that do not contribute to the final output of the program.

Considering a functional programming language with a call-by-name evaluation strategy we can distinguish two kinds of useless code that are exemplified by the following. Take the expression $\mathsf{prj}_1\langle M, N\rangle$, where $\langle -, -\rangle$ is the pair formation operator and prj_1 is the projection on the first component

- the operations prj_1 and $\langle -, -\rangle$ are *useless* code since they could be eliminated without influencing the final output of the program,
- the expression N, instead, is *dead* code since it will never be evaluated.

Obviously dead code is also useless, but not vice-versa. The removal of dead code produces a reduction in the size of a program. The removal of useless code may also reduce its evaluation time.

The same concepts can be defined also for call-by-value functional languages (like ML). Under call-by-value, useless code is more time wasting, since there is less dead code. In fact, an expression like N in the above example is evaluated

W. Taha (Ed.): SAIG 2000, LNCS 1924, pp. 172–189, 2000.

and therefore it is not dead but only useless (assuming that N is terminating and does not produce side-effects).

Typically, useless code is introduced when programs are generated in some indirect way, like translation from constructive proofs to programs, or when we do intensive reusing of libraries of subprograms. In general, it is undecidable whether a piece of code is useless or not, yet we may detect useless code in many interesting subcases. In this paper we describe a type-based technique for useless-code elimination.

It is difficult to trace back the beginning of any scientific idea. This is particularly true for type-based approaches to useless-code detection in higher-order programs. At least two different communities, mostly unaware of each others, worked in parallel on this topic: people working on logical frameworks, and people working on functional programming languages. Yet, the results they got were somehow related. In this section we will sketch the background for the logical framework community up to the early nineties. We will also compare it to the background of functional languages community in the same period.

To our knowledge, the first to think about useless code in computation were the logicians Troelstra and Kreisel in the seventies, see [30,19]. Their goal (motivating the logical framework community even today) was translating constructive proofs of a given formula A, i.e., proofs not using the excluded middle rule, into a program P, "realizing" what the formula A says. For instance, a proof of

$$F \;=\; \forall l_1 : \mathsf{list}.\exists l_2 : \mathsf{list}.(l_2 \text{ is a sorted version of } l_1)$$

should be translated into a program $SORT\colon (\mathsf{list} \to \mathsf{list})$, sorting lists. A mechanical translation is easy to define: constructive formal proofs are lambda terms, and they may be interpreted as functional program just by simplifying mathematical formulas to types[1]. Troelstra remarked that such a translation produced programs with plenty of useless code. In the example of the sorting map, from a proof of F you get a program generating both a sorted list and *a proof that such a list is sorted*. In [30], Troelstra defined a "modified realizability": a translation from proofs to programs encompassing the first algorithm to detect and remove useless code. We only mention here that a proof was turned into a vector of programs, and useless code, when present, was represented by the empty vector. We emphasize that Troelstra approach was not intended to be used as an algorithm, but rather, it was intended to be a guideline for people interested in turning, case-by-case, a proof into a program.

In 1980, Beeson [2] designed (still on paper) an updated version of Troelstra "realizability". Around 1985, Mohring [23,22] started to implement it in the system Coq [29]. Coq is a system designed to develop formal proofs in an interactive way, and extract programs out of them. In Mohring's work there was a major improvement with respect to Troelstra's idea: types were split into two classes, Spec, the types of (possibly) useful code, and Prop, the types of (surely) useless

---

[1] Here is the complete inductive definition of a forgetting map from first order formulas to types: $|a|$ (any atomic formula) $= U$ (a singleton type), $|A \to B| = |A| \to |B|$, $|A\&B| = |A| \times |B|$, $|\forall x : \sigma B| = \sigma \to |B|$, $|\exists x : \sigma B| = \sigma \times |B|$.

code. Each type, say the type int of integers, had two versions: a useful one, int : Spec, and a useless one, int : Prop. Detecting useless code meant to assign a type in Prop to a given subexpression in a type-consistent way. Since then, all type-based algorithms detecting useless code work in this way.

Implementation needs forced many compromises, with respect to Troelstra's original idea. In the original Coq system each variable had just one type. Thus, there was no way of having a variable with type int : Spec (useful) on some occurrence and int : Prop (useless) on some other occurrence. If a variable was marked as useful on some occurrence, this marking propagated on every other occurrence of the same variable. This forced, by a chain effect, to mark as useful many more expressions than one should have. A natural solution is to consider int : Spec a subtype of int : Prop, hence allowing a variable to have type int : Spec as its principal type, yet the same variable could have type int : Prop on some occurrences. The main difference with Troelstra approach, however, was the fact that detecting useless code was *not* automatic: the user had to add the markings Prop and Spec on each type by hand.

Manual marking had the advantage of making the user aware of the program hidden in a proof at each stage of the design of the proof itself. Yet, adding Prop and Spec everywhere was quite cumbersome. This motivated a work by Takayama, see [28], who wrote down in detail the algorithm implicit in the modified realizability, as presented in Goad's thesis, see [16]. Takayama discovered that the algorithm removed some useless code, but it produced also an exponential duplication of useful code! As we said, Troelstra had not in mind a practical algorithm.

By building over the work of Takayama, Berardi, see [3,4,5], designed an extension of Mohring's marking, including subtyping and an algorithm to detect and remove automatically useless code. This algorithm was afterwards improved by the other authors of this paper, see [9]. The major contribution of this line of work was the proof that, there are *optimal* markings which allow to detect the maximum amount of useless code. Such optimal markings may be computed in linear time in the proof that the original program is well typed. As expected, if we erase the expressions that are marked as useless, we get a program which has the same input/output behaviour of the original one.

In the meanwhile, people in the functional language community started to study the same topic under the name of *useless variable elimination*. This was part of a general interest in compilation techniques and transformation algorithms for functional programs. Apparently, they were unaware of the work of the logical framework community, and they started studying the topic from scratch. From that period (late '80, beginning of '90) we quote Shivers thesis [27] (about control-flow analysis in SCHEME), introducing a useless-variable elimination technique which is essentially a simplified version of Mohring's marking mechanism, with markings on variables rather than on types. This method is less general, because markings on types may describe several intermediate steps between a useful and a useless variable: a variable v of type int × int × int, that is, a tuple of 3 integers, may be marked in $2^3 = 8$ different times if we mark types. The marking on each occurrence of int tells us whether the corresponding component of v is useful or not. We may, instead, mark v only in two ways if we put the marking directly on v. This means that we may only express whether v is useful or not, and, in this latter case, we are forced to keep each component of v, even if some are not used.

The technique described in [27] is based on control flow analysis and works for higher-order untyped functional programs. This approach has been recently reformulated and proved correct in [31]. Being based on control flow analysis, this method has, in the worst case, cubic time cost.

The imperative language compiler community has also been working on UCE for a long time using essentially data flow analysis techniques, and most compiler textbooks contains sections on this topic [1,32] (see also [21]). The algorithms developed in this framework do not handle higher-order functions, but they handle inlining. Some of the simple examples considered in this paper would be handled by an imperative compiler with inlining (β-reduction). Of course, careful tuned heuristics are needed to guide the inlining process. On the other hand, more complex examples, like the one in Section 2.2, require different techniques, like those described in this paper.

2   Basic Technique for Type-Based UCE

We give here a short introduction of the type based technique for useless-code elimination. Our aim is to give the basic ideas underlying the use of type inference techniques in useless-code analysis. We present the system in its simplest (and less powerful) form. In the next section we introduce a number of extensions that lead to more powerful analyses.

A type system is designed to associate to each component (subterm) M of a program a *type* that represents a property of the meaning of M. The association of types to terms is controlled by a formal set of *typing rules* which are an essential part of the type system. Types are built from a set of *basic* types representing the primitive properties we want to talk about and closed under a set of *type constructors* corresponding to the data structures of the language. In our case we are talking of core functional languages containing the integer numbers and the basic operations of λ-abstraction, application, conditional and fixpoint. Therefore we assume that the basic data type constructor is the function space constructor $\rightarrow$[2].

Types are designed to represent properties related to the classification of meanings as sets of values. For instance, int represents the property of being a integer number and int $\rightarrow$ int that of being a function from values of type int to values of type int. If we choose to take other primitive properties, we get type systems which are suitable to reason about other properties of the language. The types intended in this more general sense are often called in the literature

---

[2] The extension to other data structures, like pairs and algebraic datatypes, has been considered, for instance, in [9,11].

annotated (see [20]) or *non-standard* (see [17]) types. We will call them simply types.

Take a core functional language (a λ-calculus with constants) with a call-by-name evaluation strategy. In the case of useless-code analysis we consider two basic types:

1. δ representing the property of subterms whose values *may* influence the final output of the program, and
2. ω representing the property of subterms whose values *do not* influence the final output of the program.

The other types are build from δ, and ω using the "→" constructor in the usual way. For instance, a term M of type $\omega \to \delta$ is a term that produces an interesting result without using its input, i.e. a constant function.

We point out that the meaning of types is intended in a relative sense, depending on the context in which the term occurs[3]. For useless-code analysis we use the type information in the following way: we look for a proof that the program has type δ (or some other type representing usefulness), trying to assign type ω (i.e. "useless"), to some parts of it. The type inference rules prevent to do this in a non-consistent way.

Consider the term $P = (\lambda x.3)M$ (where M is any term) we can associate the following types to the subterms of P:

$$((\lambda x^{\omega}.3^{\delta})^{\omega \to \delta} M^{\omega})^{\delta} . \tag{1}$$

Informally the above decoration of P means that we can classify P to be useful (with type δ) assuming that both x and M are useless. Note that types match in the usual way: the term $\lambda x^{\omega}.3^{\delta}$ of type $\omega \to \delta$ is applied to the term M of type ω. The term P has also other decorations, like $((\lambda x^{\delta}.3^{\delta})^{\delta \to \delta} M^{\delta})^{\delta}$. However, the decoration (1) is the *optimal* one, since it allows to detect the maximum amount of useless code.

What we have presented so far does not depend on the fact the language considered is typed or not in the usual sense. However, there are strong motivations to apply the technique to typed languages instead of untyped ones.

1. On one hand, when the structure of the types considered becomes more complex allowing subtyping or other useful type constructors, like conjunction, the type checking can become very expensive and, in the case of conjunction also undecidable.
2. On the other, in general the underlying language is already a strongly typed language. This happens in the case of most functional languages (like ML) or when the program to optimize is extracted from a formal proof in a logical framework based on type theory.

---

[3] This notion of type is similar to the Hindley-Milner notion of polymorphism, where a term can have different types in different contexts.

In the following we assume that the underlying simply typed language has a unique base type int. In this case types δ and ω represent evaluation properties of terms of type int. A possible notation for this is to consider two variants int^δ and int^ω of int, where δ, and ω are now seen as *annotations* of type int^4. For ease of notation we will identify types and annotations, writing for instance $\omega \rightarrow \delta$ for $\text{int}^\omega \rightarrow \text{int}^\delta$. We also call this annotated types simply types, using sometimes the adjective *standard* when referring to types in the usual sense. If ϕ is an annotated type then $\epsilon(\phi)$ (the *underlying* type of ϕ) is the standard type obtained from ϕ by erasing its annotations.

We now give a quick account of our approach. For the complete formal development we refer to [13].

2.1   The Basic Inference System

For any standard type ρ let $\rho(\delta)$, $\rho(\omega)$ be the type defined by annotating each occurrence of int with δ, ω. Note that the arguments of a function whose result is useless are certainly useless: so if $\rho = \rho_1 \rightarrow \cdots \rightarrow \rho_n \rightarrow \text{int}$ all its annotations of the form $\phi_1 \rightarrow \cdots \rightarrow \phi_n \rightarrow \omega$ represent useless code and are semantically equivalent to $\rho(\omega)$. These types are called ω-*types*. In the following we always consider types modulo equivalence between ω-types.

We introduce a partial order relation between types defined by reflexivity and a unique axiom scheme

$$\begin{aligned}
&(\text{Ref}) \quad \phi \sqsubseteq \phi \\
&(\omega) \quad \quad \phi \sqsubseteq \rho(\omega) \quad (\epsilon(\phi) = \rho)
\end{aligned} \tag{2}$$

We assume that to each constant c in the language is associated a basic type $\tau(c)$. For instance, $\tau(+) = \delta \rightarrow \delta \rightarrow \delta$ meaning that to get a meaningful result out of a sum we have to use both its arguments. A type environment Σ is a set of assumptions of the shape $x : \phi$, where ϕ is consistent with the standard type of x. The type inference rules are given in Fig. 1. In the inference system we explicitly decorate each term with the type assigned to it, writing M^ϕ instead of the more usual notation $M : \phi$. In this way a decorated term codifies a deduction of its typing, keeping trace of the type assigned to all its subterms in the inference process. With M^ϕ we denote in general a completely decorated term. Note that to a term M of standard type ρ we can assign only types whose underlying type is ρ.

The inference rules are the standard ones except for the axioms (Var) and (Con) which allow to assign an ω-type to a variable or constants. It is easy to prove that this is enough to assign an ω-type to any term from any type environment, i.e. $\Sigma \vdash M^{\rho(\omega)}$ is provable for all type environments Σ.

If a variable x^ρ (where ρ denotes the standard type of x) does not occur in a term M the types of M do not depend on the assumption on x. In this case in a deduction $\Sigma \vdash M^\phi$ we can assume without loss of generality that the

---

[4] Alternatively we could consider δ and ω as *subtypes* of int

$$(\text{Var})\ \Sigma, x : \phi \vdash x^{\psi}\ \ (\phi \sqsubseteq \psi)$$

$$(\text{Con})\ \Sigma \vdash c^{\psi}\ \ (\tau(c) \sqsubseteq \psi)$$

$$(\to \text{I})\ \frac{\Sigma, x : \phi \vdash M^{\psi}}{\Sigma \vdash (\lambda x^{\phi}.M^{\psi})^{\phi \to \psi}} \qquad (\to \text{E})\ \frac{\Sigma \vdash M^{\phi \to \psi} \quad \Sigma \vdash N^{\phi}}{\Sigma \vdash (M^{\phi \to \psi} N^{\phi})^{\psi}}$$

$$(\text{Fix})\ \frac{\Sigma, x : \phi \vdash M^{\phi}}{\Sigma \vdash (\text{fix}\, x.M^{\phi})^{\phi}}$$

$$(\text{If})\ \frac{\Sigma \vdash N^{\delta} \quad \Sigma \vdash M_1{}^{\phi} \quad \Sigma \vdash M_2{}^{\phi}}{\Sigma \vdash (\text{ifz}\, N^{\delta}\, \text{then}\, M_1{}^{\phi}\, \text{else}\, M_2{}^{\phi})^{\phi}}$$

Fig. 1. Rules for Type Assignment

type assigned to x in Σ is an ω-type. The following rule is then derivable in the system:

$$(\to \text{I}')\ \frac{\Sigma \vdash M^{\psi}}{\Sigma \vdash (\lambda x^{\rho(\omega)}.M^{\psi})^{\rho(\omega) \to \psi}} \quad \text{if } x \text{ does not occur in } M$$

This principle combined with the fact that all terms have an ω-type is the basic tool of our analysis.

As an exercise use the inference rules to decorate the term

$$(\lambda x : \text{int} \to \text{int}.3)(\lambda y : \text{int}.(+\ y\ 2)) \tag{3}$$

in such a way that the type of the term is δ and that both x and $\lambda y : \text{int}.(+\ y\ 2)$ are decorated with type $\omega \to \omega$.

The analysis of the system requires the introduction of a semantics for the language. We assume a standard call-by-name operational semantics given along the lines of [24]. Let $\cong$ represent the ground observational equivalence induced by this semantics, i.e. defined by: $M \cong N$ iff, M, N have the same type ρ and for all context $\mathcal{C}[]$ of type int with a hole of type ρ capturing the free variables of M and N, $\mathcal{C}[M]$ and $\mathcal{C}[N]$ have the same value.

The soundness of the inference system is proved in [13]. A corollary of the soundness theorem, Theorem 6.3 of [13], that justifies the simplification algorithm, can be stated for closed terms in the following way.

Theorem 1 (Soundness of the Simplification). *Let M be a term of standard type ρ and $M^{\rho(\delta)}$ be the decorated version of M derived from the rules in Fig. 1. Then $M \cong M'$ where M' is any term obtained from M by replacing any subterm to which in $M^{\rho(\delta)}$ is assigned an ω-type with any other term of the same underlying type.*

For instance, referring to the example (3) we have that

$$(\lambda x : \text{int} \to \text{int}.3)(\lambda y : \text{int}.(+\ y\ 2)) \cong (\lambda x : \text{int} \to \text{int}.3)D$$

where D is any term of standard type int $\rightarrow$ int, for instance $\lambda y : $ int.0 or even a free variable.

Now, let M^ϕ be a decorated term in which ϕ is the final type assigned to M. There may be many decorations of M producing the same final type ϕ. Among these there is an *optimal* one in the following sense.

Theorem 2 (Optimal Decorations). *Let M a term of standard type ρ. Between the decorations of M with final type ϕ derivable from the rules of Fig. 1 there is an optimal one, M^ϕ, such that all subterms of M which have a non ω-type in M^ϕ have a non ω-type in any other decoration of M with final type ϕ derivable from the rules of Fig. 1.*

This means that, when $\phi = \rho(\delta)$, i.e. when we assume that the final result of the computation is useful, there is a maximum amount of useless code that can be detected by the inference system. Such code is represented by the subterms which have an ω-type in the optimal deduction of $M^{\rho(\delta)}$.

Theorem 1 justifies the following optimization algorithm.

Definition 1 (Simplification Mapping O$(-)$). *Let M a term of standard type ρ, and let $M^{\rho(\delta)}$ be an (optimal) decoration of M with final type $\rho(\delta)$. Then $O(M)$ in the term obtained from M by erasing in $M^{\rho(\delta)}$:*

- *all subterms having an ω-type,*
- *all λ-abstractions binding a variable with an ω-type, and*
- *all standard subtypes whose annotation is an ω-type.*

It is proved, Theorem 6.10 of [13], that the transformation is well defined and preserves the final type of the term. As a consequence of the soundness theorem and of the well-foundedness of the transformation $O(-)$ we have that $O(M)$ is observationally equivalent to M. For example (omitting some types in the decoration):

$$O(((\underline{\lambda x^{\omega \rightarrow \omega}}.3^\delta)\underline{^{(\omega \rightarrow \omega) \rightarrow \delta}}\underline{(\lambda y^\omega.(+\ y\ 3))^{\omega \rightarrow \omega}})^\delta) = 3$$

where we have underlined the components of the term erased by the transformation $O(-)$. Note that the transformation O can change (simplify) the types of internal subterms.

There is an algorithm to find optimal decorations. We describe it through an example.

Assume that we want to decorate the term

$$N \;=\; (\lambda x : \text{int} \rightarrow \text{int}.(x(\text{succ}\ 1)))(\lambda y : \text{int}.3)$$

in which succ represent the successor function. We go through the following steps.

1. Build a decoration schema of the term, in which each type variable corresponds to an occurrence of the type int. For each occurrence of a term

variable or of a constant we use a fresh set type variables. The decoration scheme for N would be the following:

$$((\lambda x^{a\to b}.(x^{\overline{a_1}\to b_1}(\mathsf{succ}^{\overline{\overline{c}}\to d}\ 1^{\overline{\overline{e}}})^{\overline{\overline{d}}})^{b_1})^{(\overline{a\to b})\to b_1}(\lambda y^f.3^g)^{\overline{f\to g}})^{b_1}\ .$$

Here we have tagged in the same way the types that must match in the applications of $(\to E)$.

2. Write a set of equations corresponding to the type matching required by rule $(\to E)$. In the example this correspond to equate the types with the same tag. Since the term is well typed (in the sense of standard types) this requires a one-one correspondence of the variables occurring in the schemes involved in the applications. For N we get, writing equations from left to right, the following set.

$$\mathcal{E}_1 = \{c = e, a_1 = d, a = f, b = g, \}$$

3. Now add the equations that force all type schemes associated to the same term variable to be equal and all constants to have standard annotations. However, in doing this we must take into account that rules (Var) and (Con) allow to assign also ω-types to variables and constants. We then introduce the notion of *guarded* set of equations, which is an expression of the form $\{a\} \Rightarrow \mathcal{E}$ where a is a type variable and $\mathcal{E}$ a set of equations. Its meaning is that the equations in $\mathcal{E}$ are meaningful only if $a = \delta$. The guard that controls the set of equations $\mathcal{E}$ obtained by equating the scheme θ' associated to an occurrence of a term variable x with the scheme θ assigned to x in its abstraction is the rightmost variable of θ'. Such variable determines whether θ' will be instantiated to an ω-type or not. Similarly for constants. In the case of our example we get this set of guarded sets of equations:

$$\mathcal{E}_2 = \{\{b_1\} \Rightarrow \{a = a_1, b = b_1\}, \{d\} \Rightarrow \{c = \delta, d = \delta\},$$
$$\{c\} \Rightarrow \{c = \delta\}, \{g\} \Rightarrow \{g = \delta\}\}$$

4. Finally we have to add the set equations

$$\mathcal{E}_3 = \{b_1 = \delta\}$$

forcing the final type of the term to be "useful". The final set of equations is then $\mathcal{E} = \mathcal{E}_1 \cup \mathcal{E}_2 \cup \mathcal{E}_3$.

5. Starting from $\mathcal{E}_3$ and applying transitivity we search for all variables forced to be equal to δ by the equations in $\mathcal{E}$. The guarded sets of equations are considered only if their guard is forced to δ. All the variables which are not forced to be δ can be equated to ω. In the case of the example we have that the variables forced to to be δ are b_1, b and g. We then get the following decoration of the term.

$$((\lambda x^{\underline{\omega}\to\delta}.(x^{\underline{\omega}\to\delta}(\mathsf{succ}^{\omega\to\omega}1^\omega)^\omega)^\delta)^{(\underline{\omega}\to\delta)\to\delta}(\lambda y^{\underline{\omega}}.3^\delta)^{\underline{\omega}\to\delta})^\delta$$

It is easy to show that the decoration obtained from the algorithm is optimal in the sense of Theorem 2.

The optimized term is obtained from the original one by erasing the subterms and subtypes corresponding to ω-types in the previous decoration, which are the ones underlined. Therefore, we have that

$$\mathbf{O}((\lambda x : \text{int} \to \text{int}.(x(\text{succ } 1)))(\lambda y : \text{int}.3)) = (\lambda x : \text{int}.x)3.$$

As for complexity we have that:

- the set of equations $\mathcal{E}$ is built in time bounded by the size of the decorated term,
- the propagation of δ can be evaluated in time bounded by the number of type variables, and
- the transformation $\mathbf{O}$ is linear in the size of the term.

Therefore the whole optimization algorithm runs in time linear on the size of the decorated term.

2.2 A Non-trivial Example from Program Extraction

In this section we show a non-trivial example of UCE[5]. This example, due to C. Mohring and further developed by S. Berardi and L. Boerio (see [4] and [8]), is based on an instance of useless code that can arise in programs extracted from proofs. It shows how, in particular contexts, a primitive recursive operator could be transformed in an iterator (or even in a conditional operator) and how the simplified term is, in general, not β-convertible to the original one.

1. The term

$$\begin{aligned} \text{rec}_\pi = {}&\lambda m : \pi.\lambda f : \text{int} \to \pi \to \pi. \\ &\text{fix } r : \text{int} \to \pi.\lambda n : \text{int.ifz } n \text{ then } m \text{ else } fn(r(\text{pred } n)) \end{aligned}$$

   of type $\pi \to (\text{int} \to \pi \to \pi) \to \text{int} \to \pi$ represents the primitive recursor operator from natural numbers to π since, for every M, F and N of the proper types:
   - $\text{rec}_\pi \, M \, F \, 0 \cong M$, and
   - if $N \Downarrow k$ and $k > 0$ then $\text{rec}_\pi \, M \, F \, N \cong F \, N \, (\text{rec}_\pi \, M \, F \, (\text{pred } N))$.
2. The term

$$\begin{aligned} \text{it}_\pi = {}&\lambda m : \pi.\lambda g : \pi \to \pi. \\ &\text{fix } r : \text{int} \to \pi.\lambda n : \text{int.ifz } n \text{ then } m \text{ else } g(r(\text{pred } n)) \end{aligned}$$

   of type $\pi \to (\pi \to \pi) \to \text{int} \to \pi$ represents a simplified form of the operator rec_π which allows to iterate n times a function g on an input m. We call this operator a "iterator". In fact, for every M, G and N of the proper types:

---

[5] The example presented uses the pair data structure. The extension of the system of Section 2.1 to handle pairs is described in [9,13].

- $\text{it}_\pi \, M \, G \, 0 \cong M$, and
- if $N \Downarrow \mathsf{k}$ and $\mathsf{k} > 0$ then $\text{it}_\pi \, M \, G \, N \cong G(\text{it}_\pi \, M \, G \, (\text{pred} \, N))$.

Consider now the types $\rho = \text{int} \to \text{int}$, $\sigma = \text{int} \to (\text{int} \times \text{int}) \to (\text{int} \times \text{int})$, and $\tau = \text{int} \times \text{int}$. We will show how to use the system of Section 2.1 to detect and remove the useless code in the term, of type ρ,

$$P = \lambda x : \text{int.prj}_1(\text{rec}_\tau \, \langle M_1, M_2 \rangle \, F \, x)$$

where

- M_1, M_2 are closed terms of type int, and
- $F = \lambda n : \text{int}.\lambda m : \text{int} \times \text{int}.\langle h_1(\text{prj}_1 m), h_2(\text{prj}_1 m)(\text{prj}_2 m)\rangle$ is a term of type σ, with free variables $h_1 : \text{int} \to \text{int}$, $h_2 : \text{int} \to \text{int} \to \text{int}$, such that, for any integer variables x, y_1, y_2:

$$F \, x \, \langle y_1, y_2 \rangle \cong \langle h_1 \, y_1, h_2 \, y_1 \, y_2 \rangle \ .$$

Using the type assignment system of Section 2.1 we can derive that

$$\{h_1 : \delta \to \delta, h_2 : \omega \to \omega \to \omega\} \vdash P'^{\delta \to \delta},$$

where (omitting the type decoration which are clear from the context):

$$P' = \lambda x^\delta.\text{prj}_1\big(\text{rec}'^{(\delta \times \omega) \to (\omega \to (\delta \times \omega) \to (\delta \times \omega)) \to \delta \to (\delta \times \omega)}_\tau$$
$$\times \langle M_1, M_2 \rangle^{\delta \times \omega} \, F'^{\omega \to (\delta \times \omega) \to (\delta \times \omega)} \, x^\delta\big) \ ,$$

- $\text{rec}'_\tau = \lambda m^{\delta \times \omega}.\lambda f^{\omega \to (\delta \times \omega) \to (\delta \times \omega)}.$
  $\text{fix} \, r^{\delta \to \delta \times \omega}.\lambda n^\delta.\text{ifz} \, n \, \text{then} \, m^{\delta \times \omega} \, \text{else} \, fn^\omega (r(\text{pred}n)^\delta)^{\delta \times \omega}$, and
- $F' = (\lambda n^\omega.\lambda m^{\delta \times \omega}.\langle h_1(\text{prj}_1 m^{\delta \times \omega})^\delta, h_2(\text{prj}_1 m)^\omega (\text{prj}_2 m)^\omega\rangle).$

By applying the transformation $\mathbf{O}(-)$ we obtain the simplified term:

$$Q = \mathbf{O}(P'^{\delta \to \delta}) = \lambda x : \text{int.it}_{\text{int}} \, M_1 \, H \, x \ ,$$

where

- it_{int}, defined at the beginning of this section is the result of the application of $\mathbf{O}(-)$ to $\text{rec}'^{(\delta \times \omega) \to (\omega \to (\delta \times \omega) \to (\delta \times \omega)) \to \delta \to (\delta \times \omega)}_\tau$, and
- $H = \mathbf{O}(F'^{\omega \to (\delta \times \omega) \to (\delta \times \omega)}) = \lambda m_1 : \text{int}.h_1 m_1$.

2.3   About the Evaluation Strategy

The UCE technique of Section 2.1 has been introduced considering a call-by-name language. However, the technique can be adapted to languages using different evaluation strategies.

First observe that, when considering terminating program without side-effects (which is the typical case for programs extracted from formal proofs) we have that, independently from the evaluation strategy of the language, the simplified programs are observationally equivalent to the original ones.

In the case of programs without side-effects, but with possible divergent subexpressions, instead, we have that the simplified programs is observationally greater than the original one, i.e. it may terminate on more inputs.

Note that, however, it is possible to keep observationally equality also in presence of possibly divergent subexpressions and side-effects (as in ML-like languages) by first performing an effect analysis which marks as "useful" the subexpression that may diverge or contain side effects. This approach has been described in [15].

3   Extensions

In this section we present some extensions to the basic type inference system of Section 2. We first consider extensions to the type system and then extensions to the term language.

3.1   Considering More Expressive Types

In this section we describe extensions of the type inference system that involve changes to the type assignment rule and/or extensions of the type syntax. The functional programming language considered is the one of Section 2.

Introducing a More Refined Subtyping. The subtyping between any type and an ω-type allows to consider variables and constants as useful on some instances and as useless on others. This subtyping is rather coarse (does not reflect the structure of standard types). For instance, take the term

$$P = \lambda f : (\text{int} \to \text{int}) \to \text{int}.(\lambda g : \text{int} \to \text{int}. + (g\ M)(f\ g))(\lambda z : \text{int}.5) \ ,$$

where M is a closed term of type int. The subterm M of P is useless code. In order to detect this useless code it is necessary to decorate the first occurrence of g with type $\omega \to \delta$. This is consistent with the fact that the subterm $(\lambda g : \text{int} \to \text{int}. \cdots)$ is applied to $(\lambda z : \text{int}.5)$ that can be decorated with type $\omega \to \delta$. However, the second occurrence of g cannot be decorated with $\omega \to \delta$ since we do not have information about f, whose type depends from the context. For instance, P could be applied to the term $(\lambda h : \text{int} \to \text{int}.h7)$. So we are forced to assume for f the type $(\delta \to \delta) \to \delta$ and both the second occurrence of g, and the term $\lambda z : \text{int}.5$ must be decorated with $\delta \to \delta$.

This means that we cannot detect the useless-code M.

In order to allow to detect more useless code we introduce a subtyping relation $\sqsubseteq^+$, that extends $\sqsubseteq$ with the contravariance on the arrow constructor. That is, we add to the rules (2) the following rule:

$$(\to) \quad \frac{\psi_1 \sqsubseteq^+ \phi_1 \quad \phi_2 \sqsubseteq^+ \psi_2}{\phi_1 \to \phi_2 \sqsubseteq^+ \psi_1 \to \psi_2} \quad .$$

With this extended subtyping $\omega \to \delta \sqsubseteq^+ \delta \to \delta$. Considering again the system of Fig 1 in which in the rules (Var) and (Con) we use this extended ordering it is possible to produce the following decoration of P:

$$\lambda f^{(\delta \to \delta) \to \delta}.((\lambda g^{\omega \to \delta}.((+^{\delta \to \delta \to \delta}(g^{\omega \to \delta} M^{\omega})^{\delta})^{\delta \to \delta} (f^{(\delta \to \delta) \to \delta} g^{\delta \to \delta})^{\delta})^{\delta})^{(\delta \to \delta) \to \delta} (\lambda z^{\omega}.5^{\delta})^{\omega \to \delta})^{\delta} \ ,$$

which shows that the subexpression M is useless. This system detects more useless code, but in the simplification algorithm we cannot do transformations that modify the types of subterms. For instance in the above example we cannot transform the occurrence of g at type $\omega \to \delta$ into an occurrence of g at type δ since we must keep consistency with the occurrence of g at type $\delta \to \delta$. We can only replace all subterms of M decorated with an ω-type with simpler subterms, e.g. a free variable acting as a place holder (see [13] for details on both the system and the simplification algorithm). Therefore, starting from the above decoration we can produce the following simplification of P:

$$(\lambda g : \mathsf{int} \to \mathsf{int}. + (g\ \mathsf{d})(f\ g))(\lambda z : \mathsf{int}.5) \ ,$$

where the useless code showed by the decoration has been replaced by a dummy place holder d.

An inference algorithm for this system can be easily obtained by modifying the algorithm presented in the previous section, considering inequalities instead of equations. This transformation can be combined with the transformation $\mathbf{O}$ defined in the previous section. In particular we should perform this transformation before, detecting the maximum of useless code, and then the transformation $\mathbf{O}$, removing the maximum of dummy place holders.

The UCE with subtying was introduced by Berardi and Boerio in [5] and presented in a framework similar to the present one in [9,13].

Introducing Type Conjunction. The types that can be assigned to instances of variables by the system of Section 3.1 must have a common subtype that is the type assigned to the variable in the environment or in their abstraction. Sometimes, however, this is a limiting factor. For instance, consider the term

$$R = (\lambda f : (\mathsf{int} \to \mathsf{int}) \to \mathsf{int} \to \mathsf{int}. + (f(\lambda x : \mathsf{int}.3)N)(f(\lambda y : \mathsf{int}.y)7)) \\ (\lambda h : \mathsf{int} \to \mathsf{int}.\lambda z : \mathsf{int}.hz) \ ,$$

where N is a closed term of type int. Since f is bound to a term that applies its first argument to the second, the subterm N is useless code. To detect this useless code we have to decorate the first occurrence of f (the one that is applied to N) with the type

$$\phi_1 = (\omega \to \delta) \to \omega \to \delta$$

The second occurrence of f, however, has to be decorated with the type

$$\phi_2 = (\delta \to \delta) \to \delta \to \delta,$$

since it is applied to the identity and to constant. Now, even though ϕ_1 and ϕ_2 are decorations that can assigned to

$$\lambda h : \text{int} \to \text{int}.\lambda z : \text{int}.hz,$$

there is no type ϕ such that ϕ is a subtype of both ϕ_1 and ϕ_2. So, in the system with $\sqsubseteq^+$, we are forced to decorate with type ϕ_2 also the first occurrence of f. The useless code N, then, cannot be detected.

By extending the syntax of types with the conjunction operator and introducing suitable rules for conjunction introduction and elimination in the system, it is possible to assume for f the conjunction $\phi_1 \wedge \phi_2$, so that the useless code N can be detected. The conjunctive type system for UCE is described in [12] (a preliminary version of the system is described in Chapter 8 of [10]).

Inference of decorations in the presence of conjunction can be very costly. A system making a restricted use of conjunction is presented in [14] (see also Chapter 9 of [10]).

3.2 Adapting the Technique to Higher-Order Typed λ-Calculi

In this section we continue the historical survey of Section 1, and we sketch how the UCE described in Section 2 has been extended to typed λ-calculi including quantification over types. The first to describe such an extension was Boerio in [7] (see also Chapter 5 of [8]): he studied useless code in Girard's system F extended with primitive for integers. In system F types may contain universal quantification, $\forall t.\rho$, and terms abstraction over type variables, $\Lambda t.M$. The motivation for extending the UCE to this language comes mainly from the fact that proofs in Coq used this kind of system. (Moreover in system F algebraic data types, such as lists and trees, can be encoded.) In [26], Prost extended this work to the higher-order polymorphism present in the lambda-cube systems.

Boerio used a notation somehow different from the present one: each type of useless code was represented by a single type constant: Unit. Here we describe his work adapting it to the notation used in this paper.

In system F (standard) types contain in addition to the arrow constructor also quantification over type variables. So now, in addition to annotate with δ, and ω the basic types (such as int) also type variables are annotated. The simplification, again, will consist in removing the subterms decorated by ω-types and the subtypes whose annotation is ω.

The rules for decorating terms as lambda abstractions, applications and constants are the usual ones. Now, the crucial case is how to deal with the introduction and elimination rules for type quantification. In a type $\forall t.\rho$, each free occurrence of t in ρ, may have label δ or ω (to express the fact that each useful object may be useless in some context)[6].

---

[6] Boerio annotated the binder variable t in $\forall t. \cdots$ always by δ (the occurrences of t in the type could then have annotations δ or ω). This restriction on annotations was not really necessary. Later, Prost in [25] remarked that we could allow to annotate the t in $\forall t. \cdots$ by ω. In this way more useless code could be detected.

If $\varLambda t.M : \forall t.\rho$ in system F, then $\varLambda t.M(\tau) : \rho[t := \tau]$. Therefore, in order to complete the rules for decorating terms, Boerio defined the annotation of $\rho[t := \tau]$ starting from the annotation of ρ, and τ. In the substitution $\rho[t := \tau]$, each t annotated with δ is replaced by τ with its original annotation, whereas the instances of t annotated with ω are replaced by τ, with annotations consisting only of ω's. This rule expresses the fact that occurrences of type variables annotated with ω are useless, hence they may be replaced by ω-types.

The main remark about this system is that the algorithm to infer decorations is rather similar to the algorithm for the simply typed λ-calculus presented in Section 2. Also in this case we may prove that each partial decoration of the term may be completed to a unique optimal decoration with the maximum amount of ω's (Theorem 2), and if the decoration annotated with δ all the type variable of the final type, then the term obtained by removing the subterms decorated by ω-types and the subtypes whose annotation is ω is observationally equivalent to the original one (Theorem 1). The optimal decoration may be computed in a feasible way.

3.3   Adapting the Technique to ML-Like Languages

In this section we describe extensions of the UCE of Section 2 dealing with programming language features like: recursive datatypes, let-polymorphism, and side-effects.

Handling Algebraic Data Types. Berardi and Boerio [6] (see also Chapter 3 of [8]) extended the UCE of Section 2 to deal directly with algebraic data types. Even though algebraic data types could be encoded in system F a direct (first order) treatment makes the optimizations clearer. A UCE extending [6] with subtyping has been proposed by Damiani [11].

Xi [33] describes a technique, based on dependent types, for detecting unreachable matching clauses in typed functional programs. This work is primarily concerned with program error detection, while the approach described in the present paper is mainly designed for program optimization. The kind of useless code considered in [33] is orthogonal with respect to the useless code detected by the techniques mentioned above.

Handling let-Polymorphism. Kobayashi [18] proposed a type-based uselesscode elimination technique for a language with let-polymorphism. The UCE of [18] is described as a variant of the ML type reconstruction algorithm. For the language without let, it generates the same simplifications as the algorithm in Section 2.1, but it is faster[7]. As explained in [18] let-polymorphism has interesting interactions with useless-code elimination: on one side polymorphism provides

---

[7] For the simply typed λ calculus, it is almost linear in the size of the undecorated term. Being based on ML-type inference, it becomes exponential when let-expressions are involved.

more opportunity for useless-variable elimination and, on the other, the simplified program may be more polymorphic than the original one. Kobayashi's UCE does not include subtyping. Therefore it does not perform the simplifications described in Section 3.1.

Handling Side-Effects. Fishbach and Hannan [15] proposed a type-based useless-code elimination technique which preserves side-effects and termination behaviour in a call-by-value language. This UCE can be described as the integration of a simple effect analysis to the system of of Section 2.1 (see the discussion in Section 2.3).

4   Future Work

Most of the work described in Section 3 is still subject to investigation. In this section we mention only the main direction we are interested in: the possibility of extending the technique of Section 2 to fragments of imperative programs. The motivations are similar to the ones for functional languages. In particular, if one produces a program with an extensive reuse of existing libraries, large piece of code could become unreachable. Moreover, many parameters could be computed for no purpose: they were used in the original code but no more in the instantiated code. If we repeatedly build new code in this way, we produce, by a chain effect, long useless computation, and slow down even the fastest computers.

Instead of decorating as "useful" the pieces of code containing side-effects, like Fishbach and Hannan in [15], the method we plan to use is the following. First translate, preserving observational equality, an imperative program into a purely functional program, for which useless-code analysis already exists. Then analyze the resulting functional code. Finally remove or trivialize in the original imperative program all parts which are sent into useless functional code. The fact that the translation preserves observational equality guarantees that such parts are useless code also in the original program. Translating from imperative to pure functional is routine: we only quote that an assignment $x := v$ would become a map from the type of memory to the type of memory, $S \to S$, changing to v only the component of S concerning the variable x; a while loop becomes a map $WHILE: (S \times (S \to \mathsf{bool}) \times (S \to S)) \to S$. And so on.

What is not yet clear is the extent at which this technique is applicable since it requires the source code of the library used. This condition is frequently met in programs extracted from proofs, or in functional programming, but not very often in imperative programming, where libraries are usually compiled code. Thus, such a simplification tool would work only in the Open Source community. Moreover, an issue that has to be considered is the comparison with the techniques developed by the imperative compiler community.

References

1. A. V. Aho, R. Sethi, and J. Ullmann. *Complilers: Principles, Techniques, and Tools.* Addison Wesley, 1986.
2. M. J. Beeson. *Foundations of Constructive Mathematics, Metamathematical Studies.* Springer, 1985.
3. S. Berardi. Pruning Simply Typed Lambda Terms, 1993. Course notes of the "Summer School in Logic and Programming", University of Chambery.
4. S. Berardi. Pruning Simply Typed Lambda Terms. *Journal of Logic and Computation*, 6(5):663–681, 1996.
5. S. Berardi and L. Boerio. Using Subtyping in Program Optimization. In *TLCA'95*, LNCS 902. Springer, 1995.
6. S. Berardi and L. Boerio. Minimum Information Code in a Pure Functional Language with Data Types. In *TLCA'97*, LNCS 1210, pages 30–45. Springer, 1997.
7. L. Boerio. Extending Pruning Techniques to Polymorphic Second Order λ-calculus. In *ESOP'94*, LNCS 788, pages 120–134. Springer, 1994.
8. L. Boerio. *Optimizing Programs Extracted from Proofs.* PhD thesis, Università di Torino, 1995.
9. M. Coppo, F. Damiani, and P. Giannini. Refinement Types for Program Analysis. In *SAS'96*, LNCS 1145, pages 143–158. Springer, 1996.
10. F. Damiani. *Non-standard type inference for functional programs.* PhD thesis, Dipartimento di Informatica, Università di Torino, February 1998.
11. F. Damiani. Useless-code detection and elimination for PCF with algebraic Datatypes. In *TLCA'99*, LNCS 1581, pages 83–97. Springer, 1999.
12. F. Damiani. Conjunctive types and useless-code elimination (extended abstract). In *ICALP Workshops*, volume 8 of *Proceedings in Informatics*, pages 271–285. Carleton-Scientific, 2000.
13. F. Damiani and P. Giannini. Automatic useless-code elimination for HOT functional programs. *Journal of Functional programming.* To appear.
14. F. Damiani and F. Prost. Detecting and Removing Dead Code using Rank 2 Intersection. In *TYPES'96*, LNCS 1512, pages 66–87. Springer, 1998.
15. A. Fischbach and J. Hannan. Type Systems and Algoritms for Useless-Variable Elimination, 1999. Submitted.
16. C. A. Goad. *Computational uses of the manipulation of proofs.* PhD thesis, Stanford University, 1980.
17. C. Hankin and D. Le Métayer. Lazy type inference and program analysis. *Science of Computer Programming*, 25:219–249, 1995.
18. N. Kobayashi. Type-Based Useless Variable Elimination. In *PEPM'00*. ACM, 2000. To appear.
19. G. Kreisel and A. Troelstra. Formal systems for some branches of intionistic analysis. *Annals of Pure and Applied Logic*, 1, 1979.
20. F. Nielson. Annotated type and effect systems. ACM Computing Surveys vol. 28 no. 2, 1996. (Invited position statement for the Symposium on Models of Programming Languages and Computation).
21. F. Nielson, H. R. Nielson, and C. Hankin. *Principles of Program Analysis.* In preparation, `http://www.daimi.au.dk/~hrn/PPA/ppa.html`, 1999.
22. C. Paulin-Mohring. Extracting F_ω's Programs from Proofs in the Calculus of Constructions. In *POPL'89*. ACM, 1989.
23. C. Paulin-Mohring. *Extraction de Programme dans le Calcul des Constructions.* PhD thesis, Université Paris VII, 1989.

24. G. D. Plotkin. LCF considered as a programming language. *Theoretical Computer Science*, 5(3):223–255, 1977.
25. F. Prost. A formalization of static analyses in system F. In H. Ganzinger, editor, *Automated Deduction – CADE-16, 16th International Conference on Automated Deduction*, LNAI 1632. Springer-Verlag, 1999.
26. F. Prost. A static calculus of dependencies for the λ-cube. In *Proc. of IEEE 15th Ann. Symp. on Logic in Computer Science (LICS'2000)*. IEEE Computer Society Press, 2000. To appear.
27. O. Shivers. *Control Flow Analysis of Higher-Order Languages*. PhD thesis, Carnegie-Mellon University, 1991.
28. Y. Takayama. Extraction of Redundancy-free Programs from Constructive Natural Deduction Proofs. *Journal of Symbolic Computation*, 12:29–69, 1991.
29. The Coq Home Page, `http://pauillac.inria.fr/coq/`.
30. A. Troelstra, editor. *Metamathematical Investigation of Intuitionistic Arithmetic and Analysis*. LNM 344. Springer, 1973.
31. M. Wand and I. Siveroni. Constraints Systems for Useless Variable Elimination. In *POPL'99*, pages 291–302. ACM, 1999.
32. R. Wilhelm and D. Maurer. *Compliler Design*. Addison Wesley, 1995.
33. H. Xi. Dead Code Elimination through Dependent Types. In *PADL'99*, pages 228–242, 1999.

Code Generators for Automatic Tuning of Numerical Kernels: Experiences with FFTW

Position Paper

Richard Vuduc[1] and James W. Demmel[2]

[1] Computer Science Division
University of California at Berkeley, Berkeley, CA 94720, USA
richie@cs.berkeley.edu
[2] Computer Science Division and Dept. of Mathematics
University of California at Berkeley, Berkeley, CA 94720, USA
demmel@cs.berkeley.edu

Abstract. Achieving peak performance in important numerical kernels such as dense matrix multiply or sparse-matrix vector multiplication usually requires extensive, machine-dependent tuning by hand. In response, a number automatic tuning systems have been developed which typically operate by (1) generating multiple implementations of a kernel, and (2) empirically selecting an optimal implementation. One such system is FFTW (Fastest Fourier Transform in the West) for the discrete Fourier transform. In this paper, we review FFTW's inner workings with an emphasis on its code generator, and report on our empirical evaluation of the system on two different hardware and compiler platforms. We then describe a number of our own extensions to the FFTW code generator that compute efficient discrete cosine transforms and show promising speed-ups over a vendor-tuned library. We also comment on current opportunities to develop tuning systems in the spirit of FFTW for other widely-used kernels.

1   Introduction

This paper presents a few findings of our exploratory work in the area of automatic software performance tuning. One specific aim of our study was to conduct a detailed empirical evaluation of the code generation component of FFTW (Fastest Fourier Transform in the West) [13,14], a software system for automatically generating and performance tuning discrete Fourier transform code. To see some hint of the full generality of the FFTW approach, we also considered an extension to the system to generate efficient discrete cosine transform (DCT) [25] implementations. Finally, we hoped to discover and propose ideas that could be used to tune automatically other important algorithms.

In the remainder of this section, we describe the overall problem that automatic performance tuning systems address, as well as one basic solution. We include a short summary of recent work in the area. In Section 2 we give an

W. Taha (Ed.): SAIG 2000, LNCS 1924, pp. 190–211, 2000.

overview of FFTW, and perform an empirical evaluation in Section 3. The current state of our work toward extending FFTW for the discrete cosine transforms is given in Section 4.

1.1   Motivation

The modular design of software applications has been motivated by the need to improve development, testing, maintenance, and portability of code. In addition, such design can enable software developers to isolate performance within one or more key subroutines or libraries. Tuning these subroutines on many platforms facilitates the creation of applications with *portable performance*, provided the routines or libraries have been tuned on the hardware platforms of interest. In this report, we refer to these performance-critical library subroutines as *kernels*. Some examples of kernels and their applications are sparse matrix-vector multiply in the solution of linear systems, Fourier transforms in signal processing, discrete cosine transforms in JPEG image compression, and sorting in database applications.

One practical example of a widely-used kernel standard is the Basic Linear Algebra Subroutines (BLAS) [18,11,10,6] standard. Highly tuned versions of the BLAS are typically available on most modern platforms. However, performance tuning by hand can be tedious, error-prone, and time-consuming. Moreover, each routine must be tuned for a particular hardware configuration, and modern general purpose microprocessors are diverse, constantly evolving, and difficult to compile for. Furthermore, compilers face the difficult task of optimizing for the general case, and cannot usually make use of domain- or kernel-specific knowledge. Therefore, we seek automated tuning methods that can be configured for a specific application.

1.2   A Scheme for Automatic Tuning

Several of the most successful attempts to automate the tuning process follow the following general scheme, first proposed and implemented in the PHiPAC project [4,5] for matrix multiplication:

1. Generation: Instead of writing kernels, write kernel generators which output kernels in a portable, high-level source language. These kernels can be specialized according to some set of parameters chosen to capture characteristics of the input (e.g., problem size), or machine (e.g., registers, pipeline structure, cache properties). In addition, a generator can apply kernel-specific transformations (e.g., tiling for matrix multiply).
2. Evaluation: With a parameterized kernel generator in hand, explore the parameter space in search of some optimal implementation. The search might consist of generating an implementation, measuring its performance, selecting a new set of parameters, and repeating this process until no faster implementation can be discovered.[1] Each implementation could also be evaluated for specific workloads.

---

[1] This could be considered a form of profiling or feedback-directed compilation.

This process could be done either at compile-time (i.e., library or kernel installation time), at run-time, or through some hybrid scheme.

In this report, we focus on the generation process. In addition to PHiPAC and FFTW, other recent automatic code generation systems for specific kernels include Blitz++ [29,30], ATLAS [33], the Matrix Template Library [26], all three of which target dense linear algebra kernels. More recently, the Sparsity system [17] has been developed for highly-optimized sparse matrix-vector multiplication and includes automatic code generation as well. PHiPAC, ATLAS, FFTW, and Sparsity address both the generation and the evaluation problems together. The remainder explore only the generation problem.

Of the above systems, however, only FFTW explicitly maintains a high-level symbolic representation of the computation (kernel) itself. One goal of this study was to understand what benefits are available by doing so.

Note that Veldhuizen, et al. [31] have compiled a list of current approaches to library construction and automatic tuning. They also coined the term *active libraries* to describe the role that automatic kernel construction and optimization play in software development.

2   FFTW

The FFTW package is a system for producing highly-optimized discrete Fourier transform (DFT) kernels using the family of FFT algorithms. In the following subsection, we provide a brief overview of how the kernels generated by FFTW fare in practice, and summarize the overall software architecture for readers who may be unfamiliar with it. In section 2.2, we describe in more detail the elements of FFTW (specifically, its code generator) that are most relevant to this study.

Note that the material in this section is largely a summary of the material in the original papers on FFTW [13]. However, all empirical measurements presented in this report were made by the authors. All experiments were performed using FFTW version 2.1.3.

2.1   Overview of FFTW

Figure 1 shows two examples of its success in outperforming commonly used alternative routines on two platforms. In the figures, the "naive" algorithm is the FFT algorithm presented in Press, et al. [24]. FFTPACK [27] is a standard library for computing FFTs and related operations. The vendor library shown on the Sun Ultra-10 platform (right) is the highly tuned commercial numerical library available from Sun Microsystems. Note that the algorithms tested compute the complex DFT in double-precision.

One key to the success of FFTW is the recursive decomposition of FFT algorithms. For instance, one way of expressing this decomposition is via the Cooley-Tukey recursive formulation [8] for a 1-dimensional N-point FFT, when

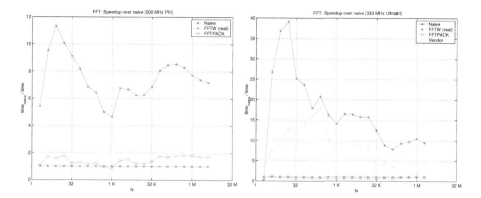

Fig. 1. (*Left*) Performance of the FFTW on a Millennium Node. (*Right*) Performance of FFTW on a Sun Ultra-10 Workstation (Configuration Details Given in Section 3).

N factors as $N = N_1 N_2$:

$$y[k_1 + k_2 N_1] = \sum_{n_2=0}^{N_2-1} \left[\left(\sum_{n_1=0}^{N_1-1} x[n_1 N_2 + n_2] \omega_{N_1}^{-k_1 n_1} \right) \omega_N^{-k_1 n_2} \right] \omega_{N_2}^{-k_2 n_2} \qquad (1)$$

where $x[n]$ is an element of the input sequence and $y[k]$ is an element of the Fourier transform, with $0 \le n \le N - 1$, and $\omega_N = e^{2\pi\sqrt{-1}/N}$. The inner sum represents a N_1-point FFT, and the outermost sum represents an N_2-point FFT.

Thus, for any non-prime value of N, we have the freedom to choose the factors N_1 and N_2. Of course, we can also continue to apply the recursion for resulting sub-problems. The FFTW system makes use of this recursive decomposition by (1) generating highly tuned transforms for use at the lowest level (base case) of the recursion, and (2) selecting the decomposition based on empirical performance measurements. Specifically, the system carries out this process through its three components:

Codelet Generator: Creates a symbolic representation of the FFT for a specific size (usually small, say, less than 128 elements), optimizes this high-level representation, and outputs efficient C code. The authors of FFTW refer to these generated implementations of the FFT as *codelets*.

Planner: At run-time, the user gives the planner a length N, and the planner factors N in various ways to get several possible decompositions, or *plans*, of the FFT. The planner then measures the speed of the various codelets to determine which plan is likely to be the fastest. Note that the plan only has to be computed once for a given value of N.[2] To reduce the complexity of exploring the various plans, the planner assumes an optimal substructure

---

[2] FFTW also contains a mechanism, referred to as *wisdom*, for storing these plans so they do not have to be recomputed in later runs.

property (i.e., a plan for an N_1-length FFT will also be fast even if it is called as a sub-problem of a larger FFT. This is not necessarily true, for instance, due to differences in the state of cache data placement). Also note that FFTW has a mode in which it uses hard-wired heuristics to guess or estimate a plan instead if the overhead of planning cannot be tolerated in a particular application.

Executor: The executor actually computes the FFT, given input data and an optimal plan.

We revisit the run-time overhead in Section 3, and omit any additional discussion of the planner and executor phases otherwise. In the remainder of this section, we describe the codelet generator.

2.2   Codelet Generator

The FFTW approach is unique among automatic code generation systems in that it maintains an explicit, high-level symbolic representation of the computation being performed. The FFTW codelet generator, written in Objective Caml, takes a length N as input and performs the following phases in order:

Generate: Generate a high-level, symbolic representation of the FFT computation, referred to as an *expression DAG*. This is like an abstract syntax tree except that it is a directed acyclic graph and not a tree. The DAG structure exposes common subexpressions. Each node is either a load or store of some input variable, or an arithmetic operation whose operands are the predecessors of the node. The data type for a node given in Objective Caml is shown in Figure 2. A visual example of an expression DAG is shown in Figure 3.

Simplify: Visit each node of the DAG in topological order, using rule-based pattern matching to perform a series of "simplifications." These simplifications are essentially local transformations to the DAG that correspond to algebraic simplifications. We describe these in more detail below.

Transpose: Tranpose the DAG. The expressions represented by FFT DAGs corresponds to a mathematical object called a linear network, which is well-known in the signal processing literature [9]. Briefly, a linear network is a graph whose nodes correspond to variables, additions, or subtractions, and whose edges correspond to multiplications. The DAG shown in Figure 3 is shown as a linear network in Figure 4. One property of a linear network is that its transpose, which is the same network with the edges reversed, corresponds to a different, albeit equivalent, dual representation of the original. In the transpose representation, opportunities for simplification are exposed that might not have been otherwise (we will examine this more closely in Section 3).

Iterate: Simplify the transposed DAG, and transpose the DAG again to return to the primal representation. This process of simplifying and transposing can be iterated if desired, although in practice there does not appear to be an appreciable benefit to doing so.

Schedule: Once all transformations have been completed, translate the DAG into a C implementation. This requires scheduling the DAG. The FFTW algorithm for scheduling is asymptotically provably optimal with respect to register or cache usage when N is a power of 2, even though the generator does not know how many registers or how much cache are available [13].

```
type node =
    Num of number
  | Load of variable
  | Store of variable
  | Plus of node list
  | Times of node * node
  | Uminus of node
```

Fig. 2. Objective Caml code defining the node data type. "number" represents a floating point constant, and "variable" an input datum, i.e., an element of x or y.

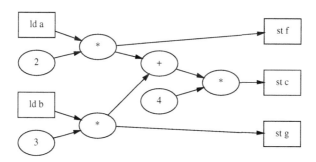

Fig. 3. An expression DAG Corresponding to the Set of Symbolic Equations $\{f = 2a, c = 4(2a + 3b), g = 3b\}$.

The simplify phase performs a small number of relatively simple transformations. These include removing additions and multiplications by $0, \pm 1$ and constant folding. It also applies the distributive property, i.e., $ax + ay = a(x + y)$.[3] The simplifier also identifies and creates common subexpressions (in the DAG, these are represented by nodes with multiple outgoing edges). Finally, it performs one DFT-specific optimization, which is to store only positive constants and propagate the minus sign on negative constants as needed. This is because

---

[3] While this could destroy common subexpressions ax and ay, the FFTW authors claim that this did not occur, although they do not know why.

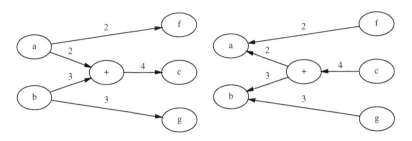

Fig. 4. The DAG of Figure 3 appears here as a linear network (*left*) and its transpose (*right*). Note that the transpose corresponds to the set of equations $\{a = 2f + 2(4c), b = 3(4c) + 3g\}$.

many compilers force loads of both positive and negative constants separately, and $+k$ and $-k$ pairs appear very frequently in FFT computations.

The Objective Caml code (roughly) which generates the symbolic form of the FFT as shown in Equation (1) is shown in Figure 5. The correspondence between the Caml code and the equation can be easily seen.

```
let rec cooley_tukey N1 N2 input sign =
  let tmp1 n2 = fftgen N1
    (fun n1 → input (n1 * N2 + n2)) sign in
  let tmp2 k1 n2 =
    exp N (sign * k1 * k2) @* tmp1 n2 k1 in
  let tmp3 k1 = fftgen N2 (tmp2 k1) sign
  in
    fun k → tmp3 (k mod N1) (k / N1)
```

Fig. 5. Roughly, the Objective Caml code that generates a function to compute a symbolic expression for $y[k]$ by Equation (1). Note that @* is an infix operator corresponding to complex multiplication, and that *exp* n k computes $e^{2\pi ik/n}$ where $i = \sqrt{-1}$.

In Figure 5, note that access to the array x being transformed is encapsulated by a function *input*. As we will see later, this helps reduce the complexity of array indexing typical in FFT and related computations. Also note that Equation (1) is only one of many possible expressions for the DFT; the function *fftgen* actually chooses one from among many such algorithms (including *cooley_tukey*) depending on the input size. When either *fftgen* or *cooley_tukey* are evaluated, each returns a Complex.expr which is a pair of nodes (corresponding to the real and imaginary parts of a complex expression). More concretely, *fftgen* has type

```
fftgen : int -> (int -> Complex.expr) ->
           int -> (int -> Complex.expr)
```

Note that Figures 2 and 5 were reproduced from [13] with modifications.

We will see how we use this machinery to develop our extensions for the discrete cosine transform in Section 4.

3   Evaluating FFTW

In this section, we show empirically the effect of two of the three major phases in the codelet generator: simplification and DAG transposition.

Evaluation studies were conducted on two platforms. The first was a Sun Ultra-10 workstation with a 333 MHz Ultra-II microprocessor and 2 MB L2 cache running Solaris 2.7. Programs on the Ultra-10 were compiled using Sun's cc v5.0 compiler with the following flags: `-dalign -xtarget=native -xO5 -xarch=v8plusa`. The vendor library used in this study was the Sun Performance Library.

The second platform was a node in the Millennium cluster [1] (a 500 MHz Pentium-III microprocessor and 512-KB L2 cache) running Linux. Programs were compiled using egcs/gcc 2.95 with the following flags: `-O3 -mcpu= pentiumpro -fschedule-insns2`. The vendor library used was the latest version of Greg Henry's tuned numerical libraries for Linux [16] which were developed as part of the ASCI Red Project. Note that due to bugs in the FFT subroutines, we do not report vendor times when input sizes exceed 32K elements.

All timing measurements were made by executing the code of interest for a minimum of 5 times or 5 seconds, whichever was longer, and reporting the average.

3.1   Simplification and DAG Transposition

The authors of FFTW observed reductions in the number of multiplications of between 5% and 25% in certain cases with DAG transposition and subsequent simplification. To see how this can occur, consider the linear network shown in Figure 4 (left). If we simplify the expression $c = 4(2a + 3b)$ to $c = 8a + 12b$, we save a multiplication. However, we cannot apply this simplification haphazardly since it is not beneficial if $2a$ and $3b$ are common subexpressions. In that case, we lose the common subexpressions $2a$ and $3b$, and may increase the overall operation count by one.

However, if we transpose the graph as shown in Figure 4 (right), we see that the simplifier will apply the distributive rule and effectively "discover" the common subexpressions. This results in the network shown in Figure 6. Notice that when we transpose again to return to the primal network, the opportunity to simplify the expression for c by "undistributing" the constant 4 does not exist anymore.

Note that if $2a$ and $3b$ had not been common subexpressions, then the constant 4 would have been propagated when simplifying the transpose, saving an operation. It seems that more complicated pattern matching could identify the difference between the two cases in which the operands either are or are not common subexpressions, obviating the need for transposition. However, such rules might be tedious or complex to develop. Thus, we believe the true benefit of the transpose is that we may use a relatively small, simple number of patterns in the simplifier. This works because the linear network representation is a suitable representation of an FFT computation.

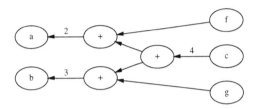

Fig. 6. The distributive rule applied by the simplifier will "discover" the common subexpressions shown in figure 4, resulting in this network.

There is a dramatic way to visualize the global effect of DAG transposition, shown in Figure 7. We modified FFTW's C unparser to output dot[4] code. While one could argue that the apparent structural differences are artifacts of the graph layout software. Nevertheless, the bottom network does appear to have discovered additional common sub-expressions, represented by the shift in the grouping structure of the graph to the network inputs.

However, one may rightly wonder what impact these transformations have on the performance realized in practice. For instance, constant folding and common sub-expression elimination are routinely implemented in optimizing compilers. Thus, one might expect these simplifications to duplicate the compiler effort.

We compared the performance of FFTW to itself on the Millennium node in three scenarios: (1) no simplification, (2) algebraic transformations, but no DAG transposition, (3) all optimizations. The results are shown in Figure 8 (*left*), normalized to the full optimization case. It appears that omitting the seemingly simple algebraic optimizations resulted in code that ran as much as two times slower than the implementation generated with full optimizations.

DAG transposition resulted in savings of up to 10% or slightly more in several cases, mostly for prime or odd sizes. Most cases in which omitting DAG transposition appears to be better than using it are generally within the timing noise threshold (we estimate this to be at most about 5% error) and therefore not significant. In those instances in which noise does not explain the finding, we believe that a change in the instruction mix may be the cause. This is because, as the FFTW authors observed, the effect of using DAG transposition is to reduce the number of multiplications. There are generally fewer multiplica-

---

[4] dot is an automatic graph layout application, available from AT&T research: http://www.research.att.com/sw/tools/graphviz

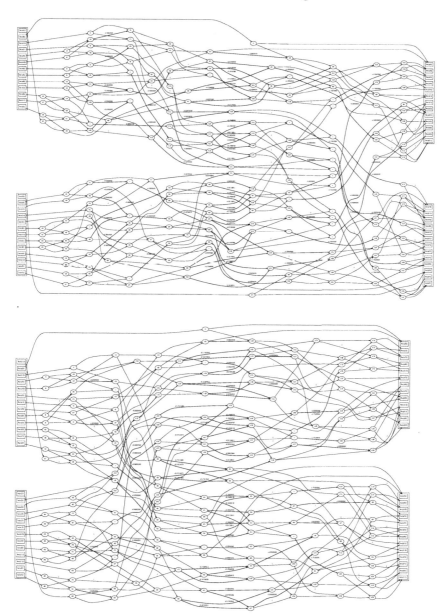

Fig. 7. (*Top*) The Linear Network Representing the Complex 13-point FFT without DAG Transposition. (*Bottom*) The result when DAG transposition follwed by an additional pass of simplification is applied to the linear network above. To reduce apparent structure which might result as an artifact of the drawing program, real inputs, imaginary inputs, real outputs, and imaginary ouputs have been grouped (shown as boxes). The boxes correspond between the top and bottom figures; however, within the boxes, the order of the nodes may not match between the top and bottom.

tions than additions, so reducing the number of multiplications only exacerbates the imbalance on architectures in which balancing adds and multiplies leads to better performance.

On the Sun Ultra-10 platform, we can observe similar trends, as shown in Figure 8 (*right*) with respect to the importance of the algebraic simplifications. However, one startling difference is that for a handful of relatively small sizes, omitting DAG transposition would have led to up to a 35% speed improvement.

Note that in both experiments, we allowed the FFTW planner to do a full search for an optimal decomposition.

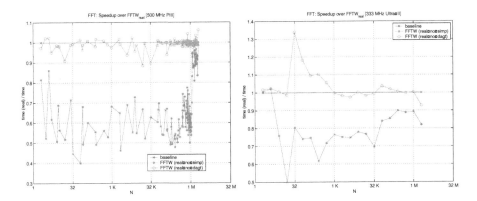

Fig. 8. (*left*) Comparison between (1) no simplification, (2) algebraic simplifications but no DAG transposition, and (3) full optimizations. Powers of 2, 3, 5, and 7 are included, as well as uniformly randomly distributed sizes between 32,000 elements and 1 million. Measurements shown for the Millennium node. (*right*) The same experiment repeated on the Sun Ultra-10 platform, (only powers of 2 shown).

3.2   Run-Time Overhead

Most FFT implementations require users to call a pre-initialization routine in which the so-called constant *twiddle factors* (the ω factors in equation (1)) are pre-computed. In practice, users perform many FFTs of the same length on different data, so it is reasonable to perform initialization in advance whose cost can be amortized over many uses. It is during this initialization phase that FFTW executes its planner, and in this section we quantify the run-time overhead incurred.

The results are shown in Figure 9 for the Millennium and the Sun Ultra-10 platforms. In both cases for each implementation, we show how many computations of the naive algorithm are equivalent to the initialization cost. Recall that FFTW has two planning modes: a "real" mode in which the algorithm tries to accurately determine a plan, and an "estimate" mode in which heuristics are applied to select a good plan. Estimation mode costs essentially the same in initialization time as that of conventional algorithms.

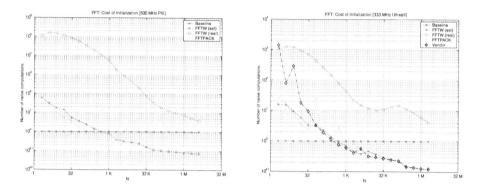

Fig. 9. Planner overhead on the Millennium node (*left*) and on the Sun Ultra-10 (*right*).

The slowdowns incurred from using the estimated plans are shown for the two platforms in Figure 10 for the Millennium and Sun Ultra-10 platforms, respectively. Note that on the Ultra-10 (for which the FFTW authors note that they implicitly tuned the heuristic algorithm), the difference between using the real vs. estimated plan is unclear. In fact, sometimes the estimated plan resulted in better performance. This is not surprising in the sense that the "real" mode does not actually find the optimal plan since it uses the optimal sub-plan heuristic to prune the search space. However, on the Millennium node, real mode does tend to find better plans, leading to a speedup of 15% to 30% for large powers of two.

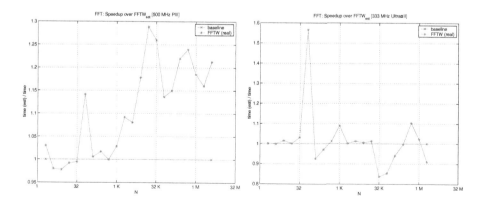

Fig. 10. Resulting performance difference between real vs. estimated run-time planning modes on the Millennium node (*left*) and the Sun Ultra-10 (*right*).

4   Fast Discrete Cosine Transforms

The results of the evaluation indicated that the generator, which includes special built-in transformations specific to the FFT, was effective in generating efficient code. Before considering generalizations to completely different kernels, it seemed natural to consider extending the system to compute a very similar transform: the discrete cosine transform (DCT).

The version of FFTW available at the time of this writing included code to generate DCT codelets, but did not have a complete DCT planner and executor implementation. However, since there are many ways to generate DCT codelets, only one of which was available in FFTW, we considered a variety of alternatives. We have also begun implementation of a DCT planner and executor. In this section, we describe the relationship between the DCT and FFT and the current status of our effort to extend FFTW.

4.1   Overview

The DCT has numerous applications in speech coding, image compression, and solving partial differential equations. For instance, both the current JPEG image file standard and the upcoming HDTV standard rely on the DCT as a funda-mental kernel. There are a variety of formal definitions of the DCT and in this report we use the formulation known as DCT-II, defined as follows. The 1-D DCT $y[k]$ of a real-valued input signal $x[n]$ is given by

$$y[k] = 2 \sum_{n=0}^{N-1} x[n] \cos\left(\pi \frac{k(2n+1)}{2N}\right) \qquad (2)$$

where $0 \leq k, n < N$, and the finite signal N is assumed to be even and symmetric about $n = N - \frac{1}{2}$, with period $2N$. An example of a signal and its extension is shown in Figure 11. Note that direct computation of equation (2) for all k has an arithmetic complexity of $O(N^2)$.

There are many ways to compute the DCT with an arithmetic complexity of $O(N \log N)$, as with the FFT. We considered two classes of methods: (1) reduc-tion of the DCT to an equivalent FFT computation and (2) purely real recursive formulations. The former allowed us to make the most use of pre-existing FFTW code generation infrastructure, while the latter should in principle lead to im-plementations with fewer arithmetic operations. We describe the algorithms we tried and their results below.

4.2   DCT-II via the FFT

We considered four algorithms which all work by reducing the DCT to an equiv-alent FFT computation:

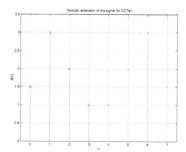

Fig. 11. The original signal (blue) of length 4 is extended (red) to be even and symmetric about $n = 3.5$ with period 8.

1. Reduction to a $2N$-point real-to-complex FFT: This is the "textbook" method [23]. Let $V[k]$ be the $2N$-point FFT of one period of the extended signal. Then the DCT-II $y[k]$ of $x[n]$ is given by

$$y[k] = 2\Re \left\{ V[k]\omega_{4N}^{-k} \right\} \qquad (3)$$

2. Reduction to one real-to-complex N-point FFT: This requires permuting the input so that the even elements $x[2n]$ appear first, followed by the odd elements $x[2n+1]$ in reverse order. If $V[k]$ is the real-to-complex FFT of this N-length permuted signal, then the DCT-II $y[k]$ is given by equation (3).
3. Reduction to one complex $N/2$-point FFT: We create a new complex signal $v[n]$ of length $\frac{N}{2}$ whose real and imaginary parts are the even and odd elements of the original signal respectively.
4. Reduction to a $4N$-point real-to-complex FFT: Consider padding the period $2N$ extended signal with zeros between every other element to obtain a length $4N$ signal. Then the first N elements of this transformed signal will be exactly the DCT-II of the original signal. This is the algorithm used in FFTW to generate DCT codelets.[5]

We might consider implementing the DCT by not changing the generator at all, and instead by just calling the pre-built FFT routines as in any of the above formulations. However, as shown in Figure 12, this is not nearly as efficient as the vendor and FFTPACK implementations on the Sun Ultra-10 for input sizes under 128K elements. Thus, we considered generating DCT-II codelets directly.

As with the FFT, each of the algorithms described above is simple to express in the code generator. Specifically, since all four algorithms involve a rearrangement of the input, we really only need to ensure that the appropriate *input* function (as in Figure 5) is supplied.

Observe that only the $4N$-point transform does not require explicit multiplication by the extra twiddle factor ω_{4N}^{-k} as in equation (3). Furthermore, the

---

[5] We actually implemented this as well, although we didn't realize our formulation was the same as the pre-existing one at the time.

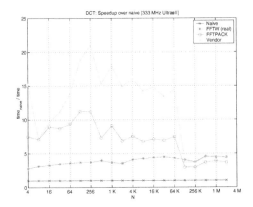

Fig. 12. Performance of the DCT-II implemented by calling the pre-built FFTW routine (i.e., without using specialized DCT-II codelets) on the Sun Ultra-10 platform.

redundancy in the $4N$ element extension exposes more common sub-expressions than the more compact reductions. Irrelevant parts of the computation are effectively pruned by both simplification and the fact that the generator only stores expressions that go to one of the desired outputs. This led to a DCT implementation that required about 25% fewer multiplications for non-power of two sizes than the more compact representations. (Power of 2 sizes produced identical implementations.)

4.3   Purely Real DCTs

Instead of reducing the DCT to an equivalent FFT computation, we can also express the DCT recursively in terms of smaller DCTs. Below, we list the three variants of these so-called purely real recursive formulations that we tried. In all cases, we assume N is a power of 2.

1. Decimation in frequency (DIF) algorithm (Yip and Rao [34]): Given an N-length sequence $x[n]$, define two new sequences

$$g[n] = x[n] + x[N - n - 1]$$
$$h[n] = \frac{1}{2}(x[n] - x[N - n - 1])$$

where $0 \le n < \frac{N}{2}$. Let $G[m], H[m]$ be the DCT-II transforms of g, h respectively. Then the even and odd elements of the DCT-II $y[k]$ of $x[n]$ are

$$y[2m] = G[m]$$
$$y[2m + 1] = H[m] + V_o[m + 1] \tag{4}$$

where $0 \le m < \frac{N}{2}$ and $H[\frac{N}{2}] = 0$.

2. Zhijin's algorithm [35]: Define g, h and G, H as above. Let $b[n] = 2h[n]$ $\cos\left(\pi\frac{2n+1}{2N}\right)$, and let $B[k]$ be its DCT-II. Then the even and odd components of the DCT-II $y[k]$ of $x[n]$ are

$$y[2m] = G[m]$$
$$y[1] = B[0]/2$$
$$y[2m+1] = B[m] - y[2m-1] \tag{5}$$

3. Restructured recursive DCT (Lee and Huang [19]): Define a recursive function $\hat{C}(x)$, which takes a sequence of x of length N and returns another length-N sequence, as follows. When the input sequence x has length 2, $\hat{C}(x)$ is the DCT-II of x. Otherwise, define two new sequences

$$x_1[k] = x[k] + x[k + \frac{N}{2}]$$
$$x_2[k] = x[k] - x[k + \frac{N}{2}]$$

where $0 \le k < \frac{N}{2}$. Then $X[k]$ be a new sequence such that

$$X[2k] = \{\hat{C}(x_1)\}[k]$$
$$X[2k+1] = \{\hat{C}(x_2)\}[k] \cdot 2\cos\left(\pi\frac{4k+1}{2N}\right) - X[2k-1]$$
$$X[-1] = 0$$

Then $\hat{C}(x) = X[0..N-1]$. To obtain the DCT-II of x, define $\hat{x}$ to be the following permutation of x:

$$\hat{x}[2k] = x[k]$$
$$\hat{x}[2k+1] = x[N-1-k]$$

Then the DCT-II of x is $\hat{C}(\hat{x})$.

As with the FFT, these can be implemented in a straightforward way in FFTW's codelet generator, thus benefitting from the simplifier/scheduler structure of FFTW's code generator. We give an example of how the first algorithm can be expressed in Appendix A.

The three variations appear similar on the surface but lead to implementations with different numbers of additions and multiplications once they have been processed by the codelet generator's optimizer, as shown in Figure 13. The execution times on both platforms are comparable for $N < 16$; for $N \ge 16$, FFT-algorithm 4 either matched or outperformed the real formulations. In comparing the three purely real codelets, we see that operation count alone does not explain the execution times. A slight difference in just one addition and multiplication on the Millennium node for $N = 16$, for instance, caused the DCT algorithm 3 to be about 15% slower than DCT algorithm 1.

		Real DCT-IIs		
N	4N-FFT	DIF	Zhijin	Lee
2	2+2	2+2	2+2	2+2
	(4)	(4)	(4)	(4)
	.14	.14	.14	.14
	.10	.10	.10	.10
4	8+6	9+5	8+6	8+6
	(14)	(14)	(14)	(14)
	.17	.18	.17	.17
	.14	.14	.14	.14
8	26+16	29+14	27+15	28+15
	(42)	(43)	(42)	(43)
	.23	.25	.24	.25
	.26	.25	.24	.25
16	72+42	81+37	77+37	80+38
	(114)	(118)	(114)	(118)
	.44	.43	.44	.45
	.52	.50	.51	.62
32	186+104	209+92	201+89	208+93
	(290)	(301)	(290)	(301)
	.86	.95	1.01	1.11
	1.22	1.32	1.33	1.27
64	456+250	513+219	497+209	512+220
	(706)	(732)	(706)	(732)
	1.87	2.68	3.25	3.10
	2.84	3.15	3.12	3.24

Fig. 13. Comparison between the 4N-point FFT-based algorithm and the three purely real recrusive DCT-II algorithms. The four rows correspond to (1) the number of real additions and multiplications (shown as $a + m$), (2) total arithmetic operations, and execution times (in μs) on (3) the Sun Ultra-10 platform and (4) the Millennium Node. The approximate timing uncertainties on the Sun Ultra-10 platform is $\pm.01$ μs, and on the Millennium node it is $\pm.02$ μs. The full set of FFTW code generation optimizations were applied in all implementations.

Figure 14 shows the raw codelet performance on the Sun Ultra-10 and the Millennium node. We show only the codelets based on FFT-algorithm 4 in both cases. Note that performance is normalized to the FFTW-based DCT-II implementation, and not a naive implementation. The drop-off at 128 and 256 is expected, since by then the fully unrolled codelet begins to exert significant register pressure on the code, leading to frequent spills.

While this appears promising, the DCT-II codelets are probably not optimal in terms of the number of operations, since they derive from complex-valued FFTs instead of a purely real-valued formulation. In the case of the 8-point DCT-II, the code included in the freely available JPEG reference implementation [2,21] only requires 29 additions and 11 multiplications. This compares to 26 additions

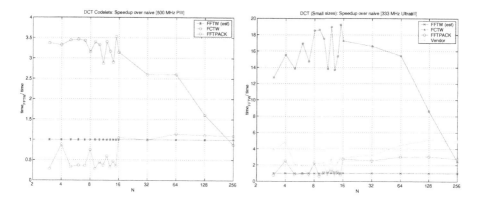

Fig. 14. DCT-II specialized codelet performance on a Millennium node (*left*) and the Sun Ultra-10 (*right*). All codelets of size less than 16 are shown, with the remaining points at powers of 2.

and 16 multiplications for the 8-point DCT-II codelet. The actual running times of the two implementations are identical to within the timing noise resolution, however, reflecting the differences in structure, pipeline usage, and scheduling of the two codes. Nevertheless, this suggests that a more efficient formulation for the DCT-II codelets is possible. We have not yet had a chance to investigate this further, but plan to do so in the near term.

The important point is that within the code generator's framework, we were able to experiment relatively quickly and simply with a large variety of implementations. The multitude of other recursive DCT-II formulations [3,7,20,22,25,32], some of which handle non-power of 2 cases, are all characterized by complex indexing schemes (unlike the FFT case), which we expect will be relatively easy to handle in the FFTW framework.

However, this work is not yet complete because we have not yet finished implementation of the planner and executor for the DCT. We also expect to complete this in the near term. Finally, we should point out that we did not examine or introduce any new simplification rules to the simplifier that would benefit the purely real formulations. Nevertheless, we believe that the visualization component we introduced will facilitate the identification of such rules.

5   Summary and Future Work

We have presented data that gives some idea of the relative merits of the various techniques employed in the FFTW codelet generator. In particular, simple FFT-specific transformations led to significantly improved final code. Moreover, for odd and prime sizes, transposition followed by additional simplification was beneficial as well. However, we saw that in a number of cases on the Ultra-10, for instance, in which DAG transposition and additional simplification reduced the efficiency of the final code. Therefore, there are a number of additional scheduling and compiler interaction issues that remain unresolved.

Nevertheless, the choice of implementation of the FFTW codelet generator was simple to extend to compute a similar transform, the DCT, and led to extremely fast codelets.

Furthermore, explicitly maintaining the symbolic representation and having multiple ways of "unparsing" it (in our case, we added the dot code output lead to an interesting visualization. This could be extremely useful in future code generation systems.

There are a number of future directions in which to take this work, which can be classified as FFTW-specific improvements, future kernel generators, and future compiler research. We make a few suggestions below.

5.1   FFTW-Specific Improvements

In addition to completing the DCT part of FFTW by implementing a planner and generator, the kernel generator could be extended to handle 2-D transforms as well. This is because specialized 2-D kernels (specifically in the DCT case) are widely used and could benefit from additional symmetries in the 2-D case.

Also, we did not discuss the codelet generator's scheduler in any detail. Briefly, the scheduler is "cache-oblivious" meaning there are no specific references or parameters that might directly relate to the number of available registers or size of the cache. An asymptotically optimal scheduling does exist, although it is not explicitly parameterized by the cache size (or equivalently the number of available registers). It would be useful to see if a cache-aware scheduler can lead to improved performance.

Finally, we did not discuss numerical stability issues. This problem is generic to any floating point kernel generator since we are now "deriving" new algorithms that may have completely different floating point behavior.

5.2   Other Kernels

This project was originally motivated by a desire to produce a specialized kernel generator for the fast wavelet transform (FWT). My initial research revealed that the FWT could benefit from a similar approach if small wavelet kernels were needed in applications. This is because wavelet transforms have similar symmetries that lead to many common sub-expressions. However, the FWT has *linear* arithmetic and I/O complexity with respect to the input size, and its recursive decomposition calls only one smaller transform at each level of the recursion. This implies that a highly tuned "kernel" for small sized transforms might not be as beneficial since each small transform is called only once. In contrast, the FFT can potentially call a small-sized transform many times at each level of the recursion (depending on how the input length factors), making the need for highly-tuned kernels for small-sized transforms much more important.

One important kernel that could benefit from FFTW codelet generator techniques is sparse matrix-vector multiplication, when the structure of the sparse matrix is known. In finite element computations, for instance, the sparse matrices often have a known block structure, where the blocks are small and symmetric. In these cases, it may be possible to generate dense matrix-vector multiply "codelets" for these blocks.[6] For example, such codelets could be specialized verisons of the "register-blocked routines" generated in the Sparsity system [17].

An important set of kernels that, like the FFT, have recursive structure are the recursive formulations of dense matrix multiply, Cholesky and LU factorization [28,15], and QR factorization [12]. Researchers have identified the importance of small kernel routines in these cases. However, we do not currently know what the right high-level representation and scheduling decisions should be.

5.3   Implications for Compilers

We do not believe that the full implications of this work in kernel generation for compiler writers will be known until more kernel generators have been written. It is clear, however, that for the time being, the flow of technology transfer will be from compiler work to kernel generation. In this sense, we feel that one important area for development in kernel generators is to find representations convenient for expressing loops (instead of just recursion as in FFTW) and associated loop transformations like tiling, unrolling, and software pipelining; many kernels may be more naturally expressed in this way.

References

1. Millennium: An hierarchical campus-wide cluster of clusters (home page). http://www.millennium.berkeley.edu.
2. Independent JPEG Group Reference Implementation, May 2000. http://www.ijg.org.
3. G. Bi. DCT algorithms for composite sequence lengths. *IEEE Transactions on Signal Processing*, 46(3):554–562, March 1998.
4. J. Bilmes, K. Asanović, C. Chin, and J. Demmel. Optimizing matrix multiply using PHiPAC: a Portable, High-Performance, ANSI C coding methodology. In *Proceedings of the International Conference on Supercomputing, Vienna, Austria*, July 1997.
5. J. Bilmes, K. Asanović, J. Demmel, D. Lam, and C. Chin. The PHiPAC WWW home page. http://www.icsi.berkeley.edu/~bilmes/phipac.
6. S. Blackford, G. Corliss, J. Demmel, J. Dongarra, I. Duff, S. Hammarling, G. Henry, M. Heroux, C. Hu, W. Kahan, L. Kaufman, B. Kearfott, F. Krogh, X. Li, Z. Maany, A. Petitet, R. Pozo, K. Remington, W. Walster, C. Whaley, and J. W. von Gudenberg. Document for the Basic Linear Algebra Subprograms (BLAS) standard: Blas technical forum. http://www.netlib.org/cgi-bin/checkout/blast/blast.pl.
7. L.-P. Chau and W.-C. Siu. Recursive algorithm for the discrete cosine transform with general lengths. *Electronic Letters*, 30(3):197–198, February 1994.
8. J. W. Cooley and J. W. Tukey. An algorithm for the machine calculation of complex fourier series. *Mathematics of Computation*, 19:297–301, April 1965.

---

[6] Indeed, the DFT is simply a matrix-vector multiply operation where the matrix is fixed and highly symmetric.

9. R. E. Crochiere and A. V. Oppenheim. Analysis of digital linear networks. In *Proceedings of the IEEE*, volume 63, pages 581–595, April 1975.
10. J. Dongarra, J. D. Croz, I. Duff, and S. Hammarling. A set of level 3 basic linear algebra subprograms. *ACM Trans. Math. Soft.*, 16(1):1–17, March 1990.
11. J. Dongarra, J. D. Croz, I. Duff, S. Hammarling, and R. J. Hanson. An extended set of Fortran basic linear algebra subroutines. *ACM Trans. Math. Soft.*, 14(1):1–17, March 1988.
12. E. Elmroth and F. Gustavson. Applying recursion to serial and parallel QR factorization leads to better performance. *IBM Journal of Research and Development*, 44(1), January 2000. http://www.cs.umu.se/~elmroth/papers/eg99.ps.
13. M. Frigo. A fast Fourier transform compiler. In *Proceedings of the ACM SIGPLAN Conference on Programming Language Design and Implementation*, May 1999.
14. M. Frigo and S. Johnson. FFTW: An adaptive software architecture for the FFT. In *Proceedings of the International Conference on Acoustics, Speech, and Signal Processing*, May 1998.
15. F. Gustavson. Recursion leads to automatic variable blocking for dense linear algebra algorithms. *IBM Journal of Research and Development*, 41(6), November 1997. http://www.research.ibm.com/journal/rd/416/gustavson.html.
16. G. Henry. Linux libraries for 32-bit Intel Architectures, March 2000. http://www.cs.utk.edu/~ghenry/distrib.
17. E.-J. Im and K. Yelick. Optimizing sparse matrix vector multiplication on SMPs. In *Proceedings of the Ninth SIAM Conference on Parallel Processing for Scientific Computing*, March 1999.
18. C. Lawson, R. Hanson, D. Kincaid, and F. Krogh. Basic linear algebra subprograms for Fortran usage. *ACM Trans. Math. Soft.*, 5:308–323, 1979.
19. P. Z. Lee. Restructured recursive DCT and DST algorithms. *IEEE Transactions on Signal Processing*, 42(7), July 1994.
20. P. Z. Lee and F.-Y. Huang. An efficient prime-factor algorithm for the discrete cosine transform and its hardware implementation. *IEEE Transactions on Signal Processing*, 42(8):1996–2005, August 1994.
21. C. Loeffler, A. Ligtenberg, and G. Moschytz. Practical fast 1-D DCT algorithms with 11 multiplications. In *Proceedings of the International Conference on Acoustics, Speech, and Signal Processing*, volume 2, pages 988–991, May 1989.
22. D. P. K. Lun. On efficient software realization of the prime factor discrete cosine transform. In *Proceedings of the IEEE International Conference on Acoustics, Speech and Signal Processing*, volume 3, pages 465–468, April 1994.
23. A. Oppenheim and R. Schafer. *Discrete-time Signal Processing*. Prentice-Hall, 1999.
24. W. H. Press, S. A. Teukolsky, W. T. Vetterling, and B. P. Flannery. *Numerical Recipes in C*. Cambridge University Press, 1992. http://www.nr.com.
25. K. R. Rao and P. Yip. *Discrete Cosine Transform: Algorithms, Advantages, Applications*. Academic Press, Inc., 1992.
26. J. Siek and A. Lumsdaine. The Matrix Template Library: A generic programming approach to high performance numerical linear algebra. In *Proceedings of the International Symposium on Computing in Object-Oriented Parallel Environments*, December 1998.
27. P. Swarztrauber. FFTPACK User's Guide, April 1985. http://www.netlib.org/fftpack.
28. S. Toledo. Locality of reference in LU decomposition with partial pivoting. *SIAM Journal on Matrix Analysis and Applications*, 18(4), 1997. http://www.math.tau.il/~sivan/pubs/029774.ps.gz.

29. T. Veldhuizen. The Blitz++ home page. `http://www.oonumerics.org/blitz`.
30. T. Veldhuizen. Using C++ template metaprograms. *C++ Report Magazine*, 7(4):36–43, May 1995.
31. T. Veldhuizen and D. Gannon. Active libraries: Rethinking the roles of compilers and libraries. In *Proceedings of the SIAM Workshop on Object Oriented Methods for Inter-operable Scientific and Engineering Computing (OO'98)*. SIAM Press, 1998.
32. Z. Wang. Recursive algorithms for the forward and inverse discrete cosine transform with arbitrary lengths. *IEEE Signal Processing Letters*, 1(7):101–102, July 1994.
33. R. C. Whaley and J. Dongarra. The ATLAS WWW home page. `http://www.netlib.org/atlas/`.
34. P. Yip and K. R. Rao. The decimation-in-frequency algorithms for a family of discrete sine and cosine transforms. *Circuits, Systems, and Signal Processing*, pages 4–19, 1988.
35. Z. Zhijin and Q. Huisheng. Recursive algorithms for the discrete cosine transform. In *Proceedings of the IEEE International Conference on Signal Processing*, volume 1, pages 115–118, October 1996.

A   DCT-II DIF Algorithm in Objective Caml

The purely real recursive algorithm can be expressed in just a dozen lines of Caml code. The resulting expression then benefits from all of the same transformations and infrastructure available to FFTW.

```
let rec dct2 n input =
  let g = let g_input = fun i ->
            (input i) @+ (input (n-i-1))
    in fun m -> dct2 (n/2) g_input m
  and h = let h_input = fun i ->
            let twiddle = (sec (4*n) (2*i+1)) @* complex_half
            in ((input i) @- (input (n-i-1))) @* twiddle
    in fun m -> dct2 (n/2) h_input m
  in fun m -> (* dct2 n input m *)
    let m2 = m / 2
    in if n == 1 then complex_two @* input 0 (* 1 element input *)
       else if (m mod 2) == 0 then (* m even *)
             g m2
       else (* m odd *)
             if m == (n-1) then (* last element *)
                h m2
             else
                (h m2) @+ (h (m2+1))
```

Note that the *input* function (not shown) provided to *dct2* is defined to only load a real element.

Generating Data Analysis Programs from Statistical Models

Position Paper

Bernd Fischer[1], Johann Schumann[1], and Tom Pressburger[2]

[1] RIACS / NASA Ames
[2] QSS / NASA Ames
Moffett Field, CA 94035 USA
{fisch,schumann,ttp}@ptolemy.arc.nasa.gov

Abstract. Extracting information from data, often also called data analysis, is an important scientific task. Statistical approaches, which use methods from probability theory and numerical analysis, are well-founded but difficult to implement: the development of a statistical data analysis program for any given application is time-consuming and requires knowledge and experience in several areas.

In this paper, we describe AUTOBAYES, a high-level generator system for data analysis programs from statistical models. A statistical model specifies the properties for each problem variable (i.e., observation or parameter) and its dependencies in the form of a probability distribution. It is thus a fully declarative problem description, similar in spirit to a set of differential equations. From this model, AUTOBAYES generates optimized and fully commented C/C++ code which can be linked dynamically into the Matlab and Octave environments. Code is generated by schema-guided deductive synthesis. A schema consists of a code template and applicability constraints which are checked against the model during synthesis using theorem proving technology. AUTOBAYES augments schema-guided synthesis by symbolic-algebraic computation and can thus derive closed-form solutions for many problems. In this paper, we outline the AUTOBAYES system, its theoretical foundations in Bayesian probability theory, and its application by means of a detailed example.

1 Introduction

Data analysis denotes the transformation of data (i.e., pure numbers) into more abstract information. It is at the core of all experimental sciences—after all, experiments result only in new data, not in new information. Consequently, scientists of all disciplines spend much time writing and changing data analysis programs, ranging from trivial (e.g., linear regression) to truly complex (e.g., image analysis systems to detect new planets). A variety of methods is used for data analysis but all rigorous approaches are ultimately based on statistical methods [BH99]. Amongst these, Bayesian methods offer conceptual advantages

W. Taha (Ed.): SAIG 2000, LNCS 1924, pp. 212–229, 2000.

in handling prior information and missing data and have thus become the methods of choice for many applications.

We believe that data analysis, especially data analysis based on Bayesian statistics, is a very promising application area for program generation. Probability theory provides an established, domain-specific notation which can form the basis of a specification language. Probability theory and numerical analysis provide a wide variety of solution methods and potentially applicable algorithms.

Manual development of a customized data analysis program for any given application problem is a time-consuming and error-prone task. It requires a rare combination of profound expertise in several areas—computational statistics, numerical analysis, software engineering, and of course the application domain itself. The algorithms found in standard libraries need to be customized, optimized, and appropriately packaged before they can be integrated; the model and its specific details usually influence many algorithmic design decisions. Most importantly, the development process for data analysis programs is typically highly iterative: the underlying model is usually changed many times before it is suitable for the application; often the need for these changes becomes apparent only after an initial solution has been implemented and tested on application data. However, since even small changes in the model can lead to entirely different solutions, e.g., requiring a different approximation algorithm, developers are often reluctant to change (and thus improve) the model and settle for sub-optimal solutions.

A program generator can help to solve these problems. It encapsulates a considerable part of the required expertise and thus allows the developers to program in models, thereby increasing their productivity. By automatically synthesizing code from these models, many programming errors are prevented and turn-around times are reduced. We are currently developing AUTOBAYES, a program generator for data analysis programs. AUTOBAYES starts from a very high-level description of the data analysis problem in the form of a statistical model and generates imperative programs (e.g., C/C++) through a process which we call *schema-based deductive synthesis*. A schema is a code template with associated semantic constraints which describe the template's applicability. Schemas can be considered as high-level simplifications which are justified by theorems in a formal logic in the domain of Bayesian networks. The schemas are applied recursively but AUTOBAYES augments this schema-based approach by symbolic-algebraic calculation and simplification to derive closed-form solutions whenever possible. This is a major advantage over other statistical data analysis systems which use slower and possibly less precise numerical approximations even in cases where closed-form solutions exist.

The back-end of AUTOBAYES is designed to support generation of code for different programming languages (e.g., C, C++, Matlab) and different target systems. Our current version generates C/C++ code which can be linked dynamically into the Octave [Mur97] or Matlab [MLB87] environments; other target systems can be plugged in easily.

This paper describes work in progress; design rationales and some preliminary results of the AUTOBAYES-project have been reported in [BFP99]. In Section 2, we give a short overview over Bayesian networks and their application for data analysis. We then proceed with a detailed description of the system architecture, the process of synthesizing the algorithm, and the steps to produce actual code. Section 4 contains a worked example which illustrates the operation of AUTOBAYES on a small, yet non-trivial example. We compare our approach to related work in Section 5 before we discuss future work in in Section 6.

2   Bayesian Networks and Probabilistic Reasoning

Bayesian networks or *graphical models* are a common representation method in machine learning [Pea88,Bun94,Fre98,Jor99]; AUTOBAYES uses them to represent the data analysis problem internally. Figure 1 shows the network for the example used throughout this paper.

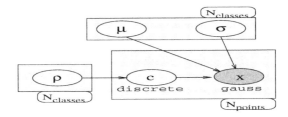

Fig. 1. Bayesian Network for the Mixture of Gaussians Example.

A Bayesian network is a directed, acyclic graph that defines probabilistic dependencies between random variables. Its arcs can sometimes be interpreted as causal links but more precisely the absence of an arc between two vertices denotes the conditional independence of the two random variables, given the values of their parents. Hence, since the example network has no arc between the vertices μ and c, the *joint probability* $P(\mu, c)$ to observe certain values of μ and c at the same time is the same as the product of $P(\mu)$ and $P(c \mid \rho)$, the conditional probability of c given ρ. The network thus superimposes a structure on the global joint probability distribution which can be exploited to optimize probabilistic reasoning. Hence, the example defines the global joint probability $P(x, c, \rho, \sigma, \mu)$ in terms of simpler, possibly conditional probabilities:

$$P(x, c, \rho, \sigma, \mu) = P(\rho) \cdot P(c \mid \rho) \cdot P(\mu) \cdot P(\sigma) \cdot P(x \mid c, \mu, \sigma)$$

The central theorem of probabilistic reasoning is *Bayes rule*

$$P(h \mid d) = \frac{P(d \mid h) \cdot P(h)}{P(d)}$$

which expresses the probability $P(h \mid d)$ that hypothesis h holds under given data d in terms of the *likelihood* $P(d \mid h)$ and the *prior* $P(h)$; the probability of the data, $P(d)$, is usually only a normalizing constant.

AUTOBAYES uses an extended version of hybrid Bayesian networks, i.e., nodes can represent discrete as well as continous random variables. Shaded vertices denote known variables, i.e., input data. Distribution information for the variables is attached to the vertices, e.g., the input x is Gaussian distributed. Boxes enclosing a set of vertices denote vectors of independent, co-indexed random variables, e.g., μ and σ are both vectors of size $N_{classes}$ which always occur indexed in the same way. As a consequence, a box around a single vertex denotes the familiar concept of a vector of identically distributed and indexed random variables.

An Example: Mixture of Gaussians

We illustrate how AUTOBAYES works by means of a simple but realistic classification example. Figure 2 shows the raw input data, a vector of real values. We know that each data point falls into one of three classes; each class is Gaussian distributed with mean μ_i and standard deviation σ_i. The data analysis problem is to infer from that data the relative class frequencies (i.e., how many points belong to each class) and the unknown distribution parameters μ_i and σ_i for each class. Although this example is deliberately rather simple, it already demonstrates the potential of generating data analysis programs; it also illustrates some of the problems.

Figure 3 shows the statistical model in AUTOBAYES's input language. The model (called "Mixture of Gaussians" – line 1) assumes that each of the data points (there are n_points – line 5) belongs to one of n_classes classes; here n_classes has been set to three (line 3), but n_points is left unspecified. Lines 16 and 17 declare the input vector and distributions for the data points[1]. Each point x(I) is drawn from a Gaussian distribution c(I) with mean mu(c(I)) and standard deviation sigma(c(I)). The unknown distribution parameters can be different for each class; hence, we declare these values as vectors (line 11). The unknown assignment of the points to the classes (i.e., distributions) is represented by the hidden (i.e., not observable) variable c; the class probabilities or relative frequencies are given by the also unknown vector rho (lines 9–14). Since each point belongs to exactly one class, the sum of the probabilities must be equal to one (line 10). Additional constraints (lines 4,6,7) express further basic assumptions. Finally, we specify the goal inference task (line 19), maximizing the probability $P(x \mid \rho_i, \mu_i, \sigma_i)$. Due to Bayes' rule, this calculates the most likely values of the parameters of interest, ρ_i, μ_i, and σ_i.

---

[1] Vector indices start with 0 in a C/C++ style.

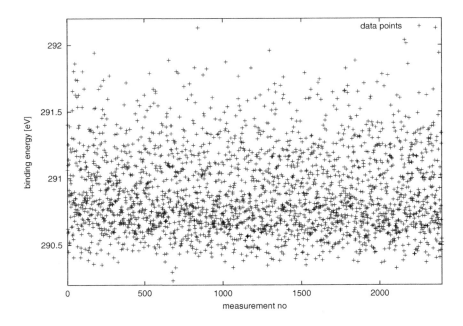

Fig. 2. Artificial input data for the mixture of Gaussians example: 2400 data points in the range $[290.2, 292.2]$. Each point belongs in one of three classes which are Gaussian distributed with $\mu_1 = 290.7, \sigma_1 = 0.15$, $\mu_2 = 291.13, \sigma_2 = 0.18$, and $\mu_3 = 291.55, \sigma_3 = 0.21$. The relative frequencies ρ for the points belonging to the classes are $61\%, 33\%$, and 6%, respectively.

3   System Architecture

The system architecture of AUTOBAYES (cf. Figure 4) has been designed for high flexibility and modularity granting easy extensibility of the system for interactive refinement of specifications. Here, we describe the main components of the system (synthesis kernel, intermediate language, back-end, and generation of artificial data). The entire system has been implemented in SWI-Prolog [SWI99]. For symbolic mathematical calculations, a small rewriting engine has been built on top of Prolog. A set of system utilities (e.g., pretty-printer, graph handling, set representations, I/O functions) facilitates the implementation of AUTOBAYES. Since AUTOBAYES requires a combination of symbolic mathematical calculation, rewriting, general purpose operations (e.g., input/output), and reasoning over graphs, Prolog is a reasonable choice as the underlying implementation language. The main reason not to choose a symbolic algebra system as for example Mathematica is its possible unsoundness. During symbolic calculation, simplifications are done by such systems without explicitly stating all assumptions. These unsound transformations can lead to incorrect results and hence incorrect programs. AUTOBAYES keeps track of all assumptions (e.g., an expres-

```
 1  model mog as 'Mixture of Gaussians';
 2
 3  const int n_points as 'number of data points'
 4        with 0 < n_points;
 5  const int n_classes := 3 as 'number of classes'
 6        with 0 < n_classes
 7        with n_classes << n_points;
 8
 9  double rho(0..n_classes - 1) as 'class probabilites'
10        with 1 = sum(idx(I, 0, n_classes - 1), rho(I));
11  double mu(0..n_classes - 1), sigma(0..n_classes - 1);
12
13  int c(0..n_points) as 'class assignment vector';
14  c ~ discrete(vec(idx(I, 0, n_classes - 1), rho(I)));
15
16  data double x(0..n_points - 1) as 'data points (known)';
17  x(I) ~ gauss(mu(c(I)),sigma(c(I)));
18
19  max pr(x | {rho,mu,sigma}) wrt {rho, mu, sigma};
```

Fig. 3. AUTOBAYES-specification for the mixture of Gaussians example. Line numbers have been added for reference in the text. Keywords are underlined.

sion being non-zero) and either discharges them during synthesis or generates assertions to be checked during run-time.

3.1 Synthesis Kernel

The synthesis kernel takes the model specification and builds an initial Bayesian network. Each variable declaration in the model corresponds directly to a network node. Each distribution declaration, e.g., $x \sim \text{gauss}(\Theta)$, induces edges from the distribution parameters Θ to the node corresponding to the random variable x; these edges reflect the dependency of the (random) values of x on the values of the parameters Θ. Building the network is relatively straightforward and requires no sophisticated dataflow analysis because the model is purely declarative. However, Θ needs to be flattened, i.e., nested random variables need to be lifted and fresh index variables need to be introduced in their place in order to represent the dependencies properly. Hence, the example declaration $x(i) \sim \text{gauss}(\mu(c(i)), \sigma(c(i)))$ induces not only the two obvious edges but three: $\mu(j) \longrightarrow x(i), \sigma(j) \longrightarrow x(i)$, and $c(i) \longrightarrow x(i)$ (cf. Figure 1). Note that x and c are still co-indexed but that each $x(i)$ now depends on all $\mu(\cdot)$ and $\sigma(\cdot)$, reflecting the unknown values of their original indices $c(i)$. A compact representation of the indexed nodes and their dependencies is achieved by using Prolog-variables to represent index variables.

Synthesis proceeds from this initial network and the original probabilistic inference task by exhaustive application of *schemas*. A schema can be understood as an "intelligent macro": it comprises a *pattern*, a *parameterized code template*, and a set of preconditions or *applicability constraints*. An example will be shown below. The pattern and code template are similar to the left- and right-hand

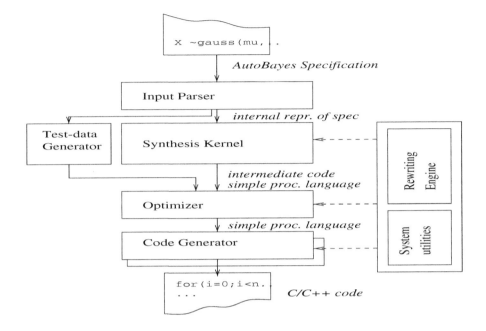

Fig. 4. System Architecture for AUTOBAYES.

side of a traditional macro definition; they comprise the syntactic part of the schema. Schema-guided synthesis, however, is not just macro expansion. Different schemas can match the same pattern, possibly in different ways. AUTOBAYES covers this search space by a depth-first, left-to-right search, with backtracking over possible multiple solutions.

The constraints refine the semantics of the schema: a schema can be understood as an axiom which asserts that the program (i.e., the appropriately instantiated template) solves the probabilistic inference task specified by the pattern *if* the constraints are satisfied; however, checking the constraints may instantiate the template parameters further. The search process mentioned above is thus a proof search; the proof is constructive in the sense that it actually generates a program (the *witness*) and does not just assert its existence.

Network Decomposition Schemas. AUTOBAYES uses four different kinds of schema. *Network decomposition* schemas are encodings of independence theorems for Bayesian networks. They describe how a probabilistic inference task over a given network can be decomposed equivalently into several simpler tasks over simpler networks and, hence, how a complex data analysis program can be composed from simpler components. The applicability constraints for these schemas can be checked by pure graph reasoning. Consider for example the following decomposition theorem.

Theorem 1 ([BFP99]) *Let U, V be sets of vertices in a Bayesian network with $U \cap V = \emptyset$. Then $V \cap descendants(U) = \emptyset$ and $parents(U) \subseteq V$ hold iff*

$$P(U\,|\,V) = P(U\,|\,parents(U)) = \prod_{u \in U} P(u\,|\,parents(u))$$

The theorem allows us to simplify the conditional probability $P(U \mid V)$ into $P(U \mid parents(U))$ (i.e., it allows us to ignore all assumptions not reflected in the network by incoming edges) and then further into a finite product of atomic probabilities (i.e., each variable depends only on the parameters of its associated distribution), provided that the applicability constraints hold over the network; here, $descendants(U)$ is defined as $children^*(U) - U$ with $children^*$ being the full graph reachability relation. This theorem then induces the following schema for maximizing the probability $P(U\,|\,V)$ with respect to a set of variables X.

schema(max $P(U\,|\,V)$ wrt X, *Template*)   :-
   $U \cap V = \emptyset$
  $\wedge\ \ U \cap descendants(V) = \emptyset$
  $\wedge\ \ parents(U) \subseteq V$
  $\rightarrow\ Template = \underline{\texttt{begin}}$
      $\langle \max\ P(\{u\}\,|\,parents(\{u\}))$ wrt $X \mid u \in U\rangle$
     $\underline{\texttt{end}}$

The schemas are written as Prolog-rules. During the search for applicable schemas, pattern-matching with the rule head (first line) is tried. When the match succeeds, the variables (U, V, X) are bound, and the body of the rule (separated by the :-) is processed. Here, the body is a logical implication. The implication's antecedents directly encode the applicability constraints as AUTOBAYES's symbolic reasoning engine contains an operationalization of the graph predicates. The schema's code template consists of a sequence of simpler maximization tasks. Their ordering is irrelevant because the $u \in U$ are independent of each other; this is a consequence of the applicability constraints. A number of similar decomposition theorems have been developed in probability theory; AUTOBAYES currently includes three different schemas based on such theorems, with the one shown above being by far the simplest.

Formula Decomposition Schemas. *Formula decomposition* schemas are similar to the network decomposition schemas above but they work on complex formulae instead of a single probability. A typical schema in this class is index decomposition. It applies to an inference task for a formula which contains possibly multiple occurrences of probabilities involving vectors and "unrolls" this task into a loop over the simpler inference task for a single vector element. Most of the applicability constraints for index decomposition can still be checked by graph reasoning but some checks involving the formula structure require proper symbolic reasoning.

Statistical Algorithm Schemas. Proper *statistical algorithm* schemas are also graph-based but they are not simple consequences of the independence theorems. Instead, their correctness is proven independently, or they are just empirically validated during construction of the domain theory. These schemas involve larger modifications of the graph, e.g., introduction of new nodes with known values, and storing the results of intermediate calculations. These schemas thus enable the further application of the decomposition schemas; however, they are much more intricate and less theorem-like. They also have much larger code templates associated and they can require substantial symbolic reasoning during instantiation. AUTOBAYES currently implements two such algorithms which are known in the literature as *expectation maximization* (or simply *EM algorithm* [DLR77]) and *k-Means*, respectively. Both schemas are applicable to general mixture models which underpin many classification tasks similar to the running example.

Numerical Algorithm Schemas. The graph-based reasoning continues until all conditional probabilities $P(U \mid V)$ have been converted into atomic form, i.e., V are all parameters of U's distribution. These can then be replaced by the appropriately instantiated probability density functions. AUTOBAYES's domain theory contains rewrite rules for the most common probability density functions, e.g., Gaussian and Poisson distributions. With this rewrite step the original probabilistic inference task becomes a pure optimization problem which can be solved either symbolically or numerically. AUTOBAYES first attempts to find closed-form symbolic solutions, which are much more time-efficient during run-time than the usually iterative numeric approximation algorithms. In order to solve the optimzation problem, AUTOBAYES symbolically differentiates the formula with respect to the optimization variables, sets the result to zero and tries to solve this system of simultaneous equations. Symbolic differentiation is implemented as a term rewrite system; however, the need to check for whether a term depends on the variable that the derivative is taken with respect to implies that some rules are conditional rewrite rules. Equation solving currently employs only a variant of Gaussian variable elimination: whenever a variable can be isolated modulo the symbolic model constants, the remaining equation is solved by a polynomial solver.

If no symbolic solution can be found, AUTOBAYES applies iterative numerical algorithm schemas, e.g., the Newton-Raphson method or the Nelder-Mead simplex algorithm. Such algorithms are also provided by general-purpose numeric libraries, e.g., [PF+92], but program generation can substantially improve this black-box style reuse, because it can instantiate actual parameters symbolically and evaluate the inlined expressions partially. This provides further optimization opportunities, often in the inner loops of the algorithms.

Control. During synthesis, these schemas are tried exhaustively in a left-to-right, depth-first manner. Whenever a dead end is encountered (i.e., no schema is applicable), AUTOBAYES backtracks. This search allows AUTOBAYES to generate program variants if more than one of the schemas are applicable and opens up possibilities to generate multiple solutions for the same problem, which then can be assessed using tests on the given data.

3.2   Generating Explanations

Certification procedures for safety-critical applications (e.g., in aircrafts or space-crafts) often mandate manual code inspection. This inspection requires that the code is readable and well documented. Even for programs not subject to certi-fication, understandability is a strong requirement as manual modifications are often neccessary, e.g., for performance tuning or system integration. However, existing program generators often produce code that is hard to read and under-stand. In order to overcome this problem, AUTOBAYES generates explanations along with the programs which make the synthesis process more transparent and provide traceability from the generated program back to the model specifiation.

AUTOBAYES generates heavily commented code: approximately a third of the output is automatically generated comments (cf. Figure 8 for an example). This is achieved by embedding documentation templates into the code templates. Future versions of AUTOBAYES will not only generate fully documented code; we are aiming at producing a detailed design-document for the generated code. This document will also show the "synthesis decisions" made by AUTOBAYES (e.g., which algorithm schema has been used) and the reasons which led to them. Open proof obligations and model assumptions will be laid out clearly.

Reliability of generated code entails that the code is robust (e.g., robustness against erroneous inputs or sensor failures). Thus, all assumptions from the spec-ification or made by AUTOBAYES which cannot be discharged during synthesis are brought to the user's attention and are listed in the documentation. Impor-tant assumptions which can be checked efficiently during run-time are converted into assertions which are inserted into the code (e.g., $N_{classes} < N_{points}$).

3.3   Intermediate Language

The synthesis kernel of AUTOBAYES generates code for an intermediate language before code for the actual target system is produced. This intermediate language is a simple procedural language with several domain-specific extensions (e.g., for convergence loops, vector normalization, and simultaneous vector assignment). Each statement of the intermediate language can be annotated. In the current version, annotations carry the generated explanations. In future versions an-notations will also be used to guide optimization and to carry out automatic instrumentation of the generated code for evaluation and testing purposes.

Using an intermediate language offers major benefits because it allows to perform code optimization independently from the selected target language and target system without excessive overhead. For example, we are able to extract loop-independent expressions without having to apply data-flow analysis to the generated code, because the structure of the loops is known from the instantiated algorithm schema.

The intermediate code is close enough to allow for a simple translation into the target language (e.g., C, C++, Matlab). The additional domain-specific constructs facilitate target-specific transformations. For example, the language construct for calculating the sum of array elements (sum) can be converted into a usual for-loop (C, C++), an iterator construct (e.g., when using sparse matrices), or a direct call of a summation-operator (e.g., when generating interpreted Matlab code).

3.4   Backend and Code Generation

The actual code-generator can be adapted easily to a specific target language and a given environment. With the help of rewrite rules all constructs of the intermediate language are transformed into constructs of the target language and printed using a simple pretty-printer. On this target-specific level, another set of optimization steps are performed (e.g., replacing of E^{-1} by $1/E$, or E^2 by $E \times E$ for an expression E). Standard optimizations (e.g., evaluation of constant expressions) are left for the subsequent compilation phase—there is no need to perform the same optimization steps as any modern compiler. The back-end also generates code for interfacing the algorithm with the target system, and to check for correct types of arguments.

Our current prototype produces C++-code for Octave [Mur97] and C-code for Matlab [MLB87]. Future work will include code-generators for design-tools for embedded systems, e.g., ControlShell [Con99] or MatrixX [Aut99].

3.5   Synthesis of Artificial Test Data

The given input specification contains enough information to generate artificial data with properties corresponding to the specified statistical model. AUTOBAYES is capable of generating code producing artificial data. For this task we use the same underlying machinery and back-end as described above. This feature of AUTOBAYES offers several benefits: using artificial data, the performance (e.g., speed or convergence) of the generated code can be evaluated and assessed; comparisons between different algorithm schemas can be made easily. Artificial data can also be used to test the generated code. For example, by using different sets of parameters, the behavior of the generated analysis algorithm can be tested for stability.

4   A Worked Example

In this section, we discuss synthesis and execution of the example described in Section 2. The specification in Figure 3 comprises the entire input to AUTOBAYES. After parsing this specification, AUTOBAYES generates the dependency graph (see Figure 1) and tries to break it down into independent parts. When trying to solve the optimization problem, the system fails to find a closed-form symbolic solution. Therefore, the EM algorithm schema is tried and instantiations are sought. This algorithm schema consists of an iterative loop which has to be executed until a convergence criterion is met. Within this loop, new estimates for ρ, σ, μ are calculated and compared to the old values. When the difference becomes small enough, the loop can be exited (cf. Figure 8).

For our example, AUTOBAYES generates a C++ file consisting of 477 lines (including comments and separation lines). This code is then compiled into a dynamically linkable function for Octave. Thus, when invoking the function "mog" (line 1 of the specification) from inside Octave, our compiled C++ code is invoked automatically. As shown in Figure 5, AUTOBAYES also synthesizes a usage line and produces a short help-text. The entire synthesis process of AUTOBAYES, including compilation of the generated C++ code takes about 35s on a G3 powerbook under Linux.

The following results have been obtained using artificial data. Starting with a total of 2400 points falling into 3 classes (cf. Figure 2), the algorithm searches for the values of mu, sigma, and rho for each class. For the final result, this run required 1163 iteration steps, taking approximately 54 sec on a G3 notebook[2]. The convergence, i.e., the normalized change of the parameters to be optimized during each iteration cycle, is shown in Figure 6.[3] AUTOBAYES automatically instruments the generated code to produce these run-time figures for debugging and testing purposes.

```
octave:2> mog
usage: [vector mu,vector rho,vector sigma] = mog(vector x)

octave:3> help mog
mog is a builtin function

Mixture of Gaussians. Maximize the conditional probability
pr([c,x]|[rho,mu,sigma]) w.r.t. [rho, mu, sigma ], given
data x and n_classes=3.
...
octave:4> x = [ ... ];
octave:4> [mu,rho,sigma] = mog(x)
mu =

   291.12
   291.28
   290.69
...
```

Fig. 5. Octave Sample Session Using Code (Function "mog") Generated by AUTOBAYES.

---

[2] This figure can change from run to run, since the algorithm starts with a random initial class assignment for each data point.

[3] This algorithm does not converge monotonically. It can reach some local minimum, from which it has to move away by increasing the error again. After some ups and downs the global minimum (i.e., an optimal estimate for the parameters) is reached and the loop ends. This behavior is typical for parameter estimation processes, e.g., as found in artificial Neural Networks [MR88].

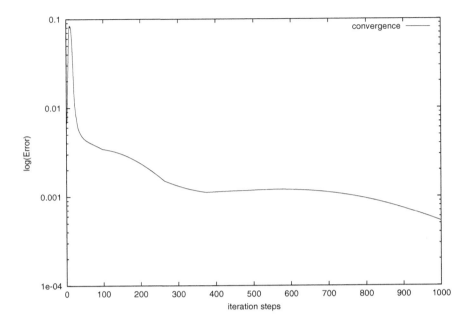

Fig. 6. Convergence behavior: differences between old and new parameters (log-scale) over iteration step. Only the first 1000 iteration cycles are shown.

Although this example has been run with artificial data, there are several real applications for this kind of model. For example, when molecules (or atoms) in a gas are excited with a specific energy (e.g., light from a laser), they can absorb this energy by excitation or by emission by one or more of their electrons, respectively. This basic mechanism generates spectral lines, e.g., in the light of stars. Single atoms usually have sharp, well-defined spectral lines but molecules which are more complex (e.g., CH_4 or NH_3) can have several peaks of binding energy, depending on their internal configuration. Thus, they can absorb (or emit) energy at different levels.

The example here (cf. Figure 7) is taken from [Ber79] and shows the spectrum of the energy of emitted photoelectrons that is directly related to the excess energy of the photon over the photoionization potential of the molecule CH_4 (for details see [Ber79], caption of Figure 67). In a simple statistical model, each of the peaks is assumed to be Gaussian distributed and the percentage of molecules being in a specific configuration is known. When we measure the binding energy for a large number of (unknown) molecules, we obtain a set of data, similar to that shown in Figure 2 above. If we suspect that the molecules might be CH_4 which has 3 distinct configurations, we can use the generated code to classify the data into these three classes and to obtain the parameters. The histogram of the data is shown in Figure 7, super-imposed with Gaussian curves using the parameter values as estimated by the program.

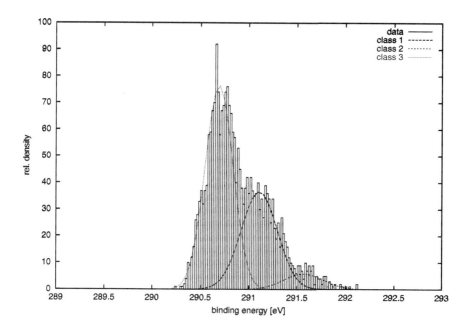

Fig. 7. Histogram (spectrum) of the artificial test data (Figure 2, number of bins = 100) and Gaussian distributions as obtained by running the generated code.

5   Related Work

Work related to AUTOBAYES appears mainly in two different fields. In the first field, statistics, there is a long tradition of composing programs from library components but there are only a few, recent attempts to achieve a similar degree of automation as AUTOBAYES does. The Bayes Net Toolbox [Mur00] is a Matlab-extension which allows users to program models; it provides several Bayesian inference algorithms which are attached to the nodes of the network. However, the Toolbox is a purely interpretive system and does not generate programs. The widely used BUGS-system [TSG92] also allows users to program in models but it uses yet another, entirely different execution model: instead of executing library code or generating customized programs, it interprets the statistical model using Gibbs sampling, a universal—but less efficient—Bayesian inference technique. BUGS, or more precisely, Gibbs sampling, could thus be integrated into AUTOBAYES as an algorithm schema.

The other field, deductive synthesis, is still an active research area. Some systems, however, have already been applied to real-world problems. The AMPHION system [SW+94] has been used to assemble programs for celestial mechanics from a library of FORTRAN components, for example the simulation of a Saturn fly-by. AMPHION is more component-oriented than AUTOBAYES, i.e., the generated programs are linear sequences of subroutine calls into the library. It uses a full-fledged theorem prover for first-order logic and extracts the program from the proof. [EM98] describes a system for the deductive synthesis of numerical simulation programs. This system also starts from a high-level specification of a mathematical model—in this case a system of differential equations—but is again more component-oriented than AUTOBAYES and does not use symbolic-algebraic reasoning. Planware [BG+98] (which grew out of the KIDS system [Smi90]) synthesizes schedulers for military logistics problems. It is built on the concept of an algorithm theory which can be considered as an explicit hierarchy of schemas.

[Big99] presents a short classification of generator techniques (albeit cast in terms of their reuse effects). AUTOBAYES falls most closely into the category of inference-based generators but also exhibits some aspects of pattern-directed and reorganizing generators, e.g., the typical staging of the schemas into multiple levels.

6   Conclusions

We have presented AUTOBAYES, a prototype system that automatically generates data analysis programs from specifications in the form of statistical models. AUTOBAYES is based on deductive, schema-guided synthesis. After constructing the initial Bayesian network from the model, a variety of different schemas are tried exhaustively. These schemas are guarded by applicability constraints and contain code-blocks which are instantiated. By way of an intermediate language, AUTOBAYES generates executable, optimized code for a target system. The current version of AUTOBAYES produces C/C++-code for dynamic linking into Octave and Matlab; future versions of AUTOBAYES will include code generation for sparse matrices and for design-tools for embedded systems (e.g., ControlShell).

We have applied AUTOBAYES successfully to a number of textbook problems where it was able to find closed-form solutions equivalent to those in the textbooks. The largest iterative solution generated so far comprises 477 lines of C++ code. Synthesis times (including compilation of the generated code) are generally well below one minute on standard hardware. We are currently testing AUTOBAYES in two major case studies concerning data analysis tasks for finding extra-solar planets either by measuring dips in the luminosity of stars [KB+00], or by measuring Doppler effects [MB97], respectively. Both projects required substantial effort to manually set up data analysis programs. Our goal for the near future is to demonstrate AUTOBAYES's capability to handle major subproblems (e.g., the CCD-sensor registration problem) arising in these projects.

AUTOBAYES has two unique features which result from using program generation (instead of compilation) and which make it more powerful and versatile for its application domain than other tools and statistical libraries. First, AUTOBAYES generates efficient procedural code from a high-level, declarative specification without any notion of data- or control-flow. Thus, it covers a relatively large semantic gap. Second, by combining schema-guided synthesis with symbolic calculation, AUTOBAYES is capable of finding closed-form solutions for many problems. Thus, the generated code for these kinds of problems is extremely efficient and accurate, because it does not rely on numeric approximations.

The explanation technique provides further benefits, especially in safety-critical areas. Code is not only documented for human understanding, but assumptions made in the specification and during synthesis are checked by assertions during run-time. This makes the generated code more robust with respect to erroneous inputs or sensor failures.

AUTOBAYES is still an experimental prototype and has to be extended in several ways before it can be released to users. In particular, further schemas have to be added and the expressiveness of the kernel with respect to the model descriptions has to be increased. However, since the schemas cannot be derived automatically from the underlying theorems, more machine support for this manual domain engineering process may become necessary, e.g., type-checking of the schemas [Bjø99]. Nevertheless, we are confident that the paradigm of schema-guided synthesis is an appropriate approach to program generation in this domain which will lead to a powerful yet easy-to-use tool.

Acknowledgements : Wray Buntine contributed much to the initial development of AUTOBAYES and the first version of the prototype. We would like to thank the anonymous reviewers for their helpful comments.

References

Aut99. MatrixX: AutoCode Product Overview. ISI, 1999. http://www.isi.com.

Ber79. J. Berkowitz. *Photoabsorption, photoionization, and photoelectron spectroscopy.* Academic Press, 1979.

BFP99. W. L. Buntine, B. Fischer, and T. Pressburger. "Towards Automated Synthesis of Data Mining Programs". In S. Chaudhuri and D. Madigan, (eds.), *Proc. 5th Intl. Conf. Knowledge Discovery and Data Mining*, pp. 372–376, San Diego, CA, August 15–18 1999. ACM Press.

BG⁺98. L. Blaine, L.-M. Gilham, J. Liu, D. R. Smith, and S. Westfold. "Planware – Domain-Specific Synthesis of High-Performance Schedulers". In D. F. Redmiles and B. Nuseibeh, (eds.), *Proc. 13th Intl. Conf. Automated Software Engineering*, pp. 270–280, Honolulu, Hawaii, October 1998. IEEE Comp. Soc. Press.

BH99. M. Berthold and D. J. Hand, (eds.). *Intelligent Data Analysis—An introduction.* Springer, Berlin, 1999.

Big99. T. J. Biggerstaff. "Reuse Technologies and Their Niches". In D. Garlan and J. Kramer, (eds.), *Proc. 21th Intl. Conf. Software Engineering*, pp. 613–614, Los Angeles, CA, May 1999. ACM Press. Extended abstract.

Bjø99. N. S. Bjørner. "Type checking meta programs". In *Workshop on Logical Frameworks and Meta-languages*, Paris, France, 1999.

Bun94. W. L. Buntine. "Operations for learning with graphical models". *J. AI Research*, **2**:159–225, 1994.

Con99. ControlShell. RTI Real-Time Innovations, 1999. `http://www.rti.com`.

DLR77. A. P. Dempster, N. M. Laird, and D. B. Rubin. "Maximum likelihood from incomplete data via the EM algorithm (with discussion)". *J. of the Royal Statistical Society series B*, **39**:1–38, 1977.

EM98. T. Ellman and T. Murata. "Deductive Synthesis of Numerical Simulation Programs from Networks of Algebraic and Ordinary Differential Equations". *Automated Software Engineering*, **5**(3):291–319, 1998.

Fre98. B. J. Frey. *Graphical Models for Machine Learning and Digital Communication*. MIT Press, Cambridge, MA, 1998.

Jor99. M. I. Jordan, (ed.). *Learning in Graphical Models*. MIT Press, Cambridge, MA, 1999.

KB+00. D. G. Koch, W. Borucki, E. Dunham, J. Jenkins, L. Webster, and F. Witteborn. "CCD Photometry Tests for a Mission to Detect Earth-size Planets in the Extended Solar Neighborhood". In *Proceedings SPIE Conference on UV, Optical, and IR Space Telescopes and Instruments*, 2000.

MB97. G. W. Marcy and R. P. Butler. "Extrasolar Planets Detected by the Doppler Technique". In *Proceedings of Workshop on Brown Dwarfs and Extrasolar Planets*, 1997.

MLB87. C. B. Moler, J. N. Little, and S. Bangert. *PC-Matlab Users Guide*. Cochituate Place, 24 Prime Park Way, Natick, MA, USA, 1987.

MR88. J. L. McClelland and D. E. Rumelhart. *Explorations in Parallel Distributed Processing*. MIT Press, 1988.

Mur97. M. Murphy. "Octave: A Free, High-Level Language for Mathematics". *Linux Journal*, **39**, July 1997.

Mur00. K. Murphy. Bayes Net Toolbox 2.0 for Matlab 5, 2000. `http://www.cs.berkeley.edu/~murphyk/Bayes/bnt.html`.

Pea88. J. Pearl. *Probabilistic Reasoning in Intelligent Systems: Networks of Plausible Inference*. Morgan Kaufmann Publishers, San Mateo, CA, USA, 1988.

PF+92. W. H. Press, B. P. Flannery, S. A. Teukolsky, and W. T. Vetterling. *Numerical Recipes in C*. Cambridge Univ. Press, Cambridge, UK, 2nd. edition, 1992.

Smi90. D. R. Smith. "KIDS: A Semi-Automatic Program Development System". *IEEE Trans. Software Engineering*, **16**(9):1024–1043, September 1990.

SW+94. M. Stickel, R. Waldinger, M. Lowry, T. Pressburger, and I. Underwood. "Deductive Composition of Astronomical Software from Subroutine Libraries". In A. Bundy, (ed.), *Proc. 12th Intl. Conf. Automated Deduction, Lect. Notes Artifical Intelligence* **814**, pp. 341–355, Nancy, June-July 1994. Springer.

SWI99. SWI Prolog, 1999. `http://swi.psy.uva.nl/projects/SWI-Prolog/`.

TSG92. A. Thomas, D. J. Spiegelhalter, and W. R. Gilks. "BUGS: A program to perform Bayesian inference using Gibbs sampling". In J. M. Bernardo, J. O. Berger, A. P. Dawid, and A. F. M. Smith, (eds.), *Bayesian Statistics 4*, pp. 837–842. Oxford Univ. Press, 1992.

```
// Mixture of Gaussians
proc(mog) {
const:  int n_classes := 3;                    // Number of classes
        int n_points := size(x, 1);            // Number of data points
input:  double x[0:n_points - 1];
output: double mu[0:n_classes-1],rho[0:n_classes-1],sigma[0:n_classes-1];
local:  ...
{ ...
  // Initialization
  // Randomize the hidden variable c
  for( [idx(pv64, 0, n_points - 1)])
    c(pv64) := random_int(0, n_classes - 1);
  // Initialize the local distribution; the initialization is "sharp",
  // i.e., q1 is set to zero almost everywhere and to one at the index
  // positions determined by the initial values of the hidden variable.
  for( [idx(pv154, 0, n_points - 1), idx(pv155, 0, n_classes - 1)])
    q1(pv154, pv155) := 0;
  for( [idx(pv156, 0, n_points - 1)])
    q1(pv156, c(pv156)) := 1;
  // EM-loop
  while( converging([vector([idx(pv157, 0, n_classes-1)], rho(pv157)),
            vector([idx(pv158, 0, n_classes-1)], mu(pv158)),
            vector([idx(pv159, 0, n_classes-1)], sigma(pv159))]) )
    {
      // Decomposition I;
      // the problem to optimize the conditional probability
      // pr([c, x] | [rho, mu, sigma]) w.r.t. the variables rho, mu,
      // and sigma can under the given dependencies by Bayes rule be
      // decomposed into independent subproblems.
            . . .
      // using the Lagrange-multiplier l1.
      l1 := sum([idx(pv68, 0, n_classes - 1)],
              sum([idx(pv66, 0, n_points - 1)], q1(pv66, pv68)));
      for( [idx(pv68, 0, n_classes - 1)])
        rho(pv68) := l1 ** -1 * sum([idx(pv66, 0, n_points - 1)],
                    q1(pv66, pv68));
      // The conditional probability pr([x] | [sigma, mu, c]) is
      // under the given dependencies by Bayes rule equivalent to
      // prod([idx(pv126, 0, n_points-1)],
      //      pr([x(pv126)] | [c(pv126), mu, sigma]))
      // The probability occuring here is atomic and can be
      // replaced by the respective probability density function.
      . . .
      for( [idx(pv64, 0, n_points-1), idx(pv65, 0, n_classes-1)])
        q1(pv64, pv65) := select(norm([idx(pv163, 0, n_classes-1)],
                exp(-1 / 2 * (-1 * mu(pv163) + x(pv64)) ** 2 *
                sigma(pv163) ** -2) * rho(pv163) * 2 ** (-1 / 2) *
                pi ** (-1 / 2) * sigma(pv163) ** -1), [pv65]);
    } } }
```

Fig. 8. Pseudo-code for the Mixture of Gaussians Example (Excerpts).

Author Index